HOW TO
FIND JOY
EVEN IF YOU HAVE A HOLE
IN YOUR BUCKET

MICHAEL BOYLE

First published in 2025 by Onyx Publishing, an imprint of Notebook Group Limited, Arden House, Deepdale Business Park, Bakewell, Derbyshire, DE45 1GT.

www.onyxpublishing.com
ISBN: 9781913206918

A CIP catalogue record for this book is available from the British Library.

Typeset by Onyx Publishing of Notebook Group Limited.

ONYX PUBLISHING

To "Mom," the Divine Mother and the source of Love through which we are ALL Together.

To my mother, father, brother, and sister. Your unwavering support and unconditional love are my foundation. Thank you.

To Tania. Through it all, together, we thrive. I love you. I am excited to keep building the future, together, for the benefit of ALL.

To Rudi, the sweet, wise love of my life. Thank you.

To Finn, "the exuberant and compassionate one." I cherish every moment we get to spend together. I love you forever.

To Sofia, who embodies the great joy of being. Thank you for your tender love. I am always your loving daddy.

To Lar and GEM.

To the many positive things I have received from my teachers and mentors, especially Dharma, Arkie, Tinker, Terry, Jed, and Dr. Joe.

To my clients. It is a humbling privilege to be the person many turn to in the hardest moments of their lives. I wrote this book for us.

To Matt. This book is part of my effort to "Live like Z."

To crippling, vegetative depression; to countless panic attacks; to decades of anxiety; to alcohol and marijuana abuse; to off-the-charts ADHD; to devastating brain injuries; to chronic illness; to lifesaving surgeries; to bad choices; and to spiritual missteps: thank you all. You have taught me well.

CONTENTS

AUTHOR'S NOTE

A note about "credit" in this book:

So many of the concepts and so much of the terminology in this book have been crystalized and shared with me, graciously and abundantly, by my mentor, Lar Short, spiritual director of Grace Essence Mandala (GEM). It would be ridiculous if I gave him specific credit every time his influence was felt in my words. There would be another hundred pages of footnotes and, "My mentor said..." Suffice it to say, words cannot even begin to describe the ways in which he and his teachings have impacted my and my family's life. Thank you, thank you, thank you.

It is not just some cliché to say that whatever of Lar's wisdom comes through these pages to the benefit of the reader is a credit to Lar and his unwavering dedication to his students. Anything jumbled up, ineffective, or out of line in this book is the product of my current limitations in development. I neither speak for Lar nor GEM in these writings, though I am profoundly grateful for them both.

Nor is it the case that everything in this book has come directly from Lar. My research, studies and pursuit of these ideas and practices over the last 25 years has been almost obsessive, and I am grateful that Lar has helped me elevate and crystalize a lot of what I was onto before meeting him.

Also, a note about information that came to light midway through the editing of this book (and that is therefore not reflected throughout): on day eight of a twenty-one-day meditation retreat I went on while waiting to receive the fifth draft of this manuscript from my publisher, I felt a stabbing pain in my back and abdomen. A few hours later, a CT scan revealed a six-inch hole in my diaphragm. Portions of my liver, gallbladder, and intestines were caught in this hole. It also came to light I had a barely functioning lung and a paralyzed diaphragm. Turns out these problems had been lying dormant since 2001, nearly a quarter century before; more than *half of my life* before. I wrote this book not knowing that this was the reason why I have been obsessed with personal healing and, as a result, helping others. I have become a master at self-care because I had to. But up until this moment, I didn't exactly know why.

The doctors, frankly, were astounded by what they found. The day after my surgery, I overheard my surgical team chatting about it with their colleagues. My lead surgeon said, "I don't know how the fuck this guy's been walking around."

Due to the complications of previous head trauma, as well as my half-functional diaphragm, my barely functioning lung, and my organs being squeezed and lodged out of place, it's taken everything I've had in me just to function.

I sought medical care for the symptoms I now know were related to this injury back when I was living in Thailand, around 2008. I was told my issues stemmed from a normal and innocuous hiatal hernia. And so I went on with my life, silently navigating my ever-present low-level chronic abdominal pain. Over the subsequent years, my nausea, fatigue, headaches, and lightheadedness became overwhelming. Because I took such good care of myself, my health parameters otherwise checked out good, as did my labs, so doctors weren't able to explain my symptoms. In fact, they were regularly judged as being "all in my head," or psychosomatic. I had a teacher who nicknamed me "Johnny Drama" due to my "hypochondriac" tendencies and emotional frustrations which, as it turns out, actually had very rational physiological origins all along.

I share this to convey the fact that I know what it's like to be dismissed, ignored, judged, and shamed. Before my diagnosis and treatment, I regularly beat myself up for not being better; for not being able to do more. That said, I also had (have) three kids, was (am) a great dad, and was chief of operations at a mental health agency that served thousands in New Mexico. I also founded a family behavioral center that still serves thousands to this day, skied advanced terrain at one of the steepest mountains in the US, and was (am) basically indomitable in my will to persevere, to do the right thing because it's the right thing to do, to serve others, and to do anything and everything I could to smile, feel okay, and provide for my family. That is how this book is now in your lap. Out of necessity, I have had to choose to be my own doctor, healer, and guide, and to find any and every tool possible to enable me to thrive, even though, aside from, and especially because of the bad stuff that happens to us all.

My wife can tell you how many times I've sobbed, wondering, "Why don't I feel better? My clients do ten percent of the stuff I teach them and feel better in one to three months. I've been doing one hundred and ten percent for fifteen years and I still feel like shit almost every day." Ironically, my almost absurdly thorough self-care routine likely prevented this injury and its solution from being discovered sooner. This realization hit me in that moment when I overheard my surgical team discussing how "wild" and "unbelievable" it was that I'd managed to live with this for so long, at such a high level of functioning. It's also ironic that, in my quest to fill a bucket with a (literal) hole in it that I didn't know about, my decades-long practical obsession with studying and practicing anything that could help someone feel better has led to ideas, tools, and ultimately a self-care system that will benefit thousands of others, yielding much better and faster results than I've experienced myself. I guess this is what they mean when they say God has a sense of humor and works in mysterious ways.

Our pain becomes our passion, and our passion becomes our power, and our power becomes our responsibility to share.

I am proud to say that the stuff you are about to learn in this book works, even if you are in the trenches. For the hundreds of people I've worked with who *don't* have a hole in their diaphragm, half a lung, and organs losing blood supply, it's worked wonders!

I am also grateful to say my perseverance in my health matters led me to a master surgeon who told me, "There is no manual for this operation. I just need to get in there and make lots of game-time decisions about what to do." What an amazing thing! After making a seven-inch incision and opening my chest with a retractor for six hours, he was able cut the scar tissue around the hole to free up my organs, as well as the scar tissue from where my liver was supposed to be, to make a cavity and put it back in its proper place, and then suture up the blown out "petals" of the diaphragm, so that everything would stay put. Since then, my diaphragm has come back to life (we weren't sure if it would, so that's hugely fortunate), my lung has become able to fully expand, and I am eager to find out just how amazing I will feel now that I am doing everything you are about to learn in this book with a fully functioning body!

In conclusion, cheers to those who have persevered; who have kept going; who have been judged; who have judged themselves; who are here to for the real talk, the real tools, and the real results you can produce by taking matters into your own hands, even if that means getting the support you need, upgrading your nervous system from survival mode to thriving mode, and making your own good luck. (I certainly think it was good luck that random stabbing pains in a meditation retreat solved a twenty-four-year-old mystery and acquainted me with a master surgeon who put Humpty Dumpty back together again!)

As is the All Together Academy motto, "Together, we thrive!" Enjoy the book, use the tools, and spread the love.

—MIKE

FOREWORD BY MAESTRO LAR C. SHORT

I have had the privilege of knowing Michael for ten years and have been a close mentor of his. Carl Jung spoke of the archetype of the wounded healer—someone who, having gone through a healing journey, can be a dependable guide for others[1]. Since then, many have sought self-actualization and self-realization through psychology and spirituality. Michael represents to me someone who has gone through the hazards associated with both, someone who fulfils the archetype of the wounded healer, and someone who has actively sought their own form of enlightenment. During his inner work, he has passed through the various gains and losses, the real and phony aspects, and the dangers in spiritual and psychological disciplines alike. He has emerged as a very competent guide for others, and he works to practically facilitate empowered modes of living, rather than spreading theoretical fundamentalism that looks for converts in the name of therapy.

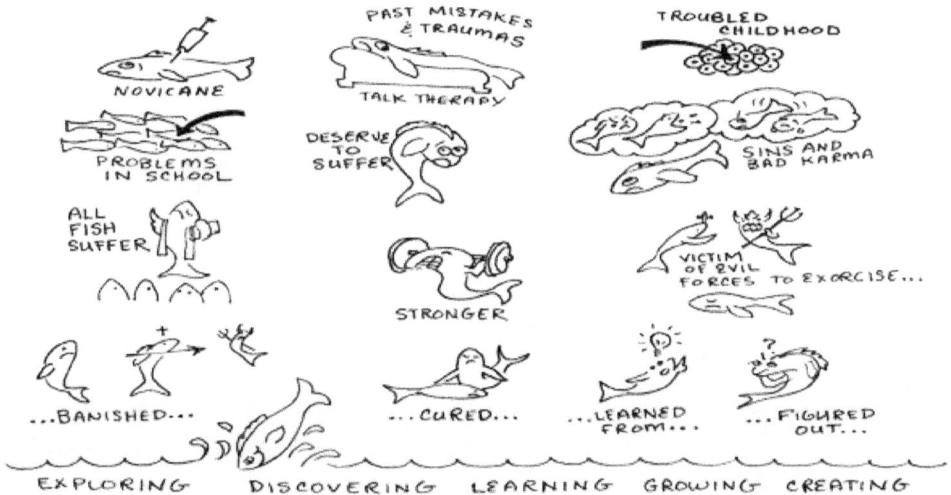

NOVICANE

PROBLEMS IN SCHOOL

ALL FISH SUFFER

...BANISHED...

PAST MISTAKES & TRAUMAS

TALK THERAPY

DESERVE TO SUFFER

STRONGER

...CURED...

TROUBLED CHILDHOOD

SINS AND BAD KARMA

VICTIM OF EVIL FORCES TO EXORCISE...

...LEARNED FROM...

...FIGURED OUT...

EXPLORING   DISCOVERING   LEARNING   GROWING   CREATING

---

1 Jung, C. G., 1951–1979, The Collected Works of C.G. Jung, R. F. C. Hull, Trans., Princeton University Press.

"Facilitating," in this context, means bringing to another ease in them being themselves. It means bringing them home to the human design of exploring, discovering, learning, growing, and creating. This is our design as humans, just like living in water is the fish's design (see previous diagram). Take the fish out of water and it suffers, and no amount of treating the symptoms of its suffering will make it thrive. Rather, one must facilitate its return to the water it was designed to live in.

Facilitating "empowered modes of living," then, means teaching one to use the skills they already inherently have to live, flourish, and thrive within their design.

I recommend Michael as a guide for true inner work to anyone who is ready to shift from being a seeker to being a finder.

—MAESTRO LAR C. SHORT
Grace Essence Mandala

INTRODUCTION

Pain is inevitable. Suffering is optional.
—The Dalai Lama[2], Haruki Murakami, and M. Kathleen Casey

Metamorphosis: A change of the form or nature of a thing or person into a completely different one, by natural or supernatural means.[3]

Metanoia: A transformative change of heart; to change the state of one's being.[4]

I REMEMBER VERY CLEARLY THE DAY my sister dared me to go to a yoga class. I was battling severe depression, had loads of East Coast skepticism about "new agey" stuff, and could never have imagined myself anywhere near a yoga studio. I was a college athlete at the time and a "tough guy," no less. I played varsity ice hockey and was surrounded by

---

2 "'Pain is inevitable. Suffering is optional,' is a quote often attributed to the Dalai Lama, Haruki Murakami, and M. Kathleen Casey, though its origin remains unclear." This acknowledges the various attributions while highlighting the lack of a definitive source.
3 As defined by Google, accessed March 2, 2025, at https://www.google.com/search?sca_esv=427fd9fc564ca397&rlz=1C5CHFA_enUS1086US1086 &q=metamorphosis&si=ACC9onyj24cUGopiOVnGD91130XTFiF2equ8HclCJMvJm2wvAzui_M bTIUFMOwGLWQHrBT3G7f-
k7SgzAFMFn5O8SBXouNnooIyJUkNRFmhP7KDBokYiyu0%3D&expnd=1&sa=X&ved=2ahUKE wjei9Duw4yKAxXhEVkFHcZbDx8Q2v4IegQIIhA4&biw=2223&bih=1053&dpr=2
4 The first part of this definition can be found at https://www.merriam-webster.com/dictionary/metanoia , accessed March 2, 2025; the latter part is a quote from my mentor Lar, presented during a verbal lecture, not publicly available.

loads of friends. I had plenty of good things going for me. That was when vegetative depression zapped my soul.

This wasn't an overnight thing. Usually, stuff that seems to happen "all of a sudden" has actually been in development for years. Case in point: when I called one of my best friends from high school to tell him that I'd been pulled from school to deal with my depression, his (loving) sarcastic remark was, "That's a shocker."

Anyway, back to yoga.

My sister had teased me about yoga—"I bet you won't even last twenty minutes"—with a smirk on her face. I'd looked at her and rolled my eyes, but she and I both knew that she had succeeded in goading my competitive spirit. I'd never been one to back down from a challenge. Well, I hadn't, until I'd become so depressed. Still, I guess a part of me knew this was a "now or never" moment.

Imagine, to my embarrassing surprise, when, after my very first yoga class, I found myself on the floor, crying with ecstatic joy. So intense was this what I could only call "heart opening" moment that from there, I ended up taking the spiritual science of yoga to further extremes than most people could ever imagine. This included seven years spent living in a mountain retreat in Thailand and an ongoing path of spiritual development I travel to this day as my number one priority. But that's a story for another time. My point is that on that mat, in my puddle of sweat and tears, I discovered my first authentic moment of true openness, maybe ever. It was certainly the first time I'd experienced this with full conscious participation as an adult. In fact, it was the first time I'd experienced it since going numb as a child (more on that later). At that moment, I told myself that I would fully commit to always cultivating this feeling of "aliveness" in my body and soul, no matter what it took. I was awake, and there was no turning back. I was on the path from severe suffering to having ALL: Awareness Loving Life. This was a monumental step in the long and continuous journey of me trying to embody whatever version of myself would offer the greatest possible benefit, not only for myself, but for others, and ALL.

It would still be quite some time, with plenty more suffering, before I would finally taste a semblance of stable peace and what I like to call "the great joy of being," but in the meantime, I started doing new things, hanging out with new people, traveling, reading inspiring books, and becoming a different person. I'm not going to lie; I was a bit obsessed with my new way of life. I would read, reread, and reread again the books I came across in a state of meditative absorption, sometimes going into a trance for hours in my favorite Davis Square, Somerville coffee shop named The Someday Café (better known to us budding beatniks as "The Somenow"). I was still a bit (okay, very) ungrounded at the time, and the people around me (including my loving family) probably thought I was going nuts, but I was on fire with a passion for growth that would take me to the edges of the cosmos in my consciousness and to corners of the world that would be impossible to describe. Many of these experiences are "off the record" (though none of them included drugs of any kind, in case you were wondering). Along the way, whole new worlds were opened to me by books that truly seemed to be divine interventions. Through what seemed to be serendipity, books like *Autobiography of a Yogi* by Paramahansa Yogananda, *Wherever You Go, There You Are* by Jon Kabat-Zinn, Peace is Every Step by Thich Nhat Hanh, Be Here Now by Ram Dass, *The Gospel of Thomas*, and dozens more came into my life and changed the course of it forever. I would read those books and write down every highlight in an old-school PalmPilot that I could carry in my pocket, and then reread the highlights repeatedly. I essentially memorized hundreds of books over the years in this way, and this really helped me to reprogram my mind.

In some ways, dear reader, it is my sincere wish that this book becomes something just as potent and transformative for you; that it has landed on your lap, or on your screen, or in your headphones, in such an auspicious and serendipitous way that it could change the course you've been on forever, for the better. My aim is for this book to boost your bottom line. In reading it, you will not only know that happiness is a skill that can be cultivated, but that it's a skill that *must* be cultivated—meaning, it will not come to you on its own, no matter how groovy your outer circumstances may be.

By coming on this journey with me, you will also come to know that not only is happiness a skill that can and must be cultivated, but that it is also *the only skill that matters most* to cultivate, because it's the only skill that enhances everything else.

The Creative-IAM (C-IAM) and the Neurochemical Roadmap to the Future You Value and Choose (NRF)

By the end of this book, you will not only be able to invoke your Creative-IAM (C-IAM) and follow your Neurochemical Roadmap to the Future You Value and Choose (NRF), but you will also have the tools and instructions you will need to navigate this territory with such skill that you won't be able to help but end up on the road to health (which, at the end of the day, is happiness).

We will delve into the C-IAM and NRF in significant detail in Part III of this book. As a brief introduction: the C-IAM is the personality structure through which you can choose to filter and organize your body, mind, and spirit. The C-IAM is juxtaposed by your Reactive-iWAS, which is a reactive personality structure based on "survival mode". Most of us mistake the Reactive-iWAS for who we are, until we come to understand that we can choose to live through and as the C-IAM instead. (All of this will make way more sense later, I promise.)

You can think of it this way: most people unconsciously form their identity as a subconscious reaction to everything that has ever happened to them. This is essentially a "victim" stance (though please note that I do not subscribe to the shaming tone that is often associated with calling someone a "victim"). What I mean by this is, most people live their lives at the mercy of anything and everything that is going on in and around them, including their entire past. In doing so, they are bound by circumstance. This leads them to operate from a place of fear, lack, or fighting for control, which eventually leaves them spent. (Have you noticed how tired you are?) They exhaust themselves so much seeking what they want and avoiding what they don't want that they end up having no energy left to actually enjoy the life they are living. On the other hand, when we develop and secure our C-IAM, we become conscious, causal, creative human beings, giving to life what we wish to receive from it, and "coming from" an inherently beneficial state of being that we can access *regardless of circumstances*. We become autonomous and free to explore, discover, learn, grow, and create in an interdependent way that benefits the self, others, and ALL (Awareness Loving Life). This way of being is characterized by joy, openness, love, kindness, awareness, gratitude, presence, and surrender (the JOLKA-GPS). In this state, we are inspired and enthused, and healing happens naturally, because our nervous system feels so safe (neurobiologically) that it unleashes an inner pharmacy of "thriving" chemistry.

The reason why our many efforts to "change for the better" or "be happy" are usually thwarted is that our thoughts, feelings, actions, and experiences default back to our Reactive-iWAS, because we haven't developed our C-IAM. In other words, we fall back to who we were; the "same old, same-old." And we are thrown around by the ups and downs of life because we haven't gained access to the state of constancy within ourselves that is A-ok no matter what is going on inside and around us. When our identities are formed as a reaction to everything, and everything is always changing, then it's no wonder we feel untethered, disconnected, at-affect, exhausted, and literally "beside ourselves."

Sound familiar?

Later in this book (in Part III), you will learn how to dismantle the false self that forms inevitably as a result of being a human being (so, no, it's not your fault, and yes, this happens to *everyone*) and in its absence, you will be able to explore, discover, learn, grow, and create your C-IAM, which is a conscious and deliberate choice to be who you really are. In this way, your new habits will have a new "being" to adhere to, organize around, and come from. Instead of gluing wings on a caterpillar and hoping it will fly (i.e., creating even "positive" habits as a bandaid to the negatively bound, reactive, counterfeit personality structure you have come to believe you are), you will enter a chrysalis, "die" as who you were, and emerge, "reborn," as who you value and choose to be: the Creative-IAM. Once you undergo this metamorphosis, you'll no longer need to cope with the problems associated with who you were, because they'll no longer exist. A butterfly, while still bound to face challenges and opportunities, no longer has caterpillar problems.

Why just cope with suffering when you can end it?

When you explore, discover, learn, grow, and create your C-IAM, you open up your Neurochemical Roadmap to the Future You Value and Choose (NRF). The NRF is a guide outlining potential "steps" and "stops" that may crop up on your journey through life (which you are navigating "as" your C-IAM). Your NRF methodically and practically gets you to where you want to be. The C-IAM is the driver, the NRF is the map, and your body, mind, and spirit are the vehicle. The C-IAM is who you are when you are at your best, and the NRF is what you do (and don't do) when you are clicking on all cylinders.

Like I said, all of this will be explained in detail in Part III of this book. While it may seem a little esoteric and lofty for now, rest assured that we will break it down bit by bit and make it easy to put into play. Before that, in Part II, we will cover an assortment of practical tools and unique ideas that will get you feeling better, today, easily, in a totally sustainable way that makes perfect sense. (Note: You are going to hear me say that a lot.) You will learn about the common roadblocks and hazards that are experienced on this journey and how to avoid them. We will talk about real-deal shortcuts that can save you time, energy, money, marriages, and maybe your family. They may even save your life. These maps, tools, and instructions have definitely saved mine, period. I went from living like I had a death wish in my twenties to where I am now. As I write, it has been over twenty years since I have had any occurrences of clinical depression. This doesn't mean that depressive patterns haven't reared their ugly head during that time, but it does mean that I now know what to do about them when they do.

Before I "did the work," these depressive episodes were chronic. They lasted years. Then, when I started using the tools I'm about to share with you in these pages, they lasted months; then weeks; then days. And now, they usually last no more than a few hours, and oftentimes just a few minutes, before I feel it, heal it, and move forward freely.

I know this stuff works. In fact, it is humbling (and kind of scary) to even think about quite how effective it actually is. I've had clients who have directly told me, "This has literally saved my life." And that's not all. It's not just that these maps, tools, and instructions have set me free from the confines of depression, PTSD, panic disorder, and head injury ramifications. Having no symptoms is awesome, don't get me wrong, but what we all really want is to love our life. Coping is amazing, but no longer needing to cope is true freedom. If these tools can take me from knocking on death's door, begging for mercy, to me writing this book in a café on the beach off the southern tip of Mexico with my powerful, creative wife and three extraordinarily resilient, wise, and healthy children (who are all enjoying a family system built on a foundation of "togetherness," love, trust, connection, and joy, aka 'secure attachment'), then consider: what could this path do for you and your family?

Some housekeeping before we begin:

To maintain client confidentiality, all names involved in the personal success stories in this book (other than those about myself and my family) have been changed.

Some chapters that are a little on the heady side have recaps at the end. Lighter chapters do not. This is deliberate. (I let you know in case you find yourself looking for a recap that isn't there!)

I am giving away tons of free resources that are referenced throughout this book. For your convenience, they are all housed in one place, at alltogether.academy/joy-bucket-tools, and will be listed on the site in the order in which they are presented in this book. You don't need to sign up for the link each time you come across a resource that piques your interest: when you sign up once, you are granted access to all the resources mentioned. I understand that some people like to keep a feeling of "flow" in their reading and therefore prefer not to go and access tools mid-read, but still, the best way to get the experiential wisdom of this book (and not just the mere knowledge it contains) is to use the tools and supplementary info in the online course I am giving you (alltogether.academy/joy-bucket-tools) along the way.

Ready? Let's dive in.

PART I
INTRODUCTION & ORIENTATION

1
WHO IS THIS BOOK FOR?

THERE IS SO MUCH NOISE IN the health and happiness marketplace these days. There's tons of great stuff in among that noise, and even more charlatan snake oil. I, for one, aim to provide you with tried-and-true maps, tools, and instructions that will allow you to discover the joy, openness, love, kindness, and awareness (JOLKA) that is characteristic of your essential self.[5] This book, if "worked," will be transformative if you fall into any of the following categories:

1. You know that you want to be truly happy and radiantly healthy (which is possible even if you have an illness, by the way) and you know that you are not yet, or you are dipping in and out of this state.

2. You are not consciously aware of your desire to be truly happy and radiantly healthy, but you do know that you are not truly happy and radiantly healthy, and that you are sick and tired of feeling sick and tired.

3. In addition to (2), you know that you are sick and tired of all the *reasons why* you believe you are sick and tired—the things that make your life "stressful" or "unhappy." You might also feel ready to be happy even though, aside from, or especially because of those reasons.

4. You fall into all these categories, and you consciously believe true happiness and radiant health to be possible, but you haven't yet found the sweet sauce. Or perhaps—and this is a big one—you

---

[5] It is ideal to embody JOLKA from a space of gratitude, presence, and surrender (your GPS). Put together, the JOLKA-GPS represents "true north." It will always let you know whether you are heading in the right direction.

believe true happiness and radiant health to be possible for others, but not for you, for various reasons.

5. You fall into categories (1) or (2), and you (consciously or unconsciously) don't believe true happiness and radiant health to be possible at all, for anyone, for various reasons.

If you are in category (5), our work together will be a little more challenging. Then again, maybe I have already excited you a touch by now—hopefully enough for you to hang in there and discover how understandable it is (from a neurochemical perspective) that you have come to these conclusions.

Regardless of which category you fall into, one of the most surprising things I've realized through my work is that almost everyone is running around like a chicken with its head cut off. And let me tell you, it's not necessarily just the people we would typically associate with suffering who are living this way. Time and time again, I have been blown away by the ubiquity of "survival mode" (SM).

I've worked with lawyers, doctors, bankers, people with advanced degrees, and people who make a lot of money—people who are at the very top of their game and are of the most impressive pedigree—and their inner lives are a mess. I've worked with soldiers, first responders, and trauma surgeons—truly heroic and courageous folks—who are crippled by fear, their relationships in turmoil. Similarly, I've worked with the homeless and helpless, the severely mentally ill, and people with the most extreme trauma one could imagine, and they, through our work together, have been able to "turn off their alarm switch," get into "thriving mode" (TM), completely eliminate symptoms, undermine diagnoses, leave medications behind (which is not a goal of mine in itself, as I find some medications personally to be very useful), and lead lives of contribution and satisfaction.

Maybe you, too, can experience lifelessness, hopelessness, helplessness, and severe depression, and still turn all of it around into a life of supreme peace centered on the great joy of being. Maybe—just maybe—there is a greater truth available to you. You'll only find out if you come along for the ride and do the work to achieve it ALL: Awareness Loving Life.

If you recognize yourself in any of the pictures I've painted so far, this book could be a gamechanger for you. One thing is for sure: this book is not something that you should just read cover to cover and then let collect dust on your bookshelf. It is a "work" book. You *must* use the tools if you want to get the results. Again, all of these can be accessed at alltogether.academy/joy-bucket-tools. This toolshed will be referenced many times in this book.

How to Find Joy
Even If You Have a Hole in Your Bucket

This book has been organized to teach you the tools and processes that will allow you to create the life you value and choose to live, even though, aside from, and especially because of the tough stuff. If you do the homework, you will go from "knowing" to "doing" to "becoming," and from "becoming" to "being," the joy, openness, love, kindness, awareness, gratitude, presence, and surrender (the JOLKA-GPS) you value and choose to embrace.

This is also a book about my journey; about a normal person experiencing both normal and extraordinary challenges and, through them, learning how to tap the uncommon potential that is common in us ALL.

All of us can rise above what is ordinary and do what is both entirely natural and extraordinary: use our state of being to thrive and heal. This is what it is ALL (Awareness Loving Life) about.

Every step of the way in this book, I really want to have your active participation, which starts with your permission. In my work with clients, this is a really big deal to me. I actually have a policy: I don't solicit, convince, "close the deal," or "market" in a typical sense. Well, at least not anymore. I used to do that stuff because I was taught by business coaches that it is what one "must" do to "succeed," but it made me sick (literally), so now, I only work with people if they've met two criteria:

They've asked me to work with them.

They're already trying, earnestly, to solve the problems they are seeking my help for, and they understand that my job is to help them get better at helping themselves.

In a certain way, by cracking open this book and reading it, you are "asking" me for help and giving me permission to share my ideas with you. But, from time to time, I'd like to make this consent more explicit. So, before we go further: are you okay with me laying down some foundational pieces that will enable the tools I am going to give you to work better? Do you mind if I tell you a bit more about my journey so that you can understand the perspective I am, and this book's content is, coming from? Does that sound good?

Thank you. Phew. I already feel better. It feels really good to give, and I am happy to be of service whenever possible. Still, no one likes to be manipulated into receiving something akin to "advice" when they are not asking for it. *No me gusta.*

Now, in case you are wondering why I am the guy to lead you through this journey, I will get into that right after a brief exercise, coming up next.

2
WHAT WE REALLY WANT

I T'S TIME WE PUT FIRST THINGS first.

Ask yourself, "What do I want?"

Don't overthink it. Just go with your instinctive answer. This can be something obvious, like, "I want more money," or "I want to be healthier," or "I want a new job."

Got something? Good. Now ask, "Why? Why do I want that?" No matter what comes up, ask, "And why do I want that?" If it feels good, keep asking, "And why that?"

It won't take long before you get to a state of being, or a sentiment expressing your core values. This is because at the bottom of all our wants is an authentic desire to feel good. We want *the state* of "happiness," or "joy," or "love." If we want money, it's because we want to feel free, or maybe feel safe. If we want a new job, it may be because we want to feel inspired. If we want a romantic partner, it's likely because we want to feel loved. If we want to heal, it could be because we want to feel energized. If we want to go on a vacation, we may want to feel excited.

This book, in a nutshell, is about putting the ends—what we truly want—*first*.

Safety, Love, Connection, Joy, Authenticity, Creativity, Freedom.

To sum up these values, I will call this "happiness." You can call it what you will. Whatever we call it, why is it "the *only* skill that matters most"? Because it's the only one that uplifts everything else. When you are happy you are a better mother, son, friend, partner, husband, colleague, boss, artist, provider, athlete, lover, and so on. When you are happy, your body heals faster, you sleep better, you get sick less often, you live longer, you make better decisions, your memory improves, food tastes better, you are inspired, you can't wait to get out of bed for a new day, and you easily and automatically contribute to the greater good.

Happiness is the bottom line. And it's time to raise the bar, for the benefit of yourself, others and ALL.

No one ever needs to, or can, have it ALL (Awareness Loving Life)— alone. Since we are going on this journey together, in the next chapter, I will catch you up to speed on how I got here, equipped with the maps, tools, and instructions I am going to share with you in this book and beyond. Together, we thrive.

3
A LITTLE BIT OF BACKGROUND

OVER THE LAST FEW DECADES, I'VE been founding and developing All Together Academy (ATA), albeit under different names and auspices. ATA is a training ground for ALL (Awareness Loving Life). There, we explore, discover, learn, grow, and create under the motto "Together, we thrive."

ATA's maps, tools, and instructions fall into three categories of human being:

- I AM: *Joyful Excellence by Design*. Have it ALL (Awareness Loving Life). This foundational level of work includes the ATA work of EATT, Embodied Aliveness Trauma Transformation.
- WE ARE: *The Relating Renaissance*. Create the chemistry.
- ALL IS: *Energy of Mind: Secular Spiritual Work for Practical People*.

This book (the IAM, and the first category) is where we will explore, discover, learn, grow, and create the Creative-IAM (C-IAM) and the Neurochemical Roadmap to the Future You Value and Choose (NRF) while learning to EATT (Embodied Aliveness Trauma Transformation) difficult experiences, so we can use their energy as fuel for excellence. The C-IAM is the foundation for a healthy and happy "WE ARE" and an expansive and grounded expression of "ALL IS." Due to my unique background, training and passion of pursuing authentic spiritual practice for 25 years and under expert guidance, ATA work also serves as a foundation for people who want to pursue a spiritual path without the (common) unnecessary obstacles that come from lack of preparation for integrating higher forces, and without getting stuck in the forest of fantasy work that is propagated in the New Age or the typical therapeutic cultural trance.

But how did this "all" come to be? Obviously, there is tons more detail than could be shared here, but here is a snapshot.

❖ 1983—On my mom's lap at age 5—I had a spiritual experience of sorts where it felt like I experienced the entire world's suffering all at once. It totally overwhelmed me and I decided then and there, "I never want to feel again."

❖ 2000- Deep, dark depression—It turns out we can make impactful decisions even when we are little and that "not feeling ever again" is not a great strategy. When we numb the bad stuff, we numb the good stuff too, and we can get to a point where we aren't sure if life is worth living.

❖ 2001—Major Awakening—The darkest hour comes right before dawn as I came home to who I really am, I realized that the purpose of life is loving, and I better get good at it!

❖ 2001—WTF!—I thought I had my big breakthrough and the tough stuff was over, but a near death ski accident resulting in a traumatic brain injury and internal damages that would wreak havoc for the next 24 years before being surgically repaired, were on my curriculum. A collapsed lung prevented me from flying home and as I got to know the ski town near Sun Valley in Idaho, I said to myself, "One day, I am going to be a therapist living in a ski town, I will have a wood burning stove, and live somewhere I can go pee outside my front door!" (I know it's weird but...)

❖ 2003—Two roads diverged in a wood—Exhibiting all the symptoms (and the typical age) of schizophrenia onset—instead of walking into a psychiatrists office and likely being medicated for life, I walked into a yoga studio where I met my wife and a practical path forward to heal myself and thrive (with lots of help!). I am grateful for it ALL.

❖ 2011—2 more bad concussions—Working manual labor to pay my way through grad school, I got smacked—hard—twice in 3 weeks. Scrambled brains. Tons of pressure. Little kids. Grad school. No money. Tiny apartment with fleas. Panic attacks. Depression. Earthquakes in the Bay Area... Get us out of here!!!

❖ 2016—Mentorship... One day after working as a therapist, peeing outside my front door facing a big, beautiful mountain, looking back in the window of our home to see my wife and kids warm around the wood-burning stove, I realized, "Holy shit! That statement I made in Sun Valley after the ski crash 15 years ago, its happened!" In Taos, NM, I rediscovered nature, raised my family in beauty, and kindled a relationship with a mentor—a true GEM— that would change everything... for good. With the JOLKA-GPS installed, I would always be able to find my way home. (To hear this wild and amazing story first hand, check out my Boyling Point podcast episode: https://www.alltogether.academy/podcasts/the-boyling-point, "What's On Fire About the Law of Attraction", not to be confused with my Blog article, "What's Bull&sh&! About the Law of Attraction" at https://www.alltogether.academy/blog.

❖ 2020—Crisis is the opportunity—After a major rupture with my wife, we "did the work, together" that not only got us back to better than ever, but also launched "The Relating Renaissance" and the "We Are" aspect of the ALL Together Academy trilogy. Now with the I AM and WE ARE intact, the "ALL IS" is still missing.

❖ 2022—Healing, Thriving, ATA is whole—Reeling from symptoms that at times had me in bed for weeks, I discover—not in theory—but through my direct experience that Joy, Openness, Love, Kindness, Awareness, Gratitude, Presence, and Surrender (the JOLKA-GPS) come from within and are 100% independent and free from circumstances and conditions, and can be accessed anytime, anyplace, regardless of what's going on inside or outside. This enables me to have the confidence to round out the 3rd aspect of the ATA pathways, Energy of Mind: Secular Spiritual Work for Practical People. I AM, WE ARE, ALL IS.

❖ 2024—Inner healing gives way to outer healing—And by inner, I mean the aspect of ourselves that can be in a state of Joy even if we are sick or in pain, and by outer, I mean my body. A Eureka moment in meditation results in a stabbing pain in my abdomen that prompts a CT scan revealing a 6-inch hole in my paralyzed diaphragm, a nearly collapsed lung, and my liver, gall bladder and intestines stuck in the hole and up near my collar bone! Through the grace and good fortune of one of the best surgeons and surgical teams in the world, my body is now able to keep up with my mind and Spirit.

I do not share this snapshot of my journey so far so that you can compare my journey or progress to yours. The point is not to compare and compete. I've had it harder than many, and I've also had it easier than many. Which side of the road you fall on relative to me is irrelevant. Comparison leads to suffering, and inspiration leads to motivation. My point in sharing this insight into my background is, I want to show you that I've done more than just study this stuff. I've lived it, and I still live it. I am currently writing these words with a stabbing pain in my side after the major surgery you read about in the Author's Note. I know how easy it is to give in and get depressed when you're facing chronic illness and living in constant pain, and I also know it is possible to be totally at peace and in a state of supreme joy *while* dealing with that pain and feeling it fully.

I practice what I teach. Through my example, I hope you also become inspired to better your best. My job is to help you, help yourself.

Another hugely important reason why you shouldn't compare my journey to yours is that many ATA clients get positive results much more quickly and easily than I did when I was living with a hole in my diaphragm and half a lung. That's the way it works: we rise on the shoulders of those who came before us. This means you can better your best thanks to what I've learned from my worst.

If you are curious, here are some of my credentials, beyond the results I've had in my personal life:

- I am a licensed marriage and family therapist (LMFT).
- I am certified in dialectical behavioral therapy (C-DBT), thought to be honest I don't know if I will keep up the racket of continuing to pay the company to maintain that certification. You all are probably as tired as I am of all the grifts out there!
- I have a Heartmath Clinical Certification for Stress, Anxiety and Self-Regulation.
- I am trained in Eriksonian Clinical Hypnosis.
- I have master's degrees in both clinical and transpersonal psychology.
- I am an authorized Inner Health Coalition/Dr. Joe Dispenza Healthcare Practitioner.
- I am certified in addictions specialties, specializing in trauma.
- I am a facilitator of advanced studies in yoga, breathwork, meditation, non-sleep deep rest, and dharma psychology.
- I hold special interests in emotional freedom technique (EFT), neurolinguistic programming (NLP), somatic trauma therapy, cognitive behavioral therapy (CBT), dialectical behavioral therapy (DBT), solution focused therapy, positive psychology, and acceptance and commitment therapy (ACT).
- I love public speaking and welcome invitations to be on your podcast or speak at your events.
- I am the founder of All Together Academy and the lead facilitator of *The Joyful Excellence Mastermind (JEM)*, *The Relating Renaissance*, and *Energy of Mind: Secular Spiritual Work for Practical People*. *Program names are subject to change, but I will always be contributing creatively to the greater good in one way or another.

Now that's out of the way, do you mind if I now tell you why I am so excited? I am excited because we are revolutionizing "mental health" with a practical path. This path not only leads to freedom from suffering and relief from symptoms, but also profound love, trust, joy, and connection. In other words, this work presents not only a means to heal, but also a foundation and bridge to the upper echelon of Maslow's hierarchy of needs (self-actualization) in a way that prepares us to safely and successfully progress into the spiritual work of "going beyond" and self-transcendence.

Mental health is the most pressing pandemic of our time, and we experience ALL (including our mental health) through our state of being. So, regardless of whether you have a mental health diagnosis or are just one of the countless people looking for love in all the wrong places and coming up short on finally feeling happy (despite having a pretty awesome life), your woes (for our practical intents and purposes) boil down to the state of your nervous system.

I hope I can communicate the potency of this realization. Your state of being permeates, creates, and *is* everything, to *you*. This means that until you touch, develop, establish, and maintain your C-IAM and travel along your NRF, you will always be blown over by circumstance, lost and without a sense of direction, meaning, or purpose. More importantly, all attempts you make to fix, understand, or patch up your life will fall short. Even "success" won't ever bring true happiness. Case in point: your life up until now.

If you look around, for all the very important progress we have made in making "mental health" a more accessible, less stigmatized topic, it is clear that our approach is not working. People are getting more overwhelmed, not less. Kids are getting less resilient, not more.

I aim to revolutionize mental health by sharing a path that is:

1. Based on creating the conditions for thriving that allow for healing to happen naturally, which works better than fixing problems (and inadvertently exacerbating them).
2. Body-based versus stuck in the head.
3. Linked to optimal performance. Mental Health *is* optimal performance and must be defined not merely by the absence of negative symptoms but by the Embodied Aliveness of joy, love, connection, creativity, skill expression, and contribution to the greater good that we all truly desire and benefit from.
4. We-Centric vs Me-Centric. There is no personal happiness disconnected from expressing our core values for the benefit of not only ourselves, but others, and ALL. This means we must be aware

of, but not dominated by, injustice, and realize that taking care of one another, and the world we share, is *self-care*.

5. Circumstance independent. The consumerist cultural trance inculcates us all with the unconscious assumption that we will finally "get" happiness once outer conditions are "just right." By cultivating the only skill that matters most and discovering "happiness" that is free from conditions and circumstances, we are then able to more skillfully and effectively navigate the outer conditions of our lives.

6. Practical, methodical, easy, natural, holistic, kind, gritty and accessible to ALL.

Why just cope with suffering when you can end it? Along the way, coping is great, but I am only interested in models of growth that are grounded in the possibility of total freedom and unconditional happiness. That is what I want for myself, that is what I want for you. Therefore, that is what you will find in these pages.

Overcoming

A note about the concept of "overcoming":

One of my best friends helped me edit this book, and he cautioned me that I should be careful to not come off as unrelatable by talking too much about "overcoming," versus being a "work in progress." I appreciated his feedback, and I think he would agree that these concepts need not be mutually exclusive. It is important to know that it's possible to both completely overcome and outgrow just about anything, *while* always viewing life as a work of art that's constantly in progress. To be clear, though, when I talk about "overcoming," I don't mean to sound arrogant or holier than thou. I am, in so many ways, a work in progress (and always will be). Still, it's important for you to know that with what you will be introduced to here (especially in Part III), you will be able to accomplish the kind of change that means you no longer have the problems you were facing previously. I am presenting a system of opportunity, the very intention and goal of which is to not only get you to a place where you can cope well with your challenges, but also (more importantly) to get you to a place where you no longer *need* to cope (because you have completely outgrown your old issues to a point where they have become irrelevant). This doesn't mean you won't face new challenges—there will always be new challenges, forever—but it does mean that in this relative world, your outer life circumstances (i.e., your physical health, career, and relationships) may (and often will) consistently become easier, smoother, "happier," freer, and more characterized by flow, play, and beauty.

I always tell my therapy clients that my job is to work myself out of a job. I mean that. It's great to have coping skills, but like I've said, it's even better to completely outgrow the problem so that it's no longer there for you to cope with.

The tools you will learn from this book are practical. They work, if you work them. You are the key ingredient. While this book is filled with many workable maps, tools, and instructions for how to use the tools, you are both the worker and what is "worked." (FYI: "Work" is "deliberate dedicated action that produces a result." "Deliberate" means "after a pause," and "dedicated" is a "choice made with sacred intention" to produce the intended result you value and choose to produce. A "choice" is a "free selection after a pause." The *pause* is a big deal, and you are going to learn why and more importantly how).

Throughout this book, you will also learn that your consciousness is always producing results. The quality of those results depends on your state of being and how it interacts with "all." Your freedom, health, happiness, and entire experience of life depends on your capacity to be in the driver's seat of your life. You must operate from your C-IAM so that you can pick and choose the NRF ingredients that will naturally bring about the best possible outcomes for you, others, and everything.

Think of your consciousness as a kitchen with unlimited ingredients and think of the present moment as the stew that naturally results from the combination of ingredients that have been cooking your whole life, up until now. In this book, you will learn that you are the master chef—the C-IAM—and that even if you've been living on a diet of crap circumstances for a long time, you can start adding new ingredients right away (and life will immediately start tasting better and better for it).

You can feel better today, easily, without any gimmicks, in a totally sustainable way that makes perfect sense.

Consciousness is both creative and unbiased. It produces whatever ingredients our state of being focuses on most. Indeed, in this book, you will repeatedly learn that laws of nature often operate on a "for better or worse" basis, and that it is up to us to choose how we use our experiences so that these laws work for (not against) our interests. One of these laws is, "What you focus on grows," again, for better or worse.

As my mom used to say to me when I was growing up, "You can't make chicken soup out of chicken shit." If the quality of your mind is shitty, your life will taste like crap. What you focus on, you become. Thank goodness there are practical maps, tools, and instructions that will allow us to become the head chef in a kitchen of unlimited ingredients!

In this book, I welcome you to my kitchen, where I cook with only the very best ingredients and treat them with loving care. These are recipes I, too, have been privileged enough to experiment with, discovering their magic, after learning them from my ancestors and mentors, the very best chefs of all time.

Mangia!

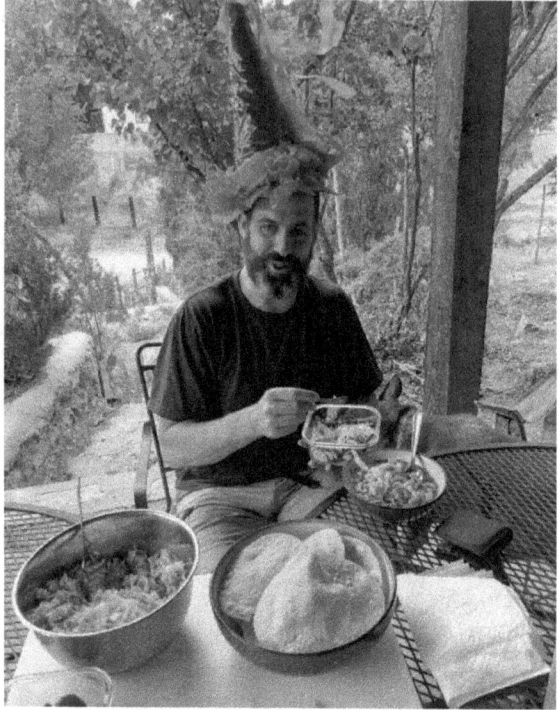

Trauma, Influence, and Personal Responsibility: A Disclaimer

Before we proceed further, please allow me to give a brief disclaimer about trauma and the influences in our lives that are beyond our control.

While we in the ATA training ground write about, speak about, and regularly use ideas and tools that can dramatically improve physical, mental, and emotional health (even if, aside from, and especially because bad stuff happens), we also understand and promote a trauma sensitive approach. What I mean by this is, we understand that there are forces and influences in people's lives that are beyond their control that can make it significantly harder for them to take matters into their own hands and improve their inner and outer conditions. Some of these influences include things like accidents, trauma, perpetration, racism, cultural factors, socioeconomics, gender norms, and sexual orientation (though this is not an exhaustive list). While we teach and encourage each other to "do the work" so we can experience PTG (posttraumatic growth), we in no way promote victim blaming, victim shaming, gaslighting, denial, or condoning of wrongdoing.

Then again, we are all imperfect beings, and I (Michael Boyle), as the founder of ATA, am well aware that I carry unconscious biases and assumptions, make mistakes, project my perceptual limitations onto others and the world, and sometimes assume I am right when I am not (or when there are also other ways to be right). So, I ask for your advanced forgiveness and maybe even the benefit of doubt, whenever relevant.

This is not to say I am not willing and ready to apologize specifically when I am in the wrong. I welcome feedback that is given in the interest of us all growing together into better, kinder, more open-hearted, and more effective stewards of ALL (Awareness Loving Life). Because after all, together, we thrive.

Another disclaimer about personal responsibility: during any time you spend implementing any of the work you are learning at All Together Academy, through this book, or in your work with me (Michael Boyle), you are responsible for your physical, mental, and emotional safety, for getting in touch with local, accessible licensed healthcare providers (if necessary), and for being aware of how to contact emergency services (if needed). Nothing we do at ATA, on the ATA website, in conjunction with Michael Boyle, or in any related books, pages, videos, PDFs, or audio clips is a replacement for professional medical or mental health care. Even though I am a licensed marriage and family therapist in New Mexico and Massachusetts, USA, ATA's work does not constitute formal psychotherapy. What you can experience here falls under the rubric of education, and you are always empowered to do or not do, to read or not read, to watch or not watch, to listen or not listen, to stop or start, or to continue or discontinue according to your needs, desires, and goals, and under the guidance of your local professional healthcare providers.

Go it? Cool. Let's get into it.

4
THE SACRED CHALLENGE

I AM EXCITED—REALLY EXCITED—THAT you're here, because we have an opportunity to make a difference that makes a difference, for ourselves, others, and ALL. Before I get too far ahead of myself, though, let's get back to why we are here now.

The ethos of this book and "the work" of All Together Academy is: if you are waiting...

- To feel better,
- For some future circumstances to take place,
- To believe in the truth of what I am going to share with you before you start implementing it,
- For proof that what I am going to share with you will work before you start implementing it,
- Or for you to "feel like" implementing the stuff I teach,

...then you will be waiting forever. The time to start feeling better is now, always and forever. So, together, let's:

1. Sit up.
2. Get focused.
3. Take a huge breath in.
4. Let the breath out.

Now that I have your attention, let's do that again. (If you actually do this, you will actually feel better, right now, easily, in a totally sustainable way that makes perfect sense.) Ready?

1. Breathe all the way out.
2. Take a big inhale.
3. Hold it in.
4. Take in a little more air.

5. Let it all out with a sigh.
6. Repeat two more times.

Did you do it? Or did you just read it and think about it? I bet even reading that moved the needle a smidge for you, but the difference that makes the difference—the difference that gets the ball rolling—lies in the doing; in rolling from "knowing" to "doing" to "becoming" to "being". Remember, you can feel better, today, easily, without any gimmicks, in a totally sustainable way that makes perfect sense, but *only if you do the work*. So, if you didn't do it, do it now. As my daughter says, "Ready, settie, go!"

Now that you are feeling better, let's dive further into this book, so I can show you how you can keep feeling better easily, in a totally sustainable way that makes perfect sense. Remember, along the way, you will find tons of free resources at alltogether.academy/joy-bucket-tools. From there, you can also access an incredible community full of others like you who are doing the work, as well as regular live classes offered by yours truly. What's more, if you read this entire book, you'll also find a discount code for twenty percent off our 30-Day Reset From Surviving to Thriving program, an independent online journey, which is a prerequisite for joining "JEM" (Joyful Excellence Mastermind) and/or private coaching with me.

The Sacred Challenge

Before you start this journey, we need to establish whether you are currently dealing with a sacred challenge. A sacred challenge can be defined as inner or outer circumstances that you sincerely feel you can't handle. The curriculum of every single life includes at least one (but usually many) sacred challenges, and these challenges are often linked together, like "levels" in a video game.

They are "sacred" because they are uniquely suited to you, in that when you overcome them, you receive the exact powers and gifts that you will need if you are to reach your highest and most beneficial potential. By working through the sacred challenge you are facing, you end up discovering a medicine, tool, secret, or key that you will need to unlock a door that contains a medicine, tool, secret, or key that you will need at another level after that.

It is imperative that you face your sacred challenges and unlock their (i.e., your) potential, so you can not only maximize the quality of your life now, but also the quality of your future.

How to Find Joy
Even If You Have a Hole in Your Bucket

These moments in life are tough! Like, legitimately hard. Hard enough that we sincerely think and feel, "I can't handle this!"

In some spiritual traditions, these challenges are considered to be a supremely compassionate gift from the mother goddess. The logic here is that the mother goddess cares so deeply about us that only she could be merciful and steadfast enough to send them our way. After all, these lessons can be so challenging that our parents likely couldn't even stomach giving us such medicine, no matter how beneficial its effects may be. Only life itself (or the mother goddess) can bring us to the precipice we must be brought to if we are to learn how to fly without wings.

Suffice it to say, this is "not every kid gets a medal" territory. Sacred challenges are challenging enough that plenty of people do not overcome them at all, and such people ultimately go to their deathbeds feeling unfulfilled, scared, and regretful. Such people fail to bring to life the unique gifts and powers that can only be discovered once they emerge, victoriously, from their sacred challenge(s).

How will these challenges show up in your life? In exactly the way you think you can't handle. How will you know you are up against a sacred challenge? You will sincerely think and feel, "I can't handle this!" and you will likely try and fail to overcome it many times before you ultimately succeed.

The content of this book outlines the gifts I have earned through overcoming my own sacred challenges. When you unleash the awesome potential that is locked inside your sacred challenges, it's not just you who benefits; it's everyone you know, and, in direct and indirect ways, all of us.

One of my mentor's teachers and my son's namesake, Rudi, lived by and taught "the rules of the game." The second rule of the game is, "If we are working, we cannot attract more than we can handle." What we face in the present moment may appear to be and often feels like more than we can handle, because it is more than we *could* have handled previously. We must work to grow into the person who can not only handle it, but also transcend it and leave it behind (for new challenges and opportunities await). If we are not growing and if we are not facing our sacred challenges, then the mother goddess (according to some belief systems) is so compassionate that she will increase the pain in our lives to urge us to wake up.

I'm guessing you've noticed this. When you don't learn your lesson, the pattern shows up again, only bigger and "badder." This feels harsh and unappealing to many, especially those who go to their deathbeds defeated. Don't be one of them! Some never realize that pain in life is inevitable but suffering is optional. While we may be physically battered and bruised, we can still master our life's curriculum and discover mental, emotional, and spiritual freedom in the process. And sacred challenges push us toward just that: psychospiritual freedom that is independent from conditions and circumstances.

No one gets a free pass from pain, tragedy, trauma, grief, or loss, and it is absolutely possible (and perhaps very much the universal purpose of each of our lives) for each and every one of us to reach our most awesome potential precisely through our sacred challenges. When we do overcome them, it is natural for us to achieve states of being that unleash wisdom, joy, and creativity for the greatest possible benefits to ourselves, others, and ALL.

This may feel confusing for now. Please keep an open mind.

What I am getting at is, freedom from suffering is not some pot of gold at the end of a rainbow. It is not "heaven" at the end of a life of hardship. It doesn't happen when everything works out the way we hope it will. Freedom from suffering is ever-now. It requires ongoing cultivation, and even though this may seem unfair, sacred challenges will keep coming, even when you are free from suffering and living a life characterized by joy and love. As the saying goes (this time in reverse), suffering is optional, but pain is inevitable. In fact, a sacred challenge will often reappear in the form of many different "levels" in your life. As I said, the challenge you overcome at level three will sometimes give you the key you'll need to enter the labyrinth at level eight, where you discover the sword you'll need to battle the beast at level eleven.

What's more, "the thing" you need—whether the key or sword—is often hiding under the rock you are trying your hardest to avoid. It is also often the case that your fear of "the thing" is so much worse than "the thing" itself. You are so afraid to turn over the rock that you torture yourself worrying about what's under there, when in actuality, it is a benevolent gift that will enable you to move forward on your journey.

When you look at life this way, it becomes clear that it is like a game— the greatest game of ALL—and in this game, specific obstacles have been placed on your path for your benefit. If you played a video game that had no obstacles, you would think it was so boring that you would never play again. Similarly, challenges are opportunities, and it is by coming up against them and making mistakes time and again that you grow the coordination, muscle, skill, and wisdom you need to finally advance to the next level.

If you are up against a sacred challenge right now, the first mistake you can make is not realizing you are in a fight for your life. One of the slogans in our family life is, "Slay the beast and do what you like the least (first)." Choose what is easy and familiar now, and your life will get harder. Choose what is harder and new now, and life will get easier over time. Sharpen your sword and use your tools like your life depends on it, because it does.

5
THE BRAIN WE ARE ALL BORN WITH

WHAT I AM GOING TO SHARE with you in the following pages may seem complex and challenging to understand, which is in large part because it is unique. What you will find, though, is that it is also quite practical and that it makes perfect sense. That realization, however, might not come until you get past the initial "I've never thought of it that way before" experience that sometimes makes us all feel a bit confused.

Later in this book, I will go into great detail about what I'm calling the "survival mode" (SM) and "thriving mode" (TM) of your nervous system and being. These are the filters for everything you will ever experience and are therefore the make-or-break elements of your life. For now, I would like to ask you a question I am known to ask quite a lot as part of my ongoing research in the laboratory of human experience: how many people do you perceive to be truly happy? How many people do you know who really "have it together" and are undoubtedly thriving most of the time (which is not to say they, or their lives, are perfect)?

I've asked this question a lot, and I've never had anyone tell me they know more than a handful. The vast majority say, "Less than three," and many say, "I don't know *anyone* I would put in that category." Does this not seem strange to you? It does to me. We all know a lot of people, so if most of the people we know are "stressed out" in some way or another, then it's fair to say that most people are not really thriving. Clearly, something about the way we are collectively approaching life isn't working! After all, we all desire happiness, do we not? Even if we have a different word for "it" than "happy," we all want "it," because somewhere in the depths of our being, we know "it" is possible. Yet here we are, pooped and confused, and wondering where our ship has sailed to. How did we get to this point? Why do we all have aching bodies, aching hearts, worried minds, and seemingly permanent exhaustion?

Simply, because we were designed this way. In a weird but totally sensible twist of fate, our brains (which were built to prioritize survival) are hardwired to focus on and exaggerate pain and suffering. Our survival mode is the default, and this default mode has a built in "negativity bias."

Just like Robin Williams told Will Hunting, this is not your fault. At the same time, though, if you want a better quality of life, it is your responsibility. If you want to make the most of your brain and body in this lifetime, you need to take deliberate, dedicated action. This will not happen by itself, nor will the happiness you seek ever come from all the "things" you are doing that you think will "make" you happy. Only you can *discover* and *cultivate* happiness.

You may have heard the ol' "happiness comes from the inside" adage and dismissed it as impractical—maybe even unrealistic—and certainly unactionable. It certainly seems a heck of a lot like happiness comes from getting most of the stuff you want and not getting most of the stuff you don't. But it turns out this is a bogus lie. Even if you are on the proverbial beach in Hawaii, you will still find something to feel frustrated, anxious, depressed, or overwhelmed about if your brain is in survival mode. Which makes sense, right? From an evolutionary perspective, we are designed to assume the stick is a snake to err to the side of safety and to be dissatisfied enough that we keep seeking greener pastures. But there is a higher-potential evolutionary option at our disposal. We can choose to stop seeking happiness outside of ourselves—to stop looking for love in all the wrong places, only to find disappointment—and to *actually find what we are looking for*, not so much in what we *get* from life as in what we *give* to it.

While I may not be "enlightened" (whatever the heck that means), I do aim to be one of the few people who are truly happy—who truly "have it together"—and that means, in part, that I want others to be truly happy. Wishing for others to thrive and being willing to contribute to that greater good is an intrinsic part of our "thriving mode" as humans. I didn't make up the motto "Together, we thrive" for no reason. We are in this together. We are literally linked. We have evolved, neurochemically, to be rewarded (with happiness) when we advance not only ourselves, but also the tribe. Thriving is contagious. However, it's easier and more automatic to catch a case of the upsets (again, for evolutionary reasons that make perfect sense). Allow me to illustrate:

Imagine a herd of elk, five hundred strong, spanning a valley, maybe in an area the size of a few football fields. While perusing the perimeter of the valley, a single elk notices a rustle in the bushes. The rustle may have been the wind... or it may have been a wolf. Either way, the elk isn't sticking around to find out!

What happens next is magic: the whole herd takes off at once!

This didn't happen through one elk communicating with another, and another, and another. That would take way too long and would likely result in the wolf (if there is one) having baby elk for dinner. Instead, there is a part of the mammalian brain that communicates nearly instantly whether it is "safe to approach" or "time to run," and it always errs on the side of "time to run." Just like when the smoke detector in your kitchen goes off when you are cooking a nice dinner that has only seared a little too much, alarms are meant to go off if there *might be* a fire, not just when they are *one hundred percent sure there is* a fire.

You and I have this same brain structure that elks do: our "alarm system" is designed to be tripped by the tiniest *possibility* of a problem. We are alarmed and primed to look for and to internalize reasons to fight, run away, or hide from everyone and everything. Not only that, but we also send off the signal that we are not safe to approach (and then wonder why we feel so lonely and misunderstood). Because of the "herd" part of your brain, the state of your nervous system is, for better or worse, contagious, and it spreads faster than any disease. The state of your nervous system communicates far more potently than any words could, instantaneously. We are all linked in an interconnected web of mutual influence.

Most people have no idea that they were born with a brain that was primed to be unhappy—and I'm not only talking about those who are prone to depression, anxiety, and whatnot (no judgment there, by the way; that's my history). If we are in "survival mode" (which many of us are, most of the time), we default to the evolutionary priority: survival now, at all costs, so that the species as a whole can live another day to procreate tomorrow.

The cost of you constantly being in survival mode includes your brains not being able to access:

- Happiness.
- Intimacy.
- Love.
- Joy.
- Company (survival mode makes us naturally selfish).
- Creativity.
- Spirituality.
- Healing.
- Positive dreams for a better future.
- Longevity (we literally shorten our lifespans when we are constantly in survival mode).

I repeat: the default mode of our evolutionary being does not give a rat's ass about us being happy, or falling in love, or writing a poem, or listening to a symphony. Its only priority is survival, so that we can procreate (love not required). Survival mode, even when only triggered by *perceived* threats or *memory-based* emotions (not actual, present- moment dangers), shunts resources away from everything we actually want, demands that we narrow our focus on the (perceived) threat, inaccurately perceives sticks as snakes, wreaks havoc on our long-term health and happiness, and has us treating ourselves, our loved ones, and everyone else, for that matter, as competitors and predators in a stance of "attack or defend."

I won't bore you by pontificating too much more here, but if you catch me in a coffee shop sometime, I will explain to you how this very mechanism is why all the world's violence has spiraled out of control. Survival mode's biological overreaction to anything and everything that is remotely triggering (and the fact that we mistake the intensity of our feelings for "truth") is literally the source of all personal and collective suffering. It's also what's making you anxious or depressed, compelling you to eat too much junk food, drink too much alcohol, think adult gummies are a suitable strategy for coping with life, giving you ADHD, boosting your blood pressure, tearing up your love life, making you desperate for likes on social media, and getting you to yell at your kids.

6

THE PATH FORWARD

Y OU PROBABLY DIDN'T KNOW BEFORE PICKING up this book that there are maps, tools, and instructions (which I am going to give to you) that you can use to train your brain to shift out of the default survival mode and into thriving mode. Just as there are normal, natural mechanisms at play in your life that are probably making you stressed, tired, and largely dissatisfied (which you will learn more about later), there is also untapped human potential in you that can be awakened. I do need to make it clear, however, that if this were easy and everyone you are watching on YouTube or following on Instagram actually knew how to *do it*, you'd know more people who are happy than the very few you can probably think of. So, I won't make you false promises or claims. You can find plenty of those on your Instagram feed. I am not selling snake oil, and I am not perfect. What I can promise you is this: I probably do the work and practice what I teach more than anyone you know. What is contained in these pages has been learned not only through professional training, but also personal experience. I can therefore promise that this work works, *if* (and only if) *you work it*.

I did not invent all the maps, tools, and instructions I will share with you here. I am grateful for the teachers who have taught me well and aim to share what I've been taught with respect and fidelity. When appropriate, I've added some of my own creative wisdom to the teachings I have been lucky enough to receive from others and some of the things I'm going to share with you here are my own authentic, unique discoveries. Irrespective, everything in this book is based on and has been proven by me and my clients' lived experience. I have applied these principles to my personal and professional life for decades, and I have only included the stuff that works wonders. Still, there's no getting around the brass tax that bears repeating: the work only works if you work it. I don't need to offer you a money-back guarantee, because that would be misplaced responsibility. You are your own money- back guarantee. If you do the work, things will get better, and you will be better, and as you continue to better your best, you and your relationships, family, friends, community, health, career, and wealth will all begin to evolve and expand. But it all starts with you.

There is nothing more or less "broken" about you than there is about anyone else (even though your "suffering story" tries to convince you that your situation is uniquely too difficult to overcome). Every human being (not just you) is born with survival mode (SM) as their default mode, which is why we all suffer and do harm to ourselves and others. The root cause of our suffering is the same for all of us, even if that suffering takes a different form in each case. The various stories and reasons we attach to our suffering to justify our survival-driven perceptions, thoughts, feelings, actions, and experiences, are, in fact, secondary to the underlying mechanism at play (survival mode).

Every human being is also born with the potential to upgrade to the thriving mode (TM) lying dormant in them, regardless of what has or hasn't happened to them.

This in itself is high-level stuff that will get you ahead of the masses, as most human beings don't even know about SM and TM. They just think life is what "happens" as they react to anything and everything that has ever happened to them. Fewer know that it is possible to go from SM to TM as their main mode of being; that they can transition from being mostly reactive and dictated by circumstance, to being mostly creative and the major dominant influence in how their life pans out. *Fewer still know* how to go from SM to TM—that is, what to practically do. *Fewer again start* the work, even if they know it's possible and they've received instructions on how to. An even *smaller minority continue* to do the work, because the survival mode default is a powerful, addictive biological imperative that is hard to outgrow. *Fewer still fully realize,* "Why just cope with suffering when I can end it and have it ALL: Awareness Loving Life?"

As mentioned earlier, I liken this entire path to playing "the greatest game of ALL." Everyone is called to play this game, but not everyone listens to the calling. Many people take their reactive identities and all the reasons why they think they can't, to their graves filled with regret. If you, on the other hand, are looking for a better quality of life; to have your cake and eat it too; to not just feel better, but to feel great; to have more fun and make a bigger positive impact; then it may just be (like many of my clients who decide to play this game with me) that you are:

- Intelligent.
- Motivated.
- Successful.

It may also be that shit has hit the fan for you, in the form of:
- A crisis or trauma.
- A mistake or misfortune.
- A loss of purpose or passion (or perhaps a "sacred challenge").

You may need to:
- Reinvent yourself.
- Get your shit together.
- Get back to being better than ever.

You may be skeptical of:
- Religion.
- Typical therapy.
- The "new age."

What is definite is that you must be:
- Open minded.
- Ready and willing.
- Action oriented.

From there, we will:
- Turn stops into steps.
- Free yourself from regret.
- Make it all worth it.

...via tools that are:
- Tried-and-true and evidence based.
- Both inside and outside the box.
- Based on the body, mind, and spirit.

As a result, you will:
- Discover who you really are and what you are here for.
- Get your mojo back.
- Feel relief, honor, and pride.

...inside a community:

- Of camaraderie and accountability.
- With the best information and tools available.

...even if:
- You're currently in the toughest spot of your life.
- You don't know what to do.

However, it's up to you to make this the best thing that ever happened for you, because:
- You can only play "the greatest game" if you choose to.
- Failure to choose is to guarantee the worst kind of loss.
- You are always either waiting (forever) or creating (always).

In doing so, you will traverse a path:
- Out of misery and mediocrity,
- Into forgiveness, freedom, and fun,
- With compassion, humor, and grit.

Why? Because:
- Nothing will ever make you happy until you make you happy.
- When you make you happy, you can accomplish anything else you value and choose to.
- Until then, anything you accomplish will feel empty of true value.

We need you to be healthy and happy, because together, we thrive! One single acorn can turn into an oak tree, which produces enough acorns to generate an entire forest of trees, each of which generates tens of thousands of new acorns, all of which unleashes a ripple effect of exponential and inherently beneficial fruit.

Alternatively, that acorn can get run over by a truck and flattened, all potential exhausted.

It's our job to put our acorn back in fertile soil, protect and nurture it, and give it the right conditions to thrive. The rest is up to nature.

The world needs you to become your own oak tree. After all, we aren't just talking about ordinary acorns and oak trees here; your acorn is totally unique, and only you can become the type of oak tree that you are. Only you can create "your" fruits and flowers. If you don't become an oak tree, the whole world, including you and the people you love the most, will miss out on the gifts that only you can share with us all.

Together, we thrive.

PART II
THE HIERARCHY OF "EVERYTHINGS"

7
THE HIERARCHY OF "EVERYTHINGS"

THE "HIERARCHY OF EVERYTHINGS" OUTLINES THE facets of our being that underpin our health and happiness, in order of importance. These are:

- State of being.
- State of breathing.
- State of thinking and feeling.
- State of relating.
- State of sleep, rest, and relaxation (SRR).
- State of pleasure, pain, and stress inoculation.
- State of moving/exercising.
- State of drinking/hydrating.
- State of eating/nutrition/digestion.

Most people who are "trying to get healthy" work on the items on this list from the bottom up, which is why most people never change. You can eat the cleanest, most organic, purest diet on the planet, but if you are doing so from survival mode, your body will turn your perfect diet into a perfect nightmare.

In the upcoming chapters, we will cover, in detail, the tools and resources you will need in order to optimize all of these "everythings" (except the state of being; that will be covered in Part III), with specific focus on the things that are mostly unique to All Together Academy. It is very easy to find hordes of information about the complications that arise from "stress," improper breathing, lack of quality sleep and rest, lack of exercise, addiction (on all levels of the continuum), dehydration, inflammation, indigestion, and poor quality food, but I am going to keep us focused on what I have found to work; on the stuff that you and I can actually do to alleviate these concerns and cultivate thriving mode. I am also going to focus more on creating solutions than on fixing problems. After all, what you focus on grows, for better or worse.

Again, this is not just stuff I've studied, or that I teach; this is how I live. I also didn't make all of this up. I am, first and foremost, a student.

Allow me to provide a summary of each of the "everythings" on this list, so you can get an idea of what to expect from the coming chapters.

State of Being

Part III will take you to the top of the hierarchy of everythings, to the state of being. There, you will activate your Creative-IAM (C-IAM), which is juxtaposed by your Reactive-iWAS (Reactive-iWAS). You will also create a Neurochemical Roadmap to the Future You Value and Choose (NRF).

As you have probably gathered by this point, this is high-level stuff. So, before that, we will make our way through the rest of the everythings. This education will form a rock- solid foundation for your state of being exploration.

Your state of being is everything.

State of Breathing

Your state of breathing is very closely related to your state of being, but they're not quite the same. Although your state of being is not dependent on anything external, the way you breathe is one of the easiest, most immediate and reliable ways in which you can influence your state of being. I've had a lot of clients think they were anxious about "this or that"—valid stuff that anyone "ought to" feel anxious about—but it also turned out that they were not breathing optimally and that their brain wasn't making good use of the ample oxygen in their blood. Some breath training later, their experience became, "Huh, the stuff that used to stress me out is still going on, but I don't feel anxious about it anymore."

There is so much good stuff about breathwork already out there, so we will keep it brief in this book.

Your state of breathing is everything.

For popular resources on this topic, see Patrick McKeown or James Nestor. For something off the beaten path that will really blow your mind, search for Dr. Anjani Teves on YouTube and learn how to breathe with every diaphragm (yes, there are many) in your whole body!

State of Thinking and Feeling

Another "everything" that is very closely related to your state of being and your state of breathing is your state of thinking and feeling. Improvement in this "everything" happens when you train your mind to slow down, you become "the noticer," pause, and bring more choice to what you think and how you feel.

With expertise in any arena comes finer levels of "distinction making." For example, my wife can listen to a song and tell you if one single note was off-key. I wouldn't have a clue about this while listening, but that doesn't mean the note *wasn't* off-key. She has just cultivated a finer degree of distinction and perception in this arena. This is very useful for her passion and career as a professional musician. Similarly, when you cultivate your awareness and energy, you, too, become able to make more subtle distinctions between your thoughts and feelings and "you." This is very useful. So, after your state of breathing, we will get into your state of thinking and feeling, so you can get your thoughts and feelings working *for* you, not *against* you (as they do when your life is under the tyranny of the survival mode's likes and dislikes).

Your state of thinking and feeling is everything.

State of Relating

After your state of thinking and feeling is your state of relating.

Relationships make or break us human beings. They're where we experience almost all the risk and reward of life. If you think about it, we are in a "relationship" with everyone and everything all the time, including ourselves.

I will share a brief synopsis of the ATA *Relating Renaissance* in Chapter 27, though I will have to leave the remainder of the state of relating content to book two of this series. (Put it on your TBR for the full deep dive!)

Your state of relating is everything.

State of Sleep, Rest, and Relaxation (SRR)

Sliding down the hierarchy of everythings, we come to sleep, rest, and relaxation (SRR).

The best psychiatrist I worked with as a colleague always prioritized sleep. At the time, we were working in a community mental health clinic serving the most critical mental health needs in a three-county region. Day in and day out, we worked almost entirely with SMI (severe mental illness). This was almost always underscored by severe, complex trauma. This doc, who was one of my clinical supervisors early in my career, would remind me when doing intakes and assessments, "We have no way of really telling what is going on with someone until they are getting enough sleep. Lack of quality sleep can masquerade as almost any other range of symptoms." Indeed, there is now tons of great research that tells us about how lack of quality sleep over time results in serious complications of all kinds, physical, mental, and emotional. This research also says that reprioritizing our life in line with good quality SRR can work like a master key that unlocks and alleviates entire ranges of symptoms and complications, without us needing to address any of them specifically.

Your state of SRR is everything.

State of Pleasure, Pain, and Stress Inoculation

Continuing down the scale of everythings is your state of pleasure, pain, and stress inoculation. Managing this everything involves becoming aware of and managing your states of pleasure and pain.

Pleasure and pain make up a huge part of your nervous system. You might think that you are geared to seek pleasure and avoid pain, but that may perhaps be more of a cultural belief than a biological truth. It turns out that there is a part of your nervous system dedicated to maintaining "the pleasure–pain balance," and it is imperative that it remains just that: balanced. When we explore this everything, I will make the argument that a huge degree of the suffering that we are witnessing nowadays is connected to the fact that we disproportionately seek pleasure, so much that we activate the innate mechanisms of pain that are attempting to achieve balance. Ironically, the more we hit the "pleasure" button, the more we activate pain. The good news is, by purposefully stepping on the "pain" side of the seesaw (within reason) when needed, we can activate inherent pleasure and feel a whole lot better, while simultaneously inoculating ourselves to stress.

Your state of pleasure, pain, and stress inoculation is everything.

State of Moving

Appropriate bodily movement (according to your needs) is another everything which I believe can solve eighty-five percent of our problems (as an educated guess).

Generally speaking, you move much more constantly than you eat or drink, which is why the quality of your movement is more influential than what you eat or drink (assuming you aren't eating and drinking poison).

Unless you are an athlete in training, you don't need a complicated, involved exercise routine to cultivate the great joy of being. If you *are* an athlete in training, you'll already have your approach down. For the rest of us who are aiming to merely be healthier and happier, we need to move more. Don't overthink it. Get up. Walk. Shake your butt. Choose the stairs. Integrate movement all through the day and don't stay stagnant for long. Stretch when you're sitting down. Get outside. Move it or lose it. Stagnancy is a death sentence; movement is life.

In this chapter, I will share some tricks of the trade for busy people and teach you the only yoga posture you will ever need. I will also offer some unique insights into what doesn't work that might throw the status quo into question.

Your state of moving is everything.

State of Drinking and State of Eating

Your state of drinking and state of eating are on the scale of everythings (meaning they are indispensable), but they are further down the list because you only change your chemistry a handful of times per day when you eat and drink. On the other hand, you are in a state of being (complete with its concomitant cocktail of neurochemistry) 24/7, 365.

How long can you go without air? About two to three minutes. Water? About two to three days. Food? About thirty days. How often are you thinking and feeling? That's why thinking, feeling, and breathing is way near the top of the scale, and even though they are absolutely vital, water is close to the end, and food is last.

While the quality of what we eat and drink can make a huge difference in our lives, a lot of us indulge in toxic emotions far more consistently and over a much longer period of time than we could ever indulge in a toxic meal for. Some people stay in a bad mood for *years*. That's tougher to digest than any candy, though eating too much candy may inflame our bad moods!

State of Drinking

Don't underestimate the importance of hydration. Being properly hydrated can be a total gamechanger. If you aren't properly hydrated, you frankly have no way of telling if your suffering is what you *think* it's all about, or if it's just that you need to meet this basic biological need. At the very least, check this off the list and get it done, so that you can determine whether or not it's part of the problem. In the process, you will feel better for having exercised the discipline needed to properly hydrate.

Your state of drinking is everything.

State of Eating

Last (and perhaps "least," but still "everything") is food. Jesus said, "We are defiled more by what comes out of our mouth [words] than what goes into it [food]," but still, we all know that nutrition is key. Like the pleasure–pain imbalance that is wreaking havoc on most of our lives, a huge amount of modern suffering can be boiled down to excess. We eat too much and we drink too much, like Dave Matthews says in his aptly named song. You can do wonders for your physical health by simply eating less and, dare I say, skipping some meals here and there. Yes, this can become a very dangerous problem if it is taken to the extreme, but when done right, it turns out that being intentional about *when* you do and don't eat can perhaps be more impactful than you being intentional about *what* you do and don't eat.

Your state of eating is everything.

The Hierarchy of Everythings is Everything

I know I am presenting a lot here. This book could be an entire graduate-level course, and will, in fact, someday serve as the foundation of a certification program for coaches, clinicians, and providers who want to use these tools and the ATA curriculum with their clients.

As you explore the maps, tools, and instructions for dialing in and up on each of the "everythings" to create truly holistic healing, health, and happiness, it is important that you remember to always ground your approach in the kindness of what you will often hear me refer to as your "grace and ease" question: "What is the next, easiest step I am willing to take, right now, in the direction I value and choose to go in?" Remember, you can feel better today, easily, without any gimmicks, in a totally sustainable way that makes perfect sense.

Before we dive in, I would like to emphasize the fact that in the following chapters, I will be proposing *principles*. Principles (in how I am using the term) are useful generalizations that, when learned, can be incorporated into your life in a way that works for you. I am not prescribing hard and fast rules and restrictions. I can offer my experience based on my training and research, colored by what works for me, but the bottom line and most important factor is whether it works for you. That's the be all and end all. Joyful excellence by design is not about right and wrong; about morality, superiority, or validity. It is about utility. The most important question for the work to, practically speaking, *work*, is not, "Is this true or untrue?" but "Is this useful or not useful?" If it is not useful, then respond with, "No!" If it is useful, respond with, "Yes!" cultivate more, and share the benefits.

Remember, you are one hundred percent responsible for checking any suggestions I make in this book with doctors, your own independent research, and so on.

The Hierarchy of Everythings: Recap and Reflection

Here are some principles you should keep in mind as you explore the following pages:

- If you follow your natural curiosity, passion, and playfulness, you will get the best results.
- If you adhere to the grace and ease question, you will get the best results. This is: "What's the next, easiest thing I am willing to do, right now, in the direction I value and choose to go in?" I can't tell you how often my clients overlook this principle, to a point where they hurt themselves, struggling with "shoulds," "ought tos," and "musts." Believe me, your work will work better (and faster) if you go slow, steady, simple, and easy. I've learned this lesson the hard way and have more physical and emotional scars than I care to talk about from going too hard, too fast.
- Drilling down on the "everything" that excites and inspires you most will greatly influence your natural desire to live in harmony with all the other "everythings." So, if I introduce you to something that excites you in the following pages, I challenge you to go down the rabbit hole, no matter how far up or low down on the scale it is. Mastering one "everything" may just yield the fruits of all the

"everythings" if you approach it with curiosity, passion, and joyful diligence (hint-hint: those are all states of being).

- There is no "one size fits all" prescription for optimal health and happiness. Borrow from what I do and adjust accordingly so it works for you, according to what is practical, doable, realistic, safe, and doctor recommended for you. Finding the best way forward for you is part of the work. I can only offer an example and share principles that you can apply to your life.

- "No" is an extremely powerful choice. "Yes" is an extremely powerful choice.

- "More" is an extremely powerful choice. "Share" is an extremely powerful choice.

- Your state of being is a powerful choice. State of being is everything.

- It is powerful to choose to do breathwork every day, multiple times a day. Breathing is everything.

- It is powerful to choose to relate, with kindness and respect, to yourself and others. Relating is everything. (*What if you treated yourself like you were your own best friend?*)

- It is powerful to choose behaviors that will optimize sleep, lucid dreams, and rest. Sleep, rest, and relaxation are everything.

- It is powerful to choose a balance between pleasure and pain. The pleasure–pain balance is everything.

- It is powerful to inoculate yourself from the damage caused by stress. Stress inoculation is everything.

- It is powerful to choose to exercise at least five days a week, to have a healthy sex and touch life, and to move your body every day and in every way that supports your physical, mental, and emotional wellbeing. Moving (and deliberately not moving) is everything.

- It is powerful to choose to drink enough water that you are well-hydrated, and to not drink too many drinks that rob your hydration, poison your body, and borrow from tomorrow to alter your feelings today. Hydration is everything.

- It is powerful to choose to eat real, nutritious food in appropriate amounts, and only when you are physically (not emotionally) hungry. Eating is everything.

- It is powerful to choose *not* to eat sometimes. Appropriate fasting generates more power, body and mind. *Not* eating is everything.

- The hierarchy of everythings does not always align with what people *think* influences their health and happiness. However, your state of being *is* everything, and so are all the other "everythings."

All these principles will make it easier for you to make powerful choices so that your state of being can become more powerful (your state of being is everything).

Along this journey, I will be sharing some snippets of experiences my clients, contacts, and loved ones have had while integrating this work into their lives and benefiting themselves, others, and ALL. Their names and identities have been changed, unless it's me or my family I'm talking about. Since I'm not only the Hair Club president, I'm also a client (who in the US doesn't remember that commercial?!), I will start with a story about myself!

The Hierarchy of Everythings: A Case Study

A few months before the story I'm about to tell you took place, my wife and children and I returned to the US after living in Thailand (where my sons had been born) in shaky circumstances. During this period, the magnitude of my role as a provider was pressing down on me. I knew things would get harder before they got easier; before I'd be able to get my family on solid ground.

We leapfrogged from rural northeast Thailand to Bangkok to Boston and then to Oakland, CA, where all four of us lived in one room of an apartment we shared with two other adults. We could barely afford my grad school, which I attended by day while working manual labor at night, but we just about managed to make it work.

At one in the morning during a long day (and night) of school and work, I was on the job when I suddenly found myself lying on my back.

What had happened? Where was I?

Turns out a large metal cable with a heavy socket designed to be plugged into huge speakers had come undone, swung through the air, and smacked me straight in the forehead. It was now hanging from the ceiling of the Oakland Coliseum; my forehead having interrupted its pendulum swing through the air. I never saw it coming.

Many years before this incident, in my career as a collegiate athlete, I'd had a lot of trouble with head injuries, as well as the depression and anxiety that often comes with that territory. After college (still before the "cable incident"), a near-fatal ski crash had left me unconscious for forty-five minutes and diagnosed with a "moderate traumatic brain injury" that would go on to complicate my life for decades. Any more concussions, big or small, were always going to be a big deal for my brain.

This one (the "cable incident") was big. I was messed up. I needed to rest and recover. But because I had been living overseas for seven years, I had not paid into the US workman's comp system, and my injury benefits would not be enough to support my family. So, I did what dads do: I went back to work to pay the bills, and I stayed in school to tend to our future prospects.

I was constantly hazy, dizzy, and nauseous, and the dark thoughts quickly started creeping in. *Dammit, I thought I was over this. Not again.* I had done so much personal work to heal from childhood depression and anxiety, and I was terrified it was coming back because of this head injury.

Three weeks after the "cable incident," in the middle of the Oakland night, I was this time on a loading dock pushing a heavy lighting truss up a ramp and into a truck when the latches came undone. The truss slid back and landed on my head.

I couldn't make this stuff up.

This was how I got my second concussion in three weeks.

This time, stuff got bad. Really bad. Every time I looked at a computer screen, I puked. Not cool when you're in grad school. I had to stay in a dark room 24/7 because any light was too intense. The sound of my kids crying felt like daggers in my skull. I began having about twenty panic attacks a day—the full on, "I'm dying right now, take me to the ER" kind. The suicidal thoughts that so often follow head injuries got louder and louder. I dealt with all of this in our one (dark) room. And at that time, "post-concussion syndrome" was not really a thing. I remember seeing a board-certified neurologist in San Francisco at major hospital who told me, "If your brain isn't bleeding there's nothing to worry about, 'post-concussion syndrome' is not a thing, it's all in your head." Well, no shit, Doc. Unfortunately, he meant in the pejorative way and I left understanding once again the difference between intelligence and wisdom, shaking my head that some doctors are the dumbest smart people I've ever met.

If this sounds like it couldn't get any worse, think again: a neighbor's cat then infested our one tiny room with fleas. (Yes, really.) Seeing my nine-month-old son's precious baby skin become covered in flea bites (and not being able to make it stop) brought on a different kind of rage from within my already-fragile state of mind. I was ready to pick a fight with God, and was pretty sure I could kick Her (or His, or Its) ass. But then, I had a breakthrough. This would be my opportunity! This would be my sacred challenge! I would have to take all that I'd learned through my personal therapy earlier in life—my spiritual work, my years of meditation, my yoga and Ayurveda studies, my graduate degrees, and my relentless passion to learn—and totally rewire and upgrade my brain. But I wasn't going to stop at healing. I was going to thrive. I was going to achieve it all or bust—*joyful excellence by design... Awareness Loving Life.*

This was my turning point. What's the point if not to be in love with life and ALL it has to offer?

How to Find Joy
Even If You Have a Hole in Your Bucket

As I write now, I have moved through all of that, which isn't to say I'm free from major challenges! I have three beautiful, healthy, resilient, and wise children, and I enjoy the companionship of an amazing, powerful, gorgeous wife. We are together, and at the time of my writing this first draft, we are living on the beach on the coast of Mexico, because I have built an online business that can support us anywhere in the world. I've worked with hundreds (probably thousands) of clients over the years. I've done my ten thousand hours and then some. I've founded, staffed, and managed a family behavioral health center that still serves thousands of families to this day. I've earned two master's degrees and hordes of certifications and specialty training. And, remember, when I was first writing this chapter I didn't even know that during that entire period in my life I had a hole in my paralyzed diaphragm and a half functioning lung!

I am sharing these things only to instill confidence in you and to say that you can do this. I have been through it, personally and professionally, and have come out on the other end thriving (and have witnessed lots of clients do the same) using the tools you are about to learn in this book. I've delved into community mental health work, trauma work, addiction, abuse, parenting, family stuff, couples' work, work with combat PTSD, cognitive behavioral therapy, somatic work, EMDR, and more. I have also navigated optimal performance, nutrition, exercise, breathwork, meditation, stress inoculation, sleep and dream work, NLP, hypnosis, flow states, spirituality, creativity, and more. My work is part therapy (empathy, nonjudgment, understanding, kindness, and experience) and part coaching (encouragement, solution focused, practical, positive, and humorous). I do it all with heart because ever since emerging from that major college depression, I've known that loving is the purpose of living.

How about you? What's your purpose? What matters *most* to *you*? A lot of people ask this question, "What is the meaning of life?" But not too many realize that life asks that question of us. Every moment, life is asking you: what's your purpose? Why are you here? Our answer, like it or not, is how we show up.

Consider, if you could feel better, today, easily, without any gimmicks, in a totally sustainable way that makes perfect sense, what would that look like for you? How would you show up?

I've learned over the years that giving is its own reward, and so to start things off, I'd like to give you the very first assignment I give to all my private 1:1 clients. It is an exercise I've borrowed and adapted from a business coach along my journey.

You can find the instructions at www.alltogether.academy/joy-bucket-tools (it is Tool #1 in your Joy Book Tools resource page). Please complete this task before moving on.

8

BREATHING IS EVERYTHING

THE QUALITY, QUANTITY, DEPTH, LENGTH, VIGOR, and fullness of your breath are among the most important factors for your health. Your breath is an immediate path into your ANS (autonomic nervous system), which governs... well, everything. If your ANS is in an optimal state, everything else will be, too, including, for example, your digestion processes. So, breathing might have more to do with your "diet" than what you eat (indirectly, and assuming you aren't eating junk every day, which would also seriously compromise your breathing!).

Years ago, when my son Rudi was about five, I talked to him about the belief held in many spiritual traditions that we have a certain number of breaths allotted to our life; no more, no less. His response was natural and immediate: "So that's why turtles live so long! Because they breathe so slow."

Exactly!

The breath carries our lifeforce, which is known all over the world as *chi*, *prana*, spirit, and so on. Accordingly, our subconscious determines what it *thinks* we want in our life based on what we spend most of our heartbeats and breaths on. In other words, we logically receive more of what we spend our energy on, whether in the form of actions, thoughts, or feelings. We can invest our most precious currency on that which gives a return of more lifeforce or energy, or we can spend frivolously on that which depletes our account, shortens our lifespan, and reduces our quality of life. The more heartbeats and breaths we spend thinking about our anxiety, or feeling like a piece of shit, or focusing on gratitude and abundance, the more the subconscious says, "Here are a whole bunch of circumstances to give you what seems so important to you."

In other words, we get from life what we give to life. We literally breathe our precious spirit into whatever we focus on and give it our life, for better or worse. We animate our life with breath. Where your attention goes, your energy flows. This means it's important to assess whether you are getting a good return on your investment. Are you spending your most precious assets wisely? Are you giving your heartbeats and breaths to the things you most value and choose to experience in your life? Or are you focusing on all the stuff you actually don't want (even if under the pretense of trying to get rid of it)?

Not only can you extend the quantity of your life by refining the quality of your breath, but you can also enhance the quality of your life by attaching significance to each breath, such that you call forward, from the base of ALL, what you value and choose to.

When you slow your breath down, you also slow your heart down. When you slow your heart down, things get quiet, and you can feel the peace and love that runs under and through everything. When you feel this, you create space to consider what you value and choose to express and experience. When you focus on what you want more of, you start to notice its presence more. When you notice it more, you feel it more. When you feel it more, you think of it more. When you think of it more, you feel it more. This is how you *generate* a good fortune.

Here's an easy experiment you can do to grok what I'm getting at. Go to the grocery store and walk around for 15 minutes (feel free to get some shopping done to make it convenient for you) with a grimace on your face. Furrow your brow, look down a lot, don't make eye contact, move away from people, hide your eyes and breath shallow and fast. Then, leave the store, or simply go another aisle, and start looking up and out at the world, smile at strangers, make eye contact, think warm thoughts, take big breaths into your heart and imagine as if your exhale can fill others with love.

Does the world change? You bet it does. But did it really? Or did YOU change?

You can initiate this positive upward spiral by going beyond your thoughts and feelings and into a space of deep breathing because when you change the state of your ANS (which governs your breathing) you send a deep signal into your body, brain *and your environment* that it is safe to love, safe to explore, safe to contribute, safe to go towards life with an open heart, and safe to let life come towards you, smiling.

There is a problem with this, though, like my client Fred (a very high-level leader in the world's effort to ward off climate disaster) realized and shared with me just yesterday. We were discussing the fact that he no longer needs to meet with me (because my job is to work myself out of a job), and during this conversation, he gave me the insight, "I realized we need the right tool for the job." What he meant by this is, if your nervous system is super-activated with fear or anger, "taking a deep breath" or "relaxing" or having someone (even yourself) tell you to "calm down" will likely just make things worse. Alternatively, when you have several different tools in your toolbox, you can "step the energy down" bit by bit so that you can get to a point where you can relax and meditate, or be a shining example to yourself and others. Here's an example:

In the panic attack protocol I teach clients, we have a multistep approach that systematically starts where our energy is at: panicked! Then, we methodically guide our nervous system down, step by step and state by state, until we reach a place of deep grace and ease. Once my clients have a taste of success with this protocol, their confidence grows, and they become less afraid of panic attacks. Once they are no longer afraid of panic and they meet previously "panic worthy" stimulation with a "bring it on, I got this" attitude, the irony is that the panic attacks seem to stop happening entirely.

Why just cope with suffering when you can end it?

The higher up we go on the hierarchy of everythings, the more it is relatively true to say that focusing on one of the everythings will optimize everything else. Accordingly, by mastering your breath, you can heal, optimize, and thrive in all the other everythings. My dad, who plays golf four to five times a week, marveled at how I can play once every ten years and we could still win a prestigious father & son tournament together. Mastering the breath is great for optimal performance in everything, from the putting green to the boardroom to the bedroom.

In this chapter, I will introduce you to three breathing techniques so you can make this kind of progress. These techniques alone yield fruits beyond belief!

As always, nothing in this chapter constitutes medical advice. All breathing practices must first be cleared between you and a medical professional and must never be practiced while you are driving, in water, or in other potentially dangerous situations. That said, the breathing practices I will share with you here are very much on the safer side of what is available in this field of practice.

Full Breath

Full breath is the foundation of all breathwork.

You might notice that when you go to take a full breath, you suck your tummy in and up and your chest and shoulders lift, and when you exhale, your belly puffs out. If so, that is exactly the opposite of how your body was designed to breathe. I cannot emphasize enough how important it is to retrain your body to instead:

1. Expand in all directions from your navel out (front, back, sides, and down into your loins) when you inhale.
2. Contract, gently, to the center behind your navel when you exhale.

Your shoulders/collar bone area should not move much at all. Also, even if you are taking a full breath such that your chest also expands, the expansion should begin in the abdominal cavity first, and *then* the chest cavity. Then, on exhalation, you can empty the chest cavity first and then the abdominal cavity, to complete exhalation and experience *slight* air hunger as you suspend before the next inhalation comes in spontaneously.

If you watch a baby breathe, you'll notice that we all start out by breathing optimally. Some researchers suggest that we may begin breathing incorrectly (and this brings all kinds of negative implications) around the age 4, due to factors such as stress, posture, diet, etc.[6] Why this happens is more than we can get into here, but a lot of it has to do with us being entrenched in survival mode, along with complications from a modern diet, both of which contribute to deformed jaw and nasal structure.

It is vital that we retrain ourselves to take full breaths in the way we were designed to. If you want to deep dive into this truly nutritious topic, James Nestor's book *Breath*[7] and Patrick McKeown's *The Oxygen Advantage*[8] are phenomenal foundations. Dr. M. Anjani Teve's (of Nine Rivers Osteopathy in upstate New York) "whole body breathing" on YouTube is the advanced curriculum, if you will[9]. Dr. Teves is a personal friend of mine, and is not as famous as the others, but she's a savant (I don't say that lightly), and you likely wouldn't ever know about her if she and I didn't happen to be friends. Her videos aren't super-polished (nor are mine!) or widespread (yet), but you will be hard pressed to find a more authentic and learned source for the science and art of breathing well.

<hr />

[6] O'Sullivan, R., & Beales, D., 2007, Changes in Breathing Patterns and Chest Wall Shape in Children: A longitudinal study. International Journal of Osteopathic Medicine, 10(1), 3–11.
[7] Nestor, J. (2020): Breath: The New Science of a Lost Art. Riverhead Books.
[8] McKeown, P. (2015): The Oxygen Advantage: The Simple, Scientifically Proven Breathing Techniques for a Healthier, Slimmer, Faster, and Fitter You. William Morrow.
[9] Anjani Teves, M. (2024): M. Anjani Teves, DO [YouTube channel]. YouTube. Retrieved November 22, 2024, from www.youtube.com/@m.anjanitevesdo8957.

The Physiological Sigh

This is one of the easiest and most well researched ways to relax your nervous system. In the *Huberman Lab* podcast[10], Andrew Huberman shares evidence that this simple breathing exercise can have dramatically positive effects on one's quality of life when done for five minutes a day[11]. Head to Lesson 2.1 in your book resources at www.alltogether.academy/joy-bucket-tools for a three-minute video of me teaching this exercise. The instructions are simple:
1. Breathe in through the nose.
2. Breathe in more.
3. Hold for a brief moment.
4. Sigh, all the way out.
5. Slight pause.
6. Repeat.

Fog Breath

You can access a video explanation and instructions for fog breathing at Lesson 2.2 in your C-IAM-Tools at alltogether.academy/joy-bucket-tools. Here are some written instructions:
1. Take a comfortable seat, with your spine erect. Make any adjustments you need before settling into stillness.
2. Make an internal or external statement of dedication/intention, or prayer about growth, letting go of something, your cultivation practice, and so on.
3. Do the physiological sigh. Repeat three times.

---

[10] Since the initial drafts of this book, some questions have been raised about Huberman's personal life choices and/or his being influenced by affiliate marketing, and/or his inviting discussion about controversial and potentially pseudo-scientific topics. Looking at this all as objectively as possible, I have chosen to leave the references I am using from *Huberman Lab* because I believe, on these topics, they represent accurate information. These references and this statement are not an endorsement of *Huberman Lab* generally as an entire body of work. These references demonstrate only that, on the specific topics to which I refer, I believe Mr. Huberman presents solid, actionable information in a digestible format.
[11] Huberman, A. (Host), August 2, 2011, Breathing Techniques to Reduce Stress and Anxiety | Dr. Andrew Huberman on the Physiological Sigh [Audio podcast episode]. In Huberman Lab.

4.   Inhale a full breath relatively quickly, without struggling. Do this fully into the belly and then into the chest for one to three seconds, ideally breathing in through the nose.

5.   Exhale, opening the mouth while making a sound like you are fogging up a piece of glass. As you exhale, allow tension to melt around your chest area (or anywhere else you notice tension). Allow the exhale to get longer and longer as you let go of more and more and tension. Do this from a space of allowing, letting go, and ease, not from struggling or "trying hard."

6.   Repeat at least five times, or as many times as feels good. Allow your exhalation to get longer and longer, keeping your inhale short by comparison. Eventually, you will activate a deep relaxation response, and you may even yawn. That's wonderful.

7.   Smile and invoke a sense of gratitude for the fact that you can work to change your state. Think of someone you know who might benefit from your positive thoughts and prayers and visualize them smiling and thriving along with you.

Pro Tip: I suggest working fog breath into your routine five times a day. To make it a habit, consider "tagging" it to something you already do regularly. This could be every time you go pee, get a glass of water, or check your email. This type of integration practice will result in you "drip feeding" relaxing, healing, and thriving neurochemistry into your day. This will nicely counterbalance the fast-paced life many of us lead. Plus, by "tagging it" to something you are already doing, like using the restroom, you literally add zero time obligation to your day. Now that's a good ROI!

Practice fog breath proactively, when you are not upset, so you can develop your muscles and it will also work when you are upset. I find with regular practice, I can change state with fog breath when I am mildly to moderately upset. When I am really jacked up, I need the power switch!

The Power Switch

Before we begin, please note that this tool is more vigorous than the others we have covered so far. You must check with your doctor before using it and make any modifications needed to ensure your safety. Remember, you are responsible for your own health.

The power switch is too complex to be explained here in writing, so head to Lesson 2.3 in your book resources at www.alltogether.academy/joy-bucket-tools to learn what this is about. This tool is for more intense moments when fog breath won't cut it and you're having a harder time changing state. See the video for theory and instructions. Assuming you have the go ahead from your doctor to do so, I suggest you practice the power switch at least once a day when everything is fine and dandy, plus whenever you are really upset. In the latter situation, you must couple this exercise with a strong resolve to free yourself from the upset. It won't work if you do it half-heartedly!

My sense is that the most difficult thing to let go of when we are employing a tool to change to a more resourceful state is the sense that we are "right" and therefore "should", "must", and "ought" to feel/stay upset about it. Says who? Will it help even if you are "right?" Or will you be even better able to successfully navigate challenges if you are in a more optimal state?

Using a power tool to change to a more resourceful state of being is the kindest and most merciful thing you can do for yourself. It is also the most effective way to handle whatever challenge you are facing, because it stops the bleeding of counterproductive reactions that limit your capacities in almost every way, so you can think clearly and act according to your values and wisdom.

Breathing is Everything: A Case Study

My son Finn had asthma when he was younger. He had a sunken chest, which doctors told us was "normal", that he would have it "forever," and that there is "nothing to do about it." Every time he got sick, it went straight to his lungs. We had to take him to the ER on multiple occasions because he wasn't getting enough oxygen, his lips were turning blue, and his breathing was too rapid. I quickly had to become an expert at counting his breaths and discerning the point at which we needed to get to the hospital.

One night, my wife and I went on a sort of date. Tania was playing a music gig, and I took the opportunity to tag along. I always love to watch Tania perform; she sings with such passion, vigor, and beauty. Finn was coming down with a cold at the time, but it was minor, and our friend Suza (who is really an auntie to the kids) is a trouper and always game for helping us out. She's raised kids herself and wasn't fazed about him being a bit sick. Plus, this was a gig that had been scheduled long in advance. We decided to go for it.

Suza called about three quarters of the way through the show and said, "I don't know what's going on, but it seems like Finn's having a really hard time breathing." I knew exactly what was happening. I hurried Tania off the stage, leaving her gear there, and we bolted to the car. I drove about eighty-five miles per hour through a windy, icy mountain road from Taos Ski Valley. There was no phone reception, so we couldn't do anything but trust that Suza would understand the text directions we'd given her about when the ER trip would be necessary.

We got home in one piece, and I was able to quickly assess the situation and do some of the stuff I had learned to do to get Finn better and able to increase his oxygen intake. All's well that ends well. Still, I was done with that stress in my life. It was too scary for us all. I needed to find a better way forward.

We had already been told there was nothing we could do to reverse Finn's situation; that we just had to learn how to live with it and use inhalers. However, in my personal life (as a father, therapist, and coach), I don't usually take that kind of stuff lying down. While some doctors are amazing, too many are just about the smartest dumb people I have ever met. By all means, do your medical due diligence—I certainly do—but gone are the times when we should just take what our doctors say on board without searching for better options, or without having already established a trusting relationship with a particular doctor who we know is up to speed with current research and a holistic, effective approach. Anyway, that's beside the point. I got to researching what the heck I could do for Finn—and us—so we would never have to go through this again. I found *The Oxygen Advantage* by Patrick McKeown[12]. *The Oxygen Advantage* makes some pretty big claims, like that you can resolve asthma and allergies with appropriate breathing techniques and the physiological changes they bring[13]. I wasn't sure about these lofty claims, but the theory and research looked compelling, and there were no downsides to what the author proposed, so I kept reading with gusto. In fact, I started practicing the methods myself—because I don't ever recommend to another what I haven't used successfully myself.

Sure enough, I got good results, to a point where I was ready to introduce it to Finn (and Rudi, because why not?). At the time, my boys were both

---

[12] McKeown, P. (2015): *The Oxygen Advantage: The Simple, Scientifically Proven Breathing Techniques for a Healthier, Slimmer, Faster, and Fitter You.* William Morrow.
[13] These concepts are discussed extensively throughout the entire book—the term asthma for example comes up about 100 times in a search, but I guess I good quote and concentration is on page 214-215. The fundamental cause of ongoing asthma symptoms can almost always be attributed to breathing too much...

playing soccer and dreaming about becoming pros (as lots of young kids do), so that was my angle: I told them that this cool breathing tool could help them be better soccer players. They were into it. More importantly, though, I did it with them. Every morning and every evening, we practiced our "steps." We made it fun and a bit competitive, though I had to add qualitative markers into the competition, like being relaxed, because struggling while doing the breath holds we were doing is counterproductive, and my kids are super- competitive. (I wonder where they get that from...)

In line with the goalposts set out in the book, we initially enjoyed just the result of Finn no longer needing seasonal allergy medicine (he used to be a sneezing mess when we went to his *Abuelita*'s house surrounded by tree blossoms). That was gone. Then, he weathered a few colds without breathing complications. Those also seemed to be gone. Then, the indentation in his chest that we had been told was a "normal abnormality" that he'd have forever seemed to pop out, and suddenly, his chest was full and robust. From that moment, we knew his asthma was gone for good.

At the time of writing this, I am now on draft four of this book, and I am still practicing these tools with my kids. Two days ago, I picked Finn and a friend up from soccer practice. It's newly spring in the Boston area, and I was parked under a tree waiting for them when a huge dump of pollen flew into our car—it was literally visible and covered us all. Finn and his friend both immediately started sneezing, their eyes watering intensely. I looked to Finn and subtly reminded him, "Use your tools." Knowing what to do (and without his friend knowing what was going on), Finn got to it. Within about one minute, he was able to rejoin the conversation, sneeze- free. His eyes were totally clear, even though they had been tearing up and red just one minute before. His nose was clear even though he hadn't blown it, and he didn't sneeze even once more. Meanwhile, his friend's eyes continued to pour. The poor boy sneezed about twenty times in the ten-minute ride to his home.

Finn is empowered to be his own healer! How cool is that?

Now, you might be saying, "Isn't this a book about mental and emotional health? Aren't you a psychotherapist? What does any of this have to do with inner self-help?" Well, touché. Still, don't you think a brain that's not getting enough oxygen might have a higher tendency to send "fear" signals that one interprets as anxiety? Don't you think a kid who has a life-threatening breathing problem every time he gets sick might develop anxiety, or might get discouraged more easily, or maybe even show signs of PTSD? Do you not think an otherwise-robust, powerful, and active kid who can't go as hard as he wants to in sports and life might get depressed?

As Finn's physical health matters cleared up (this was our goal), so did his anxiety about it all. Because he was now able to play with more vigor, he grew more exuberant. Despite receiving many grim life (for his entire life, not life or death) sentences from many "expert doctors," Finn had a direct experience that told him he was empowered enough to make dramatically positive changes in his body, mind, and emotions through moderate, well researched discipline. Do you think this might have helped his confidence? You bet it *does!*

Friends, the body and the mind are two sides of the same coin. They are contiguous, and they are different doorways into our relationship with ourselves. My niche as a psychotherapist and my expertise in the "mind" may concern the "inner world" of humans, but I have discovered that the body-based tools are the easiest to use and have the strongest ripple effects. There is no amount of cognitive reframing you can do to overcome "anxiety" if your brain is afraid that it's not getting enough oxygen!

This breath deficiency is more normal than you'd think—so what if we don't have as much of a "mental health" epidemic as we do one of disordered breathing? I like to think of it this way because it's a much easier challenge to work with than the infinitely complex stories we tell ourselves about "why" we feel anxious.

I've had client after client after client raise their BOLT (Blood Oxygen Level Test) score (see *The Oxygen Advantage* for details) to robust levels after their work with me and also say, "Huh, that stuff that used to stress me out is still going on, but I don't feel anxious about it anymore." Remember, the stories and reasons we use to justify and explain our symptoms are often secondary to the primary cause of them. If we alleviate the primary cause, the stories justifying the suffering become irrelevant. No longer do you think, *I must be anxious about the presentation at work,* when you discover that all along, your body has just been trying to send you a message to solve the real problem: the neurochemical imbalance that has come from you not breathing appropriately. All of a sudden, those butterflies you feel before the presentation illicit a story of "This is important to me, and I am excited about it!"

Of course, this is a known "reframe" for when we feel anxious, telling ourselves its "exciting and important to me." But, without the deeper neurochemical state change, cognitive reframing can sometimes be akin to gaslighting ourselves! Instead of putting icing on a shit-cake, I'd rather make it chocolate and delicious from the bottom up!

Breathing is Everything: Recap and Reflection

- The quality, quantity, depth, length, vigor, and fullness of your breath are among the most important factors of your health.
- You literally breathe your precious spirit into whatever you focus on and give it your life, for better or worse. What you focus on grows. Are you devoting your life to what you value and choose to receive more of? Are you getting a good return on the investment of your most precious assets (time, energy, attention, heartbeats, and breaths)?
- By training yourself to breathe longer, fuller, deeper, smoother, and easier, you can literally extend the quantity of your life (and absolutely improve the quality of it along the way).

Your tasks for this chapter are:
- Practice the full breath exercise every day.
- Follow Dr. Huberman's advice: try the physiological sigh for five minutes a day (plus here and there, whenever you think of it). You, too, can reap the benefits of this (very easy) exercise.
- If you want to activate a deeper state of "parasympathetic" dominance for healing, resting, digesting, and rejuvenating, turn off that alarm switch with fog breath. "Tag" it to something you already do and get in at least five sessions per day, and you will feel the good vibes permeating throughout your day.
- If you are more upset, you might need a stronger tool. Try the power switch proactively, or if you are really triggered.

9
THINKING AND FEELING IS EVERYTHING

YOUR THOUGHTS AND FEELINGS ARE DISTINCTLY different from your state of being and from who you are, which is more generally defined as an "Aware-Will." However, most people identify as their most familiar thoughts and feelings. "I am anxious," is an example of this. It is imperative that you instead 1) recognize the distinctions between your thoughts and feelings, your state of being, and who you are, 2) understand them, and 3) learn how to "come from" who you really are and express the states of being you value and choose.

We will develop all of this in much more depth, with practical exercises, in Part III of this book. What you need to learn for now is how you can experience these distinctions on the most basic level. Ready? Let's go.

Here it is in a nutshell: you can cultivate the ability to notice your sense of self as distinct from your thoughts and feelings, which you, as Aware-Will, can include and "host" - through meditation.

Hate meditation? Don't want to do it? That's fine. Stay with me.

Many people (often due to poor instructions or misguided ways of starting out) build up a resistance to meditation at some point or other. They think, *Meditation is hard*, or *I've tried it before and I can't do it. My mind is too busy*. This is unsurprising, as these people usually think they need to have a quiet mind to meditate, or that meditating means "not thinking." This is an impossible expectation that is sure to result in frustration and, ultimately, quitting. Furthermore, people usually start trying to "meditate" by doing so for twenty or thirty minutes at a time. However, even ten minutes is likely too long at the beginning. Naturally, these people discover that their mind is very busy and that the practice feels far from relaxing, and so they think, *I can't do that*.

You become what you practice, for better or worse. This means that if you attempt to "meditate" for thirty minutes but are, in fact, distracted and agitated for twenty-nine out of those thirty, what you have really practiced is distraction, not meditation. You would instead be much better off taking a "tiny habits" approach (which you will learn about in Part III) to your new goal of regular meditation. This means meditating for the one minute you can really stay on point for, and not bothering with the other twenty-nine. Then, you can add thirty seconds at a time, but only when it feels good to continue and you are in a state of Aware-Will.

As far as techniques go, there are countless types of mediation. The portable pause of extra and open attention (an exercise we'll discuss in—say it with me!—Part III) is the foundation of them all, so, regardless of how you want to approach meditation (such as through an app like Headspace, which I think is pretty solid), I would first recommend that you learn about extra and open attention. If you don't want to wait until Part III to learn this technique, you can access thorough instructions, for free, in Lesson 3 of your book resources, titled "Extra and Open Attention." Head to www.alltogether.academy/joy-bucket-tools and give it a go.

Through meditation, you can observe the subtle distinction between your thoughts and feelings and your state of being, discovering yourself as an Aware-Will that is not defined or limited by your habitual thoughts and feelings. The space of Aware-Will often goes unnoticed altogether or is not appreciated in its significance, which really can't be overstated. In this discovery, you realize *you are not your thoughts and feelings*. Your state of being as "Aware-Will" lies *beyond* thoughts and feelings. It can appear to take on the *characteristics, colors, and flavors* of thoughts and feelings, but, you, at your core are *not* your thoughts and feelings—even the ones you have come to identify with as "me," such as "I am anxious", "I am a lawyer", or "I am unlovable."

The proof that you are not your thoughts and feelings lies in the fact that you can notice your thoughts and feelings arising within you. Therefore, you are not your thoughts and feelings. You are that which notices them (as Awareness) and can choose what to do next, irrespective of them (as Will). You are an Aware-Will.

Learning how to operate from this space of Aware-Will is the difference between being creative versus being reactive; between being a cause versus being an effect; between being empowered versus being a victim—even if, aside from, and especially because bad stuff happens and all manner of thoughts and feelings ramble through our Awareness space all the time. When you operate from a space of Aware-Will, you develop the capacity to not only perceive thoughts and feelings as the temporary and passing conditions that they are, but to also deliberately choose what thoughts and feelings you want to give your attention and energy to, let go of, transform, or act upon. In this way, thinking and feeling become *aspects* of who you are that you can, with training, use to your advantage. You can even go as far as creating more useful packages of thoughts and feelings, "identities," which are signifiers for a complex of beliefs and perceptions that end up generating your experience. We will get to that in part III where you will develop and discover your Creative-IAM, and learn more about Identity → Belief → Perception → Experience.

Even though you are not your thoughts and feelings, your thoughts and feelings have a significant, practical, and immediate impact on your body, mind, perception, and experience. This is why your state of thinking and feeling is high up on the scale of everythings. It is not the same as your state of being, but it is so close in that it directly influences your experience, for better or worse. I could make an argument for why it should be higher on the hierarchy of everythings, above state of breathing, but thoughts and feelings are so subtle and fast that they can be difficult to work with directly. So, some of the more indirect routes to "thought and feeling management" are more effective. For example, when you slow your breath (higher on the scale) in particular ways, your thoughts slow down naturally. As your thoughts slow down and you experience more "flow," you discover yourself as an Aware-Will that, almost by accident, the JOLKA-GPS is revealed.

The non-circumstance dependent states of Joy, Openness, Love, Kindness, Awareness—Gratitude, Presence and Surrender I am referring to with the JOLKA-GPS are ornaments of your Aware-Will that arise automatically when you are "coming from" who you really are, as an Aware-Will. Your ability to rely on this circumstance-independent inner refuge could not be more profound. This is the foundation for a freedom I believe all humans long for. If I know I AM, and I can *always* return to, my sense of Self as Aware-Will, which is inherently experiencing and expressing JOLKA-GPS, regardless of what's going on inside or around me, then I am no longer in a co-dependent relationship with life trying to "get my needs met." I am now independently able to relate interdependently by *choice*, as who I am really am, with others and the world, in the most beneficial way.

It may take some practice for you to identify more closely with Aware-Will than with your thoughts and feelings about what has or hasn't happened to you, but this will come with meditation (which, according to some definitions, translates as "to become familiar with"). When meditation is practiced consistently over time, you become more familiar with who you really are, as an Aware-Will.

There are no downsides to this work, and the benefits that come with it are unendingly positive. After all, the reactive thoughts and feelings we all grapple with daily amount to all kinds of upset, are often based on inaccuracies (because the default survival mode we are all born with is designed to perceive a stick as a snake and to react accordingly), and are compelling us to do all sorts of stuff we end up regretting. We mistake our misperceptions for truth, identify our thoughts and feelings not only as "true" but also as who we are, and say, "See, I am right" when our confirmation bias finds evidence to prove our thoughts and feelings. When we "come from" a place of anger, we identify, "I am angry," and therefore justify why we give someone the finger during a bout of road rage. When our brain isn't getting the right balance of oxygen and carbon dioxide (recall what we talked about in the previous chapter) and so sends a signal that something is wrong, we associate this alarm with something that is going in our life ("I must be anxious because of that test I have tomorrow"). These are both examples of us identifying secondary thoughts and feelings as the cause of what we are experiencing; as the dictator of our identity ("I am anxious") and the rationalizer of our actions ("I, as 'anxious,' am going to skip that test").

Everyone experiences the various components of our *being*, such as thought-words, images, emotions, sensations, and experiences as "identity-makers." Day in and day out, these components of experience are smooshed together. They seem to occur so simultaneously that we unconsciously consider these fragments of experience to be "who we are" and "what reality is." Until, that is, we start meditating and learning to come from a place of Aware-Will. Through meditation, we can slow the frames down enough to see that there is space between them. And when we notice the space between our thoughts and feelings, we can grow curious about who is doing the noticing. As we explore this, we realize, "That's who I really am! I am the awareness that notices the frames of thoughts, emotions, sensations, and experiences. I am not the thoughts, feelings and experiences themselves." With practice, we "disidentify" with our thoughts and feelings, because we first notice, and then grow familiar with, who we really are (an Aware-Will). In this way, through meditation, we can develop an actual method for "not taking things personally."

Usually, when someone tells you to "not take something personally," they are gaslighting you. In the context of meditation, though, "not taking things personally" becomes a tangible goal to work toward. It comes with the realization of, "Oh, I am not my thoughts and feelings! I can choose, as an Aware-Will, to act according to my values and to create a new and better experience, regardless of what I think and feel." This is something I was able to discover and deeply embody after the enormous thoracic surgery I had in the summer of 2024. I was in so much pain, and in such a low-energy state that my mind was generating all sorts of thoughts and feelings we normally associate with depression. I felt hopeless and helpless. I felt like it could never get better. I thought things like, "I am better off dead," "I might as well give up." I was in such a bad place that even when my wife was lovingly trying to support me in remembering the teachings I have learned and share with others, it *felt* like gaslighting, it *felt* like she was not "seeing me", not "hearing my truth," like she was "dismissing" or "invalidating my experience." Until I realized this was an *opportunity*! The real deal is that in these moments we are the only ones who can *choose* for ourselves because we will interpret everything, even the good intentions and wisdom coming from our loved ones, through the lens of our personal hells. I had to make the choiceless choice to get beyond my thoughts, feelings, and even the very painful sensations in my body and I was so grateful to discover that what I am telling you here is capital T-True. The JOLKA-GPS is always shining, even if, aside from, and especially because bad stuff happens.

Here's a metaphor to illustrate:

We often get caught up in thinking that we are the *waves* of our experience (which is a very topsy turvy way to live). In doing so, we forget that we are, in fact, *the ocean itself* (not the waves). We are infinite and mighty and able to experience and express all sorts of wave patterns. The ocean is not its waves. Though it can experience rising and falling wave patterns—it can even experience raging storms—none of these ever make the ocean more or less "itself," nor do they disturb or threaten the ocean's stability or constancy as, "I AM ocean (or "ocean-ness")." Similarly, we can experience the waves of our lives, even the most tumultuous ones within and without, and still not be limited, defined, or disturbed by these temporary fluctuations. When we get caught up in the topsy turvy conditioning of life, we get turned upside down and around and we forget who are really are: the mighty ocean itself.

Why We Identify as Our Thoughts and Feelings: The Thinking-Feeling Feedback Loop

I would like to introduce you to the thinking-feeling feedback loop. This introduction will be brief, since this concept is more relevant to book three of this series (*Energy of Mind: Secular Spiritual Work for Practical People*).

Here we go:

Every time you think a thought, it produces "chemicals" that we call "emotions" or "feelings" (we call them "feelings" because we feel them, as sensations). So, thinking a thought produces sensations. But here's the rub (and the opportunity): these sensations don't depend on the "truth" or "reality" of the thoughts that triggered them. Example: if you think about a juicy, succulent orange bursting in your mouth right now, you will likely start salivating. In fact, I bet I just made you salivate while you were reading about thinking about it. If not, try it now: slow down, feel your body, close your eyes and think about a juicy orange bursting in your mouth. Notice the saliva activation in your mouth right now? You can activate your body's digestion process by thought alone, in a simple instant. Here's the kicker: sometimes we think thoughts that are not entirely true, are not true at all, or are not useful or beneficial to ourselves or others, and we still feel them very intensely (I'll explain why later) and we mistake *intensity* for "truth".

Here's how it works:

If I am walking in the woods and I see a stick that looks sort of like a snake from the corner of my eye, my body will "sound the alarm" and activate survival mode. (Remember, our inner alarm system is designed to always sound in the face of what *could* be a threat, not just in the face of what is *definitely* a threat.) This emergency response is important, as it's how we survive in life-or-death situations, but it is rather trigger-happy in people who are in survival mode often (aka, people who are "stressed"). I am not just talking about people who are obviously reeling from trauma or have a "diagnosis." I am talking about most of us. I am talking about you; there I said it. So, in the face of any doubt whatsoever, you, me and everyone you know are designed to instantly and automatically perceive the stick as a snake. This will trip my alarm system, even though it's actually a stick, and as a result, fear will course through my veins (as if it is actually a snake). I will react to the stimulus by pulling away and keeping all my attention *narrowed* on the "threat." Among all this panic, the rest of the environment will fall away from my conscious awareness as I zero in on the "snake."

This all happens in less than a second, automatically.

My "thinking brain" will then monitor the "fear" sensations in my body and confirm, "Yup, lots of fear going on in there. It *must* be a snake." Upon this "confirmation" that the thing I saw "must" be a snake, I will start to feel more fear. My heart rate will increase; my breath will get shallow and rapid; my focus will narrow more acutely; I will tense my muscles (especially around my vulnerable areas, like my eyes, stomach, chest, genitals, and neck); and my body will prepare to fight, run, or hide. While monitoring all these worsening "fear" sensations, my "thinking brain" will think more about why I "must" be afraid (to justify these feelings): *What if it's venomous? I'm nowhere near a hospital.* These concomitant thoughts now generate more "fear" sensations. And on and on the cycle goes!

Through this process, I have gotten stuck in a thinking-feeling loop: I think what I feel, and I feel what I think. This loop generates intensity, which I mistake for truth. It *feels* true, and so it "must be" true.

This can be an adaptive process when we're talking about the specific example of walking in the woods. Better safe than sorry, right? It's not the end of the world if, when focusing on the "snake" to my right, I miss the beautiful joy hawk that just landed on a treetop to my left. But when we take this mechanism out of the woods and into day-to-day life, where there aren't often snakes who are trying to poison you, we miss out on *all* the majestic hawks—that is, all the joy, love, connection, safety, inspiration, wisdom, and beauty—that we don't have the capacity to notice when we are focused on "snakes." As a result, this mechanism wreaks havoc in our marriages, in our parenting, when we are at work, and when we are stuck in traffic. It also has us defending our "selves" (our thoughts and feelings we identify with) as if our life depends on it, to the point where we feel personally threatened if someone doesn't validate "our truth" (which we intensely feel is "right"). When this mechanism runs rampant (as it does for everyone who doesn't know about it and work to resolve it), we are at the mercy of survival mode's false alarms and misperceptions moment after moment, day after day, week after week, month after month, and year after year.

I don't know if you fully believe me when I say this happens to everyone. I mean *everyone*. Again, that means you (and, not judging, it means me, too). If you have not deliberately upgraded your default mode from survival mode to thriving mode, then you are also at the mercy of this mechanism, day in and day out and it's hurting you, the people you love, diminishing your quality of life, and detracting from the future you value and choose.

Consider for a moment a less obvious "threat" than a snake in the woods. Let's say when you wake up one morning, you notice that you are feeling anxious. Your mind doesn't like the fact that it doesn't immediately know why it feels anxious, so it starts scanning your environment (inner and outer) to find reasons why you "must" be feeling anxious.

Let's say you haven't been sleeping very well lately. Cortisol is one of the main hormones responsible for waking us up in the morning, and if we haven't been getting the deep sleep and rest that we require for "neural sweeping" to happen, we get a lot of "stress" residue buildup in the brain. This means we don't start the day with a clean slate. Instead, the cortisol we all require to wake normally and naturally puts us over the edge, and we start the day by feeling "anxious." So, your feeling of anxiety when you woke up that morning was triggered by this spike in cortisol that is designed to wake you, me, and everyone else, from sleep. You don't know this, though, and your brain is not a fan of uncertainty in the face of unpleasant stimuli. So, it starts to connect your anxiety with that pain in your belly (*Is it cancer?*), or that tightening in your chest *(Is it the presentation that's due at work?)*, or your financial situation (*It must be the credit card bill*), or your relationship issues (*It's the problems in my marriage*). That you simply haven't slept well and are getting an overdose of cortisol is a perfectly logical explanation for why you're feeling anxious. To make things worse, all these inner and outer experiences are interpreted through the lens of the negativity bias, so your mind sees the worst possibilities in each of these problems. This generates more sensations, i.e. more cortisol, that you mistake as "proof" of your conclusions.

Here's a summary of this process, so you can conceptualize it clearly:

1. Survival mode demands that you narrow your focus on "threats" (real, perceived, literal, or ideological). When you do so, you are blinded to other possibilities and solutions. (This is a fact.)
2. Then, you get stuck and ruminate on the "worried" thoughts, feelings and sensations that come with these "threats."
3. This amplifies the "worried" feelings and sensations you're feeling.
4. This leads you to confirm, "That's it! It must be a real threat. That's why I must feel anxious."
5. These anxious feelings, over time, "confirmed" as "real," get strung together to form an identity that is based on reactive thoughts and feelings, and you end up with a reactive personality structure, (e.g., "I am anxious").
6. Through the Identity → Belief → Perception → Experience mechanism (which you will learn about in depth in Part 3), anxiety becomes a filter through which you experience the world and which you defend as "my truth."
7. To justify your truth, your thinking mind searches for evidence as proof, "See, the world is worthy of my *being* anxious, it really is full of snakes, it must be full of snakes, and I know they're snakes because I have a panic attack and a stomach ulcer to prove it."

Can you see why it is so important for you to learn how to distinguish yourself from your thoughts and feelings and to not define yourself by these transitory, often-inaccurate phenomena?

You can discover this distinction for yourself by meditating (as we have covered) and by engaging in a simple mental exercise: consider whether your thoughts and the feelings they generate are *useful*, rather than whether they are "true." The "truth" is far more relative than we may like to admit, and besides, clear thinking is that which is useful. So, ask yourself, "Does the way I am thinking right now produce the feelings and sensations that nourish me, or poison me? Will the way I am thinking and feeling right now logically result in more of what I want to experience in the future, or less of it?"

The Three Poisons

In Dharma traditions from "the East," what we call "negative emotions" are spoken of more brashly as "poisons." This term is used deliberately to connote how harmful it is to stay stuck in states of upset.

I am only going to touch briefly on this philosophy here. It constitutes a lifetime of study and, once again, is a topic that will be covered in more depth in book three of this series.

Poison #1: "Me" = Separate = Fear

Of all the "poisons," there are three main ones that lead to all "toxic emotions." The origin of all the "poisons" (and therefore the things that cause human beings to suffer) is fear, and fear arises naturally from the root sense of a separate self.

In other words, you feel fear when you perceive yourself as a being that is separate from everything else. When I perceive myself as an isolated "me," my experience is "Me + Everything Else = All." Naturally, when I compare this "me" to literally everything else, I feel separate, distinct, discrete, small, alone, and impotent. This sense of self naturally gives rise to the original fear, which dharma traditions call "ignorance," or, as translated by Buddhist scholar, teacher, and practitioner Bob Thurman, "mis-knowing[14]." This mis-knowing spawns fear, and from fear, all other types of suffering. Fear:

1. Which activates the tendency towards survival mode...
2. Which gets me to perceive "sticks" as "snakes..."
3. Which gets me to react as if the stick is a snake...
4. Which triggers real venom to course through my veins...
5. Which gets me to identify with the thoughts and feelings that are associated with self-preservation at all costs ...

---

[14] Thurman, R. A. F. (Host). (2015, June 25). Buddhist Inner Sciences: Mis-knowing— Ep. 22 [Audio podcast episode]. In *Bob Thurman Podcast*. Tibet House US.

6.   Which (ironically) reinforces my sense of "separateness..."
7.   Which (ironically) reactivates my original fear and spirals into all types of suffering and disease...
8.   Which (ironically) cuts me off from the feelings of safety and connection that empower my creativity and joy...

And around and around I go on the not-so-merry-go-round of cyclic suffering (known as "*samsara*").

Survival mode is, amounts to, and reinforces the original mis-knowing "me"-consciousness that triggers this entire cycle.

It is characterized by "win-lose," "lose-win," and "lose-lose" mindsets that are based on fear and self-defensive reactions to fear (fighting, running away, and hiding—aka "fight, flight, freeze") as well as self-defensive reactive personality structures. All of these are compounded by filtering experience through a negatively-biased lens that makes us easily convinced of being right, with an automatic tendency of projecting our "truth" on self, others and the world while interacting with and reacting to others' survival mode mis-knowing, reactive personalities and projections just the same.

Have you noticed the madness?

On the other hand, thriving mode is, amounts to, and reinforces "we"-consciousness, whereby I am one with and a contiguous part of ALL and we are all together, as interconnected parts of a miraculous whole. In this space, we recognize that we are not only waves, but that we are part of the interconnected ocean, that the ocean is also who we are and who everyone else is, and that we can experience all of our individual uniqueness as waves while simultaneously relaxing into our "sameness," with the knowledge that we all come from and return to the ocean and at our core the ocean is really who we are. This sense of "we" lends itself to feeling safe and supported such that we are willing and able to explore, with a genuine interest in contributing to the "win-win", participating in value exchanges, with a sense of meaning and purpose. As a result, in thriving mode, we find that experience is characterized innately by joy, openness, love, kindness, awareness, gratitude, presence, and surrender (the JOLKA-GPS).

Fear is, of course, very healthy and necessary when you are facing an actual threat in real time. But long-term human suffering does not arise from this kind of fear. Long-term human suffering comes from your wires getting crossed and your survival mechanisms protecting the life of your ego; your stories; your identities; your misperceptions; your "truth." Consider the equation we just talked about (Me + Everything Else = All). It's no wonder you feel small, separate, and afraid. Yet that "me" is not who you really are, it is actually about what's happened to you encapsulated as a description about your experiences and reactions. It is a description about life, not life itself. You are *Life* itself, always arising as Awareness, free to choose as Willingness. The "me-story" is a conglomerate of thoughts and feelings that have developed as a reaction to anything and everything that has ever happened to you, believing it to be who you are, and worthy of defending by activating survival neurochemistry that is (ironically) wearing you out and preventing you from feeling the joy you sense is your birthright (because in thriving mode, it is). Clearly, this is neither a sustainable, nor a desirable way to live. Yet, it is "*normal.*" *Everyone* is looking for love in all the wrong places, except those who are finding it where it's always been.

Poison #2 and Poison #3: Fighting for Control and Embodying "Lack"

From the original idea that we are separate from everything else (and the fear that arouses) comes the other two poisons: fighting for control, and a pervasive sense of "lack." The latter is what I am teaching my kids to recognize as a "never enough" mindset. I remind them of this when they inevitably ask for one more cookie, one more show, and so on. When identified with our lack, we grasp delusionally at the notion that more will eventually make me happy.

We often think that the antidote to the problems in our lives lies in us either being in control, or in us filling our perpetual sense of "lack" with "stuff" (e.g., achievements, material items, relationships, and consumption of all kinds). However, to experience a life of joyful excellence by design, we need to realize that all our suffering arises from us 1) identifying as our thoughts and feelings and 2) failing to realize that we are an Aware-Will that is connected to everything else and is already full of everything we need to thrive. We are, in our very essence, much more than enough. Indeed, there is no amount of more that will ever fulfill the one who is drunk on the poison of their mis-perceived lack. And, fighting for control to preserve the very false sense of a limited self that is the reason why we feel so out of control in the first place, is why we feel like dogs chasing our own tails hustling 'round and 'round until we collapse on our mats with barely a taste of satisfaction.

Understanding these concepts is a very far cry from living them, and the action-based, body-centric tools in this book will allow you to build a foundation for experiencing these philosophical explanations as your direct experience of life. Doing this work ongoing is taking place in the ALL Together Academy training grounds as you read this. As you do the work and use the tools, you will discover that just as the three poisons are a natural and inevitable result of you feeling small, separate, afraid, and lacking, as you fight for control, the JOLKA-GPS is a natural and thrilling expression of connection and ease that arises when coming from who you really are and value and choose to be. From the sense of safety you discover in "we"-consciousness and from your growing capacity to take refuge in the constancy of yourself as Aware-Will, you can explore, discover, learn, grow, and create the life you value and choose to. When you recognize yourself as being an Aware-Will, you can choose to operate from your values-based creative identity (your C-IAM) and not from your reactive identity (the Reactive-iWAS) (explained in part III). This reveals the JOLKA-GPS and provides the right conditions for your acorn to become an Oak Tree that gives off enough acorns to populate forest after forest. By becoming who you are—you automatically and inherently contribute to the greater good.

Together, we thrive.

Moving Beyond Thoughts and Feelings: Acceptance and Pivoting

Your first step to pivoting to a more optimal state is eliminating the idea of "truth" as something that is absolute. Over-validating the "truth" of what you are thinking and feeling can be a disabling type of false compassion, because it is not compassionate to stay in a state of suffering, especially one dominated by the brain's negativity bias.

How do you do this? Well, it's another ironic thing, the first step to pivoting towards creating the future you value and choose is accepting what is. So, it's not that we deny, dismiss, invalidate, or ignore—that wouldn't work at all, and I will explain why. We start with total, radical acceptance of our reactive thoughts and feelings, but we just don't stay there! After acceptance has taken place, you need to *move*. As I remember a meme I once saw saying, "If you are in hell, don't stay there!"

We need solid grand to pivot *on*, and acceptance gives us the solidity we need to step in a better direction and pivot to a more beneficial state of being. Acceptance is the basis of kindness and a life of joyful excellence by design. If you are resisting your experience, you are amplifying your suffering. Pain X Resistance = Suffering. Resistance is a multiplier. The more resistance there is, the more suffering there is. Plus, if we are angry about our anger, not only have we multiplied anger, but we are still relating to our experience from survival mode, "fight". If we are afraid to look at our fears, we are relating to our experience from survival mode, "flight." And if we are hiding from life or numbing out, we are relating to our experience from survival mode, "freeze."

Fully accepting, "I as an Aware-Will notice I am feeling angry" (which is very different from I AM angry, or you *make me* angry) is our first step because its coming from one of the thriving mode's innate JOLKA-GPS virtues—Awareness. From Awareness, I can now choose to exercise my Will to be creative. But if I am resisting my experience, hating it, rejecting it, denying it, avoiding it, running from it, ignoring it, numbing it, I am still in survival mode, which is inherently reactive, subject to the negativity bias and stuck on the not so merry go 'round.

Resistance can look like lots of things, but it always includes judgments about what's happening, and conclusions based on those judgments. Alternatively, when you accept your pain as it is and do not resist it by telling stories about your pain (such as how much you hate your pain or what it says about you, others, or the world), you eliminate suffering from the equation. This frees up lots of energy—energy you can use to move to a more optimal state.

Pain X Non-Useful Story About Pain = Suffering.

Once you drop the story that is draining your vitality or stop the bleeding (as I like to think of it), you can start to scab over, and the healing process begins. The healing process starts when we accept our pain and feel it directly, on the level of sensations in our body, without adding stories about why we are in pain, how did the pain start, will the pain ever end? When we learn, assisted by our meditation practice, to "be with" the sensations of pain, as an Aware-Will, we will find things start to open up automatically and we start to notice more possibilities. I would again like to emphasize, acceptance of what is happening is important, but you can't get stuck there because you are liable to ruminating that will end up poisoning you. The difference that makes a difference, as modalities like ACT (acceptance and commitment therapy) are proving, is to accept what has happened to you, and then *pivot* toward your values, contribution, and participation.

In Part III, we will develop an entire set of maps, tools, and instructions that will reveal *what* you, uniquely, can pivot toward and *how* you can go about doing so, so that there is no guesswork and so you know exactly what to do in the face of tough times. As Dr. Joe Dispenza often says, "When it's hardest is when it matters the most." Accept the bad stuff and then commit to your values. That kind of "therapy" works. It's when you get stuck in Storyland trying to fix, figure out, over-validate, and defend "your truth", or you resist, avoid, ignore, deny, run and hide from what you know you must face, you can see why the mental health pandemic is getting worse and not better as people vacillate between indulging in, and numbing from, their suffering.

Macho culture wants you to deny *x* and pretend it doesn't exist ("Suck it up, you're fine"). Therapy culture wants you to figure out where *x* came from, how it got here, and whose fault it is. Self-help culture wants you to fix *x* at all costs. Consumerism wants to amplify *x*, so you keep buying salves and solutions. Corporate culture wants to exploit *x* and occasionally give you a bonus for grinding harder. None of this works, because all these approaches are based on you staying stuck on *x*. Instead, you need to pivot toward *y*. But you first need to accept, "I'm stuck on *x*," so that you have solid ground to stand on as you look to move toward *y* (the future you value and choose to create).

If you would like to watch a throwback video I did on this topic, you can find that in Lesson 4 of your book resources at www.alltogether.academy/joy-bucket-tools. Here, I offer an advanced perspective on the popular Human Resources version of the "EQ" concept.

Thinking and Feeling is Everything: Recap and Reflection

- You are not your thoughts and feelings. Your state of being, or who you are, lies beyond thoughts and feelings. It can appear to take on the *characteristics, colors, and flavors* of thoughts and feelings, but is, in its nature as Awareness, independent of those thoughts and feelings the same way a mirror accurately reflects but is not materially changed by what it reflects. The proof that you are not your thoughts and feelings lies in the fact that you, as "Awareness," can notice your thoughts and feelings arising within you, like a mirror would, if sentient, notice what it was reflecting without being disturbed by what it is reflecting. Therefore, you are not your thoughts and feelings. You are that which notices them (Aware) and can choose what to do next irrespective of them (Will).
- When mis-identified as who you think you are and when not coming from your nature as an Aware-Will unmoved by what you notice in your Awareness, you think what you feel and you feel what you think in a self-enforcing "loop" that makes you think (and feel), *See? I'm right.* Confused and enamored by the intensity of the sensations driven by the mis-perceived thoughts, you mistake intensity of feeling for "truth."
- When you identify as your story about who you are, you use survival mode to defend this identity (not your actual life) and spend all

sorts of "upset" energy on "being right" that the stick is actually a snake and therefore it "makes you" upset.

- Because your story-self (which is based on your thoughts and feelings) is so unreliable and unstable despite your attempts to solidify it by assigning a sense of identity to it (I AM angry), and because you have to use real survival mechanisms to constantly defend your (false) self 's "truth," identifying as this story about yourself actually does you real harm, because of the near-constant state of stress is generates.

- Correctly identifying (through doing the work) the fact that your false self (generated from your thoughts and feelings, which through repetition and/or intensity form beliefs) is false and ephemeral brings a sense of peace, safety, and trust in yourself as Aware-Will, which is constant, steady, always available, reliable and allows for the recognition of inherent Joy, Openness, Love, Kindness, Awareness, Gratitude, Presence and Surrender. Taking refuge in what is always the case (Aware-Will), you can afford to take a chance in life and explore, discover, learn, grow, and create something better.

- Becoming better at "fighting for control" (i.e., more effectively defending your false self from a place of fear) or trying to fill your unfillable void of "lack" with "more" stuff will never work.

- When you 1) come to know and believe that you are safe much or most of the time, 2) explore, discover, learn, grow, and create as an Aware-Will more often, and 3) express your values through your chosen identity (your C-IAM) along your Neurochemical Roadmap to the Future You Value and Choose (your NRF), your experience becomes more and more oriented to the JOLKA-GPS (joy, openness, love, kindness, awareness, gratitude, presence, and surrender). These states of being are intrinsic, in that they arise *from you being you*. The more you understand and take advantage of this, the more imperturbable you become. You are already fulfilled, so you are now free to interact with others in the world *sans* neediness and with creativity, spontaneity, and effectiveness.

- Survival mode says and confirms that "Me + Everything Else = All." This makes you feel small, separate, and afraid. But that "me" was created by your imagination, using the thoughts and feelings you've had in fear-based reaction to anything and everything that has ever happened to you. These thoughts and feelings perpetuate the cycle of individual and collective suffering in the world.

- Thriving mode activates "we"-consciousness and your desire and capacity to contribute to and participate in the collective "win-win-win" This dynamic facilitates you being of the greatest possible benefits to yourself (win), others (win), and ALL (win).
- Consistent meditation practice gives the "portable pause" and space you need to experience these philosophical principles as direct, actionable, workable, and useful truths. Reactivity (survival mode), by definition, leaves no room for choice, and choice, by definition, can only come after a pause. In our spiritual training gym, where we study with my mentor, we remind ourselves with a slogan hung on the wall that the bottom line of doing the work to thrive is to "Continuously cultivate the portable pause of extra and open attention," and the first order of business is to "change state."

Homework

Continue to learn about extra and open attention, the foundation of ALL meditation techniques, in our online learning community, at www.alltogether.academy/joy-bucket-tools for free. After watching the intro video in Lesson 3.1 of your Joy Bucket tools, you can start practicing with the playlist of ten ten-minute guided meditations in Lesson 3.2.

10

SLEEP, REST, AND RELAXATION (SRR) IS EVERYTHING

E VERYTHING ARISES FROM NOTHING. LIFE COMES from darkness. Possibilities await in the unknown. Stillness and silence are pregnant with potential. Yet we live in a culture that forces and craves compulsive "doing" and constant stimulation. This makes us sick and crazy and bars us from the benefits and fruits that arise from deep, dark, quiet, mysterious stillness.

To live life to the fullest, we must *cultivate* rest and bask in the stillness and silence of the unknown. When we get good at this, we enter a state of deep safety that feels like a womb of awesome potential. From this space, we can reset and emerge new, fresh, and open to the awe and wonder of a life characterized more by spontaneity than by the drudgery most of us are accustomed to.

You may think this sounds funny. We need to cultivate rest? Resting is a skill we can "get good at?" Shouldn't that just be something we take for granted? Isn't rest something we just crash into once we're exhausted from a productive day? Oh, the irony. How productive and beneficial we could be if we learned to drink from the fountain of spacious serenity that lies within! Besides, if anything worth having is worth working for (and deep rest is essential, believe me), isn't it worth cultivating as a skill on purpose?

In this chapter, I am going to paint a picture of what I do to cultivate sleep and rest. Please don't judge me as nuts or shame yourself when you see that I have quite an extensive health cultivation routine. I've been at this for twenty-five years, and it is my passion and joy. Plus, my tendencies toward depression and anxiety, along with my complications from head trauma and severe chronic illness, have inspired me to become a professional at self-care. Instead of thinking, *Wow, I don't do much of that. I am not enough,* try thinking, *Wow, I don't do much of that, so adding any of it into my life—even just one thing—will be awesome movement in the right direction!* Also know that all the things I do every day have been built into my life through me asking the grace and ease question: "What is the next, easiest thing I am willing to do right now?" It wouldn't make much sense for you to strain yourself as you work to cultivate deep rest, so I invite you to approach this "everything" with similar grace and ease.

Something else to note: struggle is the opposite of rest, so once you stop struggling and start cultivating rest, you may feel more tired. This is not actually the case. You are now just feeling how tired you have really been. When I first became more adept at learning how to turn off my alarm system (more about that in Part III), I actually needed more rest than I do now, at the time of writing (barring my surgery recovery, of course; I have needed lots of sleep during that). I've also found this to be the case for lots of my clients who have healed from trauma or being chronically stressed out.

When your alarm switch is on much of the time, your body does not allow you to rest deeply, or sometimes to even register how tired you really are. From the perspective of a brain that just wants to survive, deep sleep is dangerous, and recognizing one's exhaustion is a vulnerability the brain thinks it can't afford to dwell on or acknowledge. "We must stay vigilant!" it yells. This means that time and time again, people who have finally learned how to turn off the alarm switch in our work together have said to me, "Am I doing something wrong? I am so tired." No, you are doing it right; you are just experiencing the aftermath of your body being in survival mode for years (which is kind of like running a marathon 24/7).

Throughout this journey, please be gentle and kind to yourself, and allow yourself to rest and rejuvenate. If you respect your body's pace and natural wisdom, you will feel vital again!

Each of the ingredients I put into the recipe below are easy to implement. It is when we add the ingredients together that we get a delicious dish! As Robin Sharma said in *The 5 AM Club*, "Seemingly small actions performed consistently over time yield staggering results."[15]

You may notice that not all these practices seem to be directly related to sleep, rest, and relaxation. However, they all contribute to profound SRR. It's all one interconnected web.

Without further ado (and with the acknowledgment that I don't always do all these things, but it's great to have options!):

---

[15] Sharma, R. (2018): The 5 AM Club: Own Your Morning. Elevate Your Life, p.123, HarperCollins.

My SRR Routine

My rest cultivation begins when I wake up at 5AM to an alarm that doesn't alarm me. For me, this is a clock that mimics the sunrise gradually, so I am not "alarmed" but gently awoken.

While still in bed, as soon as I remember to, I put my hands on my heart and invoke gratitude for life. Then, while still in bed, I pandiculate. I simultaneously and organically stretch, twist, flex, shake, and yawn like a dog or cat does, allowing my body to move however it wants to.

I sit up, and before putting my feet on the ground, I put my palms together at my heart in the classic prayer position and say, "I allow myself to meet this day with love and gratitude." I smile (whether I feel like it or not) and then (and only then) place my feet on the ground to start the day. (Do you know it takes more muscles to frown than it does to smile? If you are tired, you can save some energy by turning that frown upside down!)

All of this only takes a few minutes. But why 5AM? Well, a few reasons.

- I am a co-CEO of a family, and my wife and I don't have a chance of leading our family as exemplars of what it is to thrive if we don't prioritize deep R&R, joy, love, gratitude, peace, space, quiet, and exercise before making breakfast and lunches, combing hair, brushing teeth, and herding kids to school.

- Waking up before or with the sunrise (when I am not recovering from an illness or injury) not only enables me to be conscious of the energies of stillness, silence, and vitality that are inherent in this time of day, but it also harmonizes my natural rhythms with nature's rhythms. My body, mind, and spirit work better when they are in harmony with nature. Nature gets up when the sun gets up, so, as a natural being, so do I. Also, if I wake up with the sun, I am infinitely more productive and have much more than enough time to be creative. Millions of years of evolution have led to our circadian rhythms being in sync with the sun and the moon. I realize "night owls" might protest this, but it's pretty safe to say (and research agrees) that our neurobiology works so much better when we follow nature's clock[16].

---

[16] Mental health: Foster, R. G., & Wulff, K., 2010, The impact of light and dark on mental health. Current Psychiatry Reports, 12(5), 417–423; Physical health: Poggiogalle, E., Jamshed, H., & Peterson, C. M., 2018, Circadian rhythms and metabolic health. Chronobiology International, 35(7), 989–1005.

- When I wake up at 5AM, I am tired by 9PM, which enables me to get to sleep before 10PM. This means my body is recharging when it is most conducive to do so (from 10PM to 2AM). There really is something to be said for, "Early to be, early to rise, makes a man healthy, wealthy, and wise."

Starting my day "on the right foot" is essential. It should be illegal for me not to! Ask my wife; I can be a jerk otherwise!

My rest cultivation continues:

- Fifteen minutes after I get out of bed (having already gone to the bathroom, brushed my teeth, washed my face with cold water, and drank twenty ounces of room temperature or warm water—see the hydration everything below), when I do gentle movement exercises, like more pandiculating, before sitting down to meditate.
- When I get out in the sunlight for at least fifteen minutes within the first two hours after sunrise, to establish my circadian rhythm. (Do not look directly at sun. Just being outside is enough. It works even if it's cloudy.)
- When I do a fog breath session every time I pee, "drip feeding" the neurochemicals of parasympathetic (rest, digest, heal) ease throughout the day.
- When I pandiculate or do other movement exercise "snacks" between seeing clients or doing chores on the weekends (more on that in Chapter 12).
- When I remember to practice extra and open attention during my day-to-day interactions (we'll cover that in Part III).
- When I intermittently fast (see Chapter 14), which resets my metabolic and hormonal activity and decreases inflammation, to set me up for deep, rejuvenating sleep later.
- When I drastically reduce my sugar and carbohydrate intake or eliminate them from my diet almost entirely, which resets my metabolic and hormonal activity and decreases inflammation, to set me up for deep, rejuvenating sleep (not to mention longevity of a quality life with my wits intact).
- When I take a cold shower, which resets my metabolic and hormonal activity and decreases inflammation, to set me up for deep, rejuvenating sleep later (but not at night because this can ironically raise my body temperature, which would be counter-productive for deep sleep).
- When I get fifteen to thirty minutes of sunshine on as much bare skin as the law allows each day, which resets my metabolic and

hormonal activity and decreases inflammation, to set me up for deep, rejuvenating sleep later.

- When I tell the people in my life how much I love them and get lots of vitamin O ("Oxytocin") by giving and receiving extra-long hugs which resets our metabolic and hormonal activity and decreases inflammation, to set us up for deep, rejuvenating sleep later.
- When I exercise every single day, which resets my metabolic and hormonal activity and decreases inflammation, to set me up for deep, rejuvenating sleep later.
- When I properly hydrate myself, which resets my metabolic and hormonal activity and decreases inflammation, to set me up for deep, rejuvenating sleep later.
- When I feel like I accomplish and kick ass throughout the day and am living a life full of meaning and purpose, which resets my metabolic and hormonal activity and decreases inflammation, to set me up for deep, rejuvenating sleep later.
- When I meditate for the second time in the day before lunch (which is my first meal of the day, per the parameters of my intermittent fasting). Note: A meditation session can be (and is perhaps even most effective when it is) short and on point. One breath, thirty seconds, one minute, five minutes... these short sessions are how we integrate timeless wisdom into our precious time here in this life[17].
- When I lay down for a fifteen-minute or thirty-minute guided power nap or some yoga nidra (we'll explore this later in this chapter) after lunch. No animal I want to emulate in nature stays awake all day uninterrupted. Some human animals labor under ludicrous cultural beliefs that siestas are somehow weak or unproductive, but nothing could be further from the truth. Take naps. The king of the jungle takes naps. Prey animals do not take naps because they are in survival mode all the time and fear they will get eaten. Besides, if you consistently wake up at 5AM, you will be ready for that afternoon nap!

---

[17] When you think about it, one of the "things" that meditation "is" is resting. It is practicing resting the body and the thinking mind, while keeping your awareness alert. It is practicing relaxing. And if you practice something, you get good at it, right? By starting my day this way, I am showing my body, mind, and spirit and the universe that resting, relaxing, and thriving is my priority, first things first!

- When I do more exercise "snacks" in the afternoon. These take just one to five minutes each time.
- When I meditate for the third time in the day after I'm done working, so that I can reset my day, body, mind, and spirit to enjoy the evening with my family. (Again, I keep this session short and sweet.)
- When I stop eating a few hours before bed, because if my body is still digesting food during sleep, it screws up my sleep hormones and my digestive processes.
- When I stop looking at screens a few hours before bed, because the blue light emitted from them fools my neurochemistry into thinking it's still daytime, which alters the circadian rhythms that govern my sleep and sabotages my capacity to get deep and rejuvenating sleep.
- When at 9PM, after reading bedtime stories and putting my kids to bed, I start my going-to-sleep routine, because being sound asleep between 10PM and 2AM is optimal for recharging and healing.
- When I consciously move more slowly and pay more attention to the stillness and quiet of the evening.
- When I wash my face with cold water, brush my teeth, and put on "sleeping clothes." (Just kidding. I'm a naked sleeper.)
- When I light candles and incense and consider the notion that sleep is sacred and worthy of a clean environment, energetically and physically.
- When I practice gentle movement exercises like pandiculating.
- When I meditate for the fourth time of the day.
- When I review my day.
- When I notice any tensions that arose during the day and release them by simply noticing them, expanding my extra and open and attention, and spreading my hands by my sides, allowing the tension to drip from my body.
- When I "rewrite the script" and imagine things that didn't go as great as they could have gone going much better. This practice is amazing. Much of the REM cycle in dream sleep is dedicated to processing the tensions that you dealt with throughout the day, so if you (as an Aware-Will) do this work consciously, then REM doesn't need to. This means your sleep is deeper (because you aren't having stress-filled dreams) and your dreams become more lucid and can contribute to you thriving (and you wake up feeling more rested). Much of the reason why we wake up tired is because

even our sleep is dominated by survival mode; it is processing the stresses of the day that we did not already digest.

- When I sit on the edge of my bed like I did in the morning (when I got up), put my hands in the prayer position, invoke gratitude for my life, and say, "I allow myself to fall sleep in a state of love and gratitude."
- When I lie down and practice fog breathing with my awareness zoned in on the heart area. I focus on gratitude and imagine my body dissolving into the darkness of infinite love.

For R&R troubleshooting, I have a notebook next to my bed, so that if my mind is busy and stressed, I can write anything important enough to remember that will keep nagging me if I don't get it down. If I keep ruminating after that, I remind my mind, "Thank you but I already handled that. You are welcome to provide original thoughts that can help me thrive, but if not, it's time for sleep."

If I am restless and cannot fall asleep within fifteen minutes, I do not "toss and turn," frustratingly hoping for sleep to magically come over me. Instead, I get up, pandiculate, and do more fog breathing for five minutes. I then lay back down with my awareness on the heart area, focusing on gratitude and imagining my body dissolving into infinite love. If I still can't fall asleep easily and while in a beneficial state, I repeat: up for five minutes of stretching and breathing. I tell myself that even in the worst-case scenario (i.e., I don't fall asleep for a few hours—which happens!), I have at least done lots of movement and breathing that is good for me. I remind myself that if I am upset (i.e., frustrated or worried) because I can't fall asleep, that means survival mode is activated, which means my animal brain believes there is danger. I know my animal brain won't let me go to sleep until it feels safe, so in this situation, I get up and do something to turn the alarm switch off. Rather than trying to override biology and force myself to (not) sleep, I work with my situation as it is and allow myself to fall back to sleep naturally.

As you can see, getting a good night's sleep starts first thing in the morning and continues with the many things you do all day long to cultivate rest and a thriving approach to life. When I grant significance to all these positive investments I make into my life and future all day long, I not only make them more valuable in the moment, but I also earn interest over time. For example, when I fog breathe while peeing, I think, *Ahh, I'm going to have such a great sleep tonight.* This means I feel the benefits now and tonight, and I get the benefit of earning compound interest day in and day out. Everything beneficial that I do benefits everything else.

Sweet dreams!

If you would like a free PDF of the module I teach private clients about optimizing sleep, you can find that in Lesson 5 of your book resources at www.alltogether.academy/joy-bucket-tools.

The Biggest Bang for Your R&R Buck

Everything we're talking about in this book is important, but if I had to choose one practice that has contributed the most to my (and clients') radical, beyond-logical, "don't need to know how, but all of a sudden I feel dramatically better, and stuff that used to bother me is simply gone" results, then that practice would be yoga nidra. I also probably have more than a few clients who are going to read this right now and laugh. Yoga nidra is one of those practices that works so well, we stop doing it. Start again!

The key instruction or goal of yoga nidra is, "Allow your body to sleep while your mind remains aware." The more you practice, the more you remain aware while you traverse brainwave states that are normally associated with dreams and deep sleep. In the meantime, you get lots of great naps, building your capacity to remain aware while your brain is in theta and delta waves.

For those who know nothing about it: yoga nidra is essentially a guided meditation for traversing the different brainwave states of consciousness (waking, dreaming, and sleeping), all while remaining lucid. This has tremendous benefits, in every way possible. The less technical explanation is that it is a kickass guided nap (but I can't help myself to say it is so much more!).

My first experience with guided naps was when I was training for the US National Hockey Team at the Olympic and Para-Olympic Training Center in Colorado Springs. I made it to the final sixty-four players in the nation, and though I didn't make the team (unfortunately), being guided down into deep sleep and back out (in those days, with a cassette tape!) in such a way where I felt totally refreshed in the space of fifteen minutes stuck with me as a valuable asset for optimal performance.

During my worst days with head trauma, I could always do yoga nidra, even if I couldn't do all the other things I wanted to do, such as play with my kids, look at a computer, move around, cook, exercise, ski, and so on. I mean, it's lying down, putting on headphones, and listening to instructions. Who can't do that? There is no excuse. You can also do it at any time: morning; middle of the day; before bed; when you can't sleep; when you wake in the middle of the night... There are no limits.

Researchers, such as Andrew Huberman, are currently catching up to what ancient wisdom has said about this for millennia and have started calling this practice "non-sleep deep rest," or NSDR (to avoid cultural complications, I presume). Whatever you want to call it, it's a total gamechanger when practiced consistently over time. I am generally more of a fan of the ancient wisdom versions and think the NSDR recordings I've tried out are a bit sterile in comparison to yoga nidra. That said, there's a ton of weekend workshop warriors out there offering yoga nidra on YouTube without a lot of training. So, find what works for you. I'll be sharing some suggestions in a moment.

I was introduced to yoga nidra many years ago, and honestly, the seeds didn't take root and blossom until recently. This isn't surprising, because I only recently started practicing it every day. Consistency is the key.

An expert in the field named Richard Miller was once invited to pilot yoga nidra with combat veterans. The Army didn't like the name "yoga nidra," so Miller named it iRest for the sake of the pilot. Here, he was playing off iTunes, iPads, and so on, and the obvious "I rest." Plus, "rest" is short for "restoration" and "i" is short for "integration," thus creating "integration-restoration"—a good name for what it does, when practiced regularly[18].

I highly recommend that you integrate iRest (yoga nidra) into your daily routine. Richard Miller also has a student, Molly Birkholm, who has lots of good free recordings on whatever platform you stream music on[19]. Ally Boothroyd's yoga nidra channel on YouTube has been my go-to everyday as of late[20]. If you want to not only practice yoga nidra but learn more about its components and how and why it works, then I recommend *iRest Meditation* by Richard Miller on Audible[21]. (I have no affiliation with any of these producers, by the way.)

Doing yoga nidra every day has a cumulative and potentially not obvious effect. I am not the only one to report the dawning awareness of, "Huh, that thought or situation that just occurred used to totally trigger me into a

[18] Laya, V., June 28, 2017, A conversation with Richard Miller. LA Yoga Ayurveda & Health. Retrieved from https://www.youtube.com/watch?v=Psl9FKh6qPg
[19] Birkholm, Molly. "Molly Birkholm." Apple Music, Apple Inc., music.apple.com/us/artist/molly-birkholm/875891735. iRest Yoga Nidra for Daily Living, IVM Music, 2014.
[20] Boothroyd, A. (2024): *Ally Boothroyd | Sarovara Yoga* [YouTube channel]. YouTube. Retrieved November 22, 2024, from www.youtube.com/c/SarovaraYoga
[21] Miller, R. (2015): iRest Meditation: Restorative Practices for Health, Resiliency, and Well-Being
[Audiobook]. Audible.

downward spiral for hours, days, weeks, and months, but just now, I barely noticed it. I wonder if the yoga nidra had something to do with it...?"

Yes, it did.

I could tell you my hypotheses about why it works. I could tell you about brainwaves; about muscle memory; about somatic therapy; about surrendering; about spirit; about unleashing the innate healing potential of your body, mind, and soul. I could tell you about it all. I could also tell you how the armed forces have integrated iRest into their day-to-day ops (anyone who goes overseas gets access and encouragement to practice it). I could tell you how I think if it helps people resolve trauma from war, it can probably help me and you. I could tell you about The Department of Defense's extensive research on the benefits of the practice in relieving combat-related PTSD [22]. But my point is this: even though yoga nidra is an "outside the box" approach, it has the stamp of approval from very "inside the box" establishments that don't mess around. Whether you look at it from the perspective of brain science or God science, the bottom line is, it works if you work it.

Sleep, Rest, and Relaxation (SRR) is Everything: A Case Study

I'm not the only person I know who has benefited tremendously from yoga nidra.

My client Margaret was juggling a lot when we were working together. She's super-smart and very up to speed with self-help stuff, but, as many of us have experienced at one time or another, life had managed to overwhelm her. She had a teenager who was struggling with severe mental illness, she was going through a really tense time in her marriage, and she was in the midst of vying for an NGO executive director position in her workplace.

Margaret and I had known each other for a while, so when I suggested she find a way to prioritize yoga nidra every day in among all of this, she didn't look at me like I was totally crazy. Instead, she ran with it. I didn't know this at the time, though.

About two months later, Margaret said, "Oh my God, Michael, I know the tools you suggest work—I mean, that's why I am here—but I must admit, I was kind of just doing the yoga nidra every day because I was

---

[22] See https://shop.irest.org/pages/veterans?_pos=1&_sid=273eb87de&_ss=r

exhausted and needed a nap. But lately, stuff that used to drive me to rage just doesn't anymore. My husband noticed that I totally didn't snap the other day about something that used to set me off every time. When he pointed it out, I was like, 'Oh my goodness, that's the yoga nidra! Just like Mike said!'"

Sleep, Rest, and Relaxation (SRR) is Everything: Another Case Study

Recently, our daughter was having more consistent nightmares than we considered "normal." There's been some huge challenges in our house lately, as I've been recovering from a huge and dicey surgery, which scared us all and presented our family with some major opportunities to practice what we teach. I have been in bed a lot, and this has left my wife to do everything herself. She's a total champ, but taking care of three kids 24/7, who need soccer rides, school lunches, groceries, and dinner, along with going to work, has been a lot. This led to tension in our home—tension that Sofia was absorbing.

Even though I was seriously compromised, I looked for ways I could contribute to our household and started taking on Sofia's bedtime routine more often. At first, I was still in a lot of physical pain myself and was easily agitated, and so I would often become frustrated. "Sofia, there's nothing to be afraid of! Just go to sleep!"

You can imagine how well this worked. *Not. At. All.*

Thankfully, I snapped out of my funk around Sofia's sleep disturbance relatively quickly and remembered the importance and power of ceremony. We constructed a quick and easy altar next to Sofia's bed, featuring a little statue of something she resonates with, along with some incense and a bell. I then helped her construct her own little ceremonial prayers. Knowing what I do about how the mind-body mechanism works regardless of one's beliefs about spiritual topics, I wanted her "prayers" to be internally empowered instead of externally dependent. So, I guided her to come up with three consistent statements of "asking" (prayer) that would also evoke from within her the mindset, confidence, and resilience she needed for this ceremony to be something she would believe would work, and that would also be internally empowering.

The first statement we settled on was:

1.   "I allow myself to have good dreams."

At first, when I asked Sofia what she wanted to say, she answered, "I don't want to have bad dreams." But, knowing the way the mind works, I asked her to consider what she *wants*, not what she doesn't. Why? Try this out: "I don't want to think about pink elephants with wings." See my point? What you focus on grows. So, I helped her focus on what she *wants* (good dreams), not what she *doesn't* want (bad dreams).

I also steered her away from "wanting" language. Once we ascertained her "want," I suggested she use "I allow" instead of "I want," because "wanting" confirms a state of "lack," and the parts of the brain that are responsible for dreams are very literal. If I say, "I want to be wealthy," that actually confirms my lack of wealth. And, as I repeat often, what we focus on grows, for better and for worse.

I also didn't suggest she make an "affirmation," because typically, those give the mind plenty of friction to argue with. "I will have good dreams," gives rise to immediate counterthoughts: "No, you won't." (And FYI, affirming things like "I am wealthy" works even worse, as the mind fights back: "No you aren't. That's bullshit.") "I allow this or that," on the other hand, tends to evoke the desired experience and not give the mind as much reason to argue back and cancel out the desired benefit.

The next statement she made (because I wanted her to be prepared and resilient in the event that she would still have an occasional bad dream) was:

2.   "Even if I have a bad dream, I allow myself to let it go quickly and not be bothered by it."

Then, finally:

3.   "I allow myself to wake up feeling great."

As I write, it's been a few weeks since we came up with these statements, and I recently said to her, "Sofia, I haven't heard you crying, and you haven't been coming into our room because of nightmares. Since you started doing the ceremony every night, have you had any?"

She giddily responded, "No, Daddy. I haven't had any."

"Really? That's amazing! None? You haven't had *any*?"

"Oh, wait," she said, "I had one."

"Really? What happened?"

"It didn't bother me at all. I went right back to sleep!" She started laughing and then gave me a high five.

For me this is an even better result than if she had zero nightmares. Instead, she got to experience her resilience. Even if, aside from, and especially because bad stuff happens, Sofia knows she can "let it go quickly and not be bothered by it."

Not only is Sofia enjoying the ripple effects of better sleep, but she is also now empowered with tools, resilience, and confidence that she can apply to other challenges that arise in her life.

A key note: she never would have learned she had these tools if she hadn't gone through the hardship in the first place. Life is our greatest teacher. If we pay attention, respond creatively, and master the curriculum, it will lead us to greater and greater health, wealth, happiness and wisdom.

Sleep, Rest, and Relaxation (SRR) is Everything: Recap and Reflection

- Deep SRR is everything. If anything worth having is worth working for, it's deep SRR.
- Deep SRR is a skill, and, like all skills, it must be cultivated.
- You can work therapists like me out of a job by really dialing in your sleep. By doing so, you can access brainwave states that process your emotional residue easily and automatically. You can learn more about what you need to know to optimize sleep in Lesson 5 of your book resources at www.alltogether.academy/joy-bucket-tools, particularly about how sleep states can help your process and resolve everything from emotional distress to traumatic memories.
- Everything beneficial benefits everything else. By practicing all my tools and making the most of life during the day, I sleep better at night, and by sleeping better at night, I am better able to make the most of life during the day.
- Yoga nidra will give you the biggest bang for your R&R buck.

What should you do next?

- To cultivate deep SRR, ask the grace and ease question: "What's the next, easiest thing I am willing to do?" Seemingly small actions done consistently over time yield staggering results. A recipe of lots of little things throughout the day adds up to a delicious dish of deep SRR.
- Practice yoga nidra/NSDR at least once a day. It is a total gamechanger that has freaky-good cumulative effects my clients have reported happening usually around the two- to three-month mark of doing it every day. Take a leap faith and just start!

11

THE PLEASURE–PAIN BALANCE IS EVERYTHING

" **A**S WE MOVE INTO THE FUTURE—especially as virtual reality becomes more readily available and intense spikes of dopamine become more and more ubiquitous—the healthy, happy, and sane will be differentiated from the walking-zombie, fettered masses by the ability to say no to oneself in the face of dopaminergic desires."

This is me paraphrasing (with a bit of my own flavor) one of my favorite sources for cutting-edge neuroscience at the time of this writing, Dr. Andrew Huberman. On what grounds does Dr. Huberman say this? Well, it all starts with "dopamine."

Dopamine

"Dopamine," as a useful generalization, is the neurotransmitter of desire and anticipation of a reward. It is not the reward itself.

Your brain wants you to go after certain things when it knows or feels you need them to survive or advance your species. So, it gives you spikes in dopamine, or feelings of pleasure, to motivate you to move in the direction of food, shelter, sex, and meaningful accomplishment.

In theory, dopamine should only motivate you to pursue courses of action that lead to true and actual satisfaction. A lot of the time, that is the case. Sometimes, though, it is not: dopamine can also motivate you to seek that which cannot and will not ever truly and meaningfully satisfy you. And it turns out that we get in a lot of trouble when we start seeking the hit for its own sake, or when we start seeking things that aren't intrinsically satisfying—trends which are spiking.

We can (and often do) get hooked on the "pleasure" that "dopamine" provides to such an extent that we never move toward true satisfaction and instead stay stuck on getting pleasure for pleasure's sake. We get stuck on getting the next object, goal, vacation, bonus, milestone, partner, donut, drug, movie, or status symbol that we think will finally satisfy us. This is a problem. When "dopamine" surges (which, in the present day, are readily available to us at all times) are triggered by stimuli that do not lead to intrinsically satisfying and beneficial rewards, you get stuck in a loop of "seeking," and in this loop, desire only begets desire. Since there is no fulfilment in the equation, you get tricked into wanting more and more of the "thing," without any actual payoff.

"Dopamine" is seeking, not finding. It is wanting, not having.

It appears that, quite simply, our brains have not adapted to the ever-present intense spikes of "dopamine" that are always within arm's reach these days. As such, many of us are innocently activating neurochemical processes that are making it impossible for us to be happy, to feel genuine pleasure, or to feel free from ongoing "anxiety" (which may really just be mini bouts of withdrawal from stimulus addiction).

> *The paradox is that hedonism, the pursuit of pleasure for its own sake, leads to anhedonia, which is the inability to enjoy pleasure of any kind*[23].

Pushing the "more dopamine" button too frequently to alleviate discomfort, boredom, anxiety, frustration, numbness, lethargy, and "depression" is what could be causing your discomfort, boredom, anxiety, frustration, numbness, lethargy, and "depression" in the first place, in the form of tiny withdrawals throughout the day that urge you to "take another hit."

Our pleasure–pain balance is totally out of whack.

The Pleasure–Pain Balance

Every time we stimulate dopamine (even through relatively innocuous behaviors like checking our email), we activate something called the

---

[23] Lembke, A. (2021): Dopamine Nation: Finding Balance in the Age of Indulgence, p. 12, Dutton Books.

pleasure–pain balance in our brain. This evolutionary design assures that we will never feel satisfied enough, so that we keep moving (aka, hunting, seeking a mate, and finding greener pastures). So, when we push the "pleasure button," there is always an equal and opposite "pain" response. Our brain literally produces endogenous pain to maintain the balance. Rats, who have a similar pleasure–pain structure to us, will literally starve to death even though food has been placed one inch from their mouth when scientists overstimulate the "pleasure" side. Without the "pain" balance, they lose the motivation to do anything[24].

This concept probably sounds familiar to us all. Who hasn't experienced a sense of disappointment or loss after enjoying something, especially something you built up big expectations about? This "letdown" after pleasure is normal, natural, and healthy! We need it! Yet many of us, in response to this, hit the pleasure button again ("More!") to escape that momentary discomfort, and this means homeostasis cannot return. Think of refreshing your FB feed, binge-watching, "one more cookie," "one more drink," "one more orgasm," "one more million dollars," and so on. This is a trap, because there is never an amount of "more" that will be satisfying, because we are designed to maintain this pleasure–pain balance. The more we seek pleasure, the more we activate pain.

This makes me think of the stories we all know about the rich and famous who are so miserable that they abuse drugs and kill themselves, despite all their fortune; about the rockstar who plays in front of fifty thousand adoring fans and thinks, *There must be something wrong with me if I don't feel happy, even with all of this.* The rockstar may seek more stimulation—more fun; a bigger thrill—to find ways to ramp up the pleasure or numb that pain, but to truly end this cycle, he needs to learn that there is nothing wrong with him at all; that the pleasure produced the pain, and if he could just sit with the pain, accept it, and let it be, balance would return, and, with it, peace, satisfaction, and gratitude for such a privileged life.

A while back, I was invited to be a guest on Matthew Del Negro's podcast, *10,000 NOs.* (Ironic, considering the practice of saying "no" is a topic we'll be discussing in the upcoming pages!) Matt is a skilled interviewer, and he was able to draw from me my story of overcoming severe depression in a way that has been compelling for many to listen to (you can

---

[24] Olds, J., & Milner, P. (1954). Positive reinforcement produced by electrical stimulation of septal area and other regions of rat brain. Journal of Comparative and Physiological Psychology, 47(6), 419-427.

find this at www.alltogether.academy/speaking). I also recently saw an Instagram Reel of Matt talking to Michael Imperioli from *The Sopranos*, and it perfectly summarizes what I am explaining about the pain-pleasure balance[25]. The huge irony here is that the only way you can actually feel satisfied is by saying "no" to yourself; by feeling the discomfort and the pain of wanting "more"; by allowing homeostasis and equanimity to return. For innocuous things, this return of balance usually takes one to three minutes. Ever noticed when eating ice cream (or indulging in something similar) that you always want more, even though the only real pleasure lies in the first lick or two? If you learn to stop, say no, and allow that craving for "more" to dissipate, then you can feel actual satisfaction as your brain comes back online just a few minutes later. *Ahh, that was just right. That was enough. I feel satisfied.* Alternatively, if you don't say "enough" to yourself, you will keep indulging until you feel stuffed, sick, and ashamed. There's no real pleasure in that!

The big problems come when we chronically hit the "more" button in tons of tiny moments throughout the day (or with more "obvious" addictions) and we grow a tolerance to the good feelings. In other words, we need more of the "thing" in order to feel the same amount of pleasure. In this situation, we get to the point where the pleasure–pain balance becomes inverted: we become unable to feel pleasure at all and we instead get stuck in pain. Anhedonia is the technical term for this (see the previous Dr. Lembke quote). Along the way, the brain (which prefers to save energy) stops producing feelgood chemicals endogenously because it posits, "Oh, he's giving me more dopamine than I can handle, so I might as well stop making it."

Without the restoration of the natural pleasure–pain balance, we get to a point where we have micro-moments of addiction withdrawal throughout the day, and so our brain sends a message that something is wrong. This is because there *is* something wrong: we aren't endogenously producing the feelgood chemicals we need to thrive and heal, and we are jonesing to get our fix. We reach for "satisfaction" again and again from all the places we will never find it; from all the places that caused the dissatisfaction in the first place.

A dose of (appropriately directed) anger can be empowering, and I don't know about you, but it pisses me off that people who know everything I am telling you right now shamelessly leverage these biological truths to purposefully get you and your kids hooked on their products. That's why I

---

[25] See https://www.instagram.com/mattydel/reel/C4N2is3OUZX

made the podcast, Stealing Their Joy: How Kids Become Perfect Consumers (www.alltogether.academy/podcasts/the-boyling-point). Be it those who make smartphones, video games, social media platforms, "like" buttons, genetically modified goods, foods stuffed with sugar or extra fat and sodium, porn, fashion trends, commercials, or drugs, they are all attempting to use your neurochemistry against you so that you make them rich and you sick—and the sicker you are, the more pipe dreams they can sell you.

This situation becomes even trickier when we consider that (as can be seen in the movie *The Social Experiment*) some of these bad actors aren't playing the part knowingly. They even think they are inventing something beneficial, and they have good intentions. Still, in too many cases, these actions are motivated by sheer greed. And yes, it does benefit them if you get sick, because they also have stock in the business of selling you a cure. It is time we start recognizing the need for "win-win" business models, where choices are made *by* people, *for* people, through thriving mode's "win-win" consciousness.

Okay, stepping down off my soapbox. Back to the practical nitty gritty of day-to-day overstimulation:

Those who feel lackluster, unmotivated, unfocused, and anxious tend to create all sorts of stories or "reasons" to explain why they don't feel good or motivated—why they feel anxious, frustrated, numb, tired, and inattentive—and they ruminate on these stories, thus creating more of the same thoughts and feelings, per the thinking/feeling loop you learned about in Chapter 9. All the while, they habitually turn back to the dopamine-stimulating behaviors that may be the underlying cause for the chemical imbalance in the first place. We go around putting out fires that don't exist by dousing them with gasoline. We fail to simply restore the pleasure–pain balance through the exercise of disciplined restraint and return to a natural state of ease and equanimity.

The real kicker? If your pleasure–pain balance mechanism leans too far into the "pleasure" zone, your brain won't only try to restore this balance through emotional pain; physical pain is fair game, too. I know people who I would bet my bottom dollar are experiencing legit intense chronic *physical* pain, or at least exacerbating an underlying condition, because they have been in survival mode too often for too long and have overstimulated their "pleasure" mechanism (often in very innocent and understandable ways, perhaps even trying to get relief from their condition!).

Sometimes, constantly looking for "relief " from "stress" becomes a common strategy for life, and we end up shooting ourselves in the foot by reaching for short term fixes that end up exacerbating distress. "Unwinding" at the end of the day with a drink, a porn habit, hours in front of the TV, late night gaming, sugar, or mindless social media scrolling may seem innocuous, but these habits may also be the very culprits you think you are avoiding, the pain you think is pleasure. This issue is becoming more and more pervasive as our brains continue to access more "dopamine" stimulation in a single day than we had for an entire lifetime for most of our evolution.

There is no point in creating elaborate "reasons" for why you don't feel good if you haven't checked off the boxes that will dramatically improve the way you feel. Even if you have some sort of illness or condition that seems to explain your symptoms, getting your pleasure–pain mechanisms back in balance will help you heal.

What are these boxes? What are the practical things you can do that will make the stories about why you are suffering less relevant and possibly irrelevant?

- Reduce emotional eating.
- More exercise.
- Better/more sleep.
- Less "dopamine."
- More meditation.
- Breath expansion.
- More time in nature.
- Mindset work.
- Prosocial connections.
- Increased stress tolerance.
- Pushing the pain button on purpose.
- Discipline from pushing the pleasure button too often.

This is what you are learning about in this part of this book, through the hierarchy of everythings—look at all the things you can do to take a comprehensive, multi-faceted, holistic approach to alleviating pain and suffering and activating healing and thriving!

Instead of working on these things and creating solutions in every way we can, we tend to want to stay focused on the problem, even to the point of exacerbating the problem with the types of distractions discussed here that ultimately make things worse. Even if there is a real problem, focusing on creating solutions is a far more effective way of working with it. Doing so either eliminates the problem altogether or puts us in a much more resourceful state to cope with life. Let's face it, the two main sources of ubiquitous stimulation that are tripping up most adults (myself included sometimes), let alone kids we are allowing to access this stuff, are screens of all kinds and processed/junk "foods." This stuff is *everywhere* and it's not going away. It requires a real strategy, and active discipline to not lose the unfair fights with artificial stimulation. This pleasure–pain balance is something all modern humans must master, lest we, too, become a part of the zombie apocalypse, settling for Netflix and pot gummies as a life worth living.

If you would like a free copy of an article about the screen side of this topic I wrote years ago, when I was the director of a family behavioral health center, you can find it in your book resources, (Lesson 6.1, Youth Internet Addiction) at www.alltogether.academy/joy-bucket-tools. This article was inspired by my witnessing first hand youth addiction to screen time, where previously vivacious teens who I know for sure were not taking "drugs" had full physiological withdrawal symptoms—sweats, insomnia, heart palpitations—from trying to stop screens cold turkey.

Before we continue, I would like to share another quote from Stanford dopamine and addiction specialist Anna Lembke:

Intimacy is its own source of dopamine. Oxytocin, a hormone much involved with falling in love, mother-child bonding, and lifetime pair bonding of sexual mates, binds to receptors on the dopamine-secreting neurons in the brain's reward pathway and enhances the firing of the reward–circuit tract.

While [intimacy] promotes human attachment, compulsive overconsumption of high dopamine goods [which could be seemingly as innocuous as checking for FB likes] is the antithesis of human attachment. Consuming leads to isolation and indifference, as the drug comes to replace the reward obtained from being in relationship with others. [26]

I've got to say, when I read this quote from Dr. Lembke, it once again reminds me a heck of a lot of what "normal" teenagers look like these days as they "relate" to each other via text about the latest TikTok while actually feeling isolated and indifferent underneath it all.

It also reminds me of the poignancy of ATA's motto: "Together, we thrive." We got this, people. Let's come together.

[26] Lembke, A. (2021): Dopamine Nation: Finding Balance in the Age of Indulgence, p. 132, Dutton Books.

Pushing the "Pain" Button on Purpose

Let's explore some things you can do to minimize the downsides of "dope-amine" and maximize the upsides of vitality and life.

Safely and moderately pushing the "pain" button activates pleasure. Therefore, my goal is for you to do challenging things in the short term so that life gets easier in the long- term. Regularly choose the easy, comfortable way in the short term, and life will get harder in the long-term.

Some context before we begin: Hans Selye, the researcher who is given some credit for coining the term "stress," was mistranslated. His work (in German) differentiated between "distress" and "eustress"[27]. Distress is catabolic (it tears things down) while eustress is anabolic (it builds things up). In modern US culture, however, it's all referred to as "stress," without this distinction between "bad stress" and "good stress." Instead, all stress has been vilified (though some, like Stanford's Kelly McGonigal in her report The Upsides of Stress,[28] still acknowledge this distinction).

Distress is when we are stuck in an "overwhelm" or "threat" mindset, while eustress results from us activating the "challenge" or "opportunity" mindset. Interestingly, the very same trigger can lead us toward either distress or eustress (and most often a mixture of both). It is our job to take the inevitable distress and trauma of life and shift toward eustress and the benefits of posttraumatic growth.

One of the biggest bangs you can get for your neurochemical hacking buck is to deliberately inoculate yourself to distress and purposefully use eustress to make you stronger, healthier, and happier. By stepping on the "pain" side of the pleasure–pain balance deliberately, safely, and moderately, you can activate your brain's balancing mechanism, which will then produce chemicals that feel good, make you stronger, help you heal, and, ultimately, help you thrive.

Calling on Dr. Lembke again:

> *With prolonged, heavy use [of "dopamine"], the pleasure–pain balance gets weighted to the side of pain. Our hedonic [pleasure] set point changes as our capacity to experience pleasure goes down and our vulnerability to pain goes up.*

---

[27] Selye, H. (1975). Confusion and controversy in the stress field. Journal of Human Stress, 1(2), 37–44.
[28] Kelly McGonigal in her report The Upsides of Stress, 2015.

With intermittent exposure to pain, our natural hedonic set point gets weighted to the side of pleasure, such that we become less vulnerable to pain and more able to feel pleasure over time. [29]

My top ways of safely pushing on the "pain" side of the balance to create endogenous, feelgood, motivating, distress-relieving "chemistry" are:

- Physical exercise (see Chapter 12).
- Intermittent fasting. I only eat (most days, because flexibility is valuable) between 12PM and 6PM. I do not consume anything that will disturb my blood sugar for eighteen hours a day (see Chapter 14).
- Cold exposure. Check out the protocols suggested by Dr. Andrew Huberman on his podcast *Huberman Lab* [30].
- Chores. Practice extra and open attention without dopamine stacking (we'll discuss both of those things shortly) while you do your chores, and discover that they are, in fact, not a chore! Participation and contribution without complaint or adornment activates a deep sense of intrinsic pleasure in the embodied presence of embracing every moment. Embracing life's details without resistance reveals a wellspring of flow that is characterized by the JOLKA-GPS (joy, openness, love, kindness, awareness, gratitude, presence, and surrender).

Random, Intermittent, Infrequent Rewards

Contrary to popular demand for immediate, predictable, near-constant rewards, behavioral science is clear on the fact that that the best way to "wire in" thriving is actually through reinforcement via random, intermittent, *infrequent* rewards[31]. If you (or your kids, or your employees) are "rewarded" every time you (or they) do something good, the brain will compare what it felt like to have the reward with what it felt like to do the

---

[29] Lembke, A. (2021): Dopamine Nation: Finding Balance in the Age of Indulgence, p. 10, Dutton Books.
[30] Huberman, A. (x): Huberman Lab [Podcast]. Huberman, Andrew. "Using Deliberate Cold Exposure for Health and Performance." Huberman Lab, 27 Dec. 2021
[31] Ferster, C. B., & Skinner, B. F. (1957). Schedules of reinforcement. Appleton-Century-Crofts.

activity, and the activity we think we are rewarding will pale in comparison[32].

Obviously, there will always be a discrepancy between the spike in pleasure that comes from rewards and the baseline pleasure and pain that comes from engaging in processes that *lead* to rewards. Therefore, if you "reward" yourself every time you complete an activity, your brain will end up comparing the spike to the life-affirming behaviors that led to "reward" and you will end up having *fewer positive feelings* about the activity or process, itself, and *less motivation* to do it. In all likelihood, your desire mechanism will cut straight to craving the reward and you will develop a tendency to want to get it without the effort.

For example, employees who get bonuses every time they go above and beyond actually perform worse and have a qualitative experience of liking work *less* than employees who are given random, intermittent, infrequent positive reinforcement for their successful outcomes.[33]

It really frustrates me that I constantly need to decondition and recondition my daughter in this respect, due to the well-intentioned behavior-controlling tools that are used at school. If our children are set up to expect, want, or need a cookie, star, sticker, or "that's a good boy/girl" every time they do something positive in order to participate successfully in life, they will more likely walk a path to failure, compulsions, and deep insecurity. I'm grateful my sweet Sofia is a champ and just the other day told me, "Dad, I hate when adults say good job for stuff that's easy. I mean do they think we are that dumb?" She knows what's up.

Dopamine Stacking

Related to the idea of random, intermittent, infrequent rewards is this: we benefit greatly when we cultivate the capacity to feel good about the effort or process of what we are doing, instead of the reward or result of what we

---

[32] Funny side note: my kids rolled their eyes to another dimension the other day when I suggested we start calling chores "opportunities." We all had a nice chuckle when my son Rudi predicted becoming a famous musician someday and, when asked about his abnormal work ethic in an interview, answering, "I had a dad who called chores 'opportunities.'" I've had the last laugh, though, because my kids do their own laundry, clean their own toilet, and know how to cook, and we genuinely enjoy our time together while cleaning the kitchen after dinner.
[33] C. B. Ferster and B. F. Skinner, *Schedules of Reinforcement* (New York: Appleton-Century-Crofts, 1957), 350–380.

are doing. It's about the journey, not the destination. So, at least some of the time:

- Do not spike dopamine *before* doing "the thing."
- Do not spike dopamine *while* doing "the thing."
- Do not spike dopamine after *doing* "the thing."

Instead, train your brain to enjoy the effort for its own sake.

"Dopamine stacking" is when you add things that stimulate "dopamine" to things you do to make them "better." Doing this all the time backfires, because your brain compares the spike (the reward) to the baseline feeling you have about that activity. So, you end up liking the activity itself less (because your brain compares it to the spike) than you would have if you'd done it without the spike, and will require more and more of the spike to be able to continue liking or tolerating the activity.

Example: if I already like to exercise but I start drinking coffee before working out and I start watching YouTube during my workout, my brain will compare the coffee and YouTube "dopamine" spikes to my unadulterated experience of exercise. As a result, I will perceive exercise as less desirable in comparison to the spikes, and in turn, I will be less motivated to exercise and will sadly end up liking exercise less. Why get all uncomfortable, sweaty, and sore when I can just drink a latte and watch YouTube without all the fuss?

Does this mean you shouldn't ever crank up the tunes while you exercise and get that rush we all know and love? No. The key is to do it intermittently and randomly, which does mean *sometimes not* adding anything and just exercising (or just folding clothes or just going for a walk) without any adornment. One way to assure "randomness" is to flip a coin, roll a die, or pick a number.

In my family, every other night, we have no music at all while we do our chores, and every *other* night, we flip a coin to see if there will be music. It turns out that on the nights when we do have music, we have a blast, because the experience feels new and fresh. On the non-music nights, we have some of the best family conversations ever, because the moving around we do while cleaning lends itself to some genuine intimacy without embarrassment (not to mention some funny jokes).

If we hated doing the dishes or the laundry so much that we watched Netflix every time so we could tolerate it, we would hate doing the dishes and laundry even more, and we would grow to *need* the crutch of the "dopamine" supplement to feel any motivation to do it at all.

The worst part of all is that eventually, we would develop a tolerance to the "dopamine" crutch, to the point where even that wouldn't motivate us. When we reach this point, we dread all the details of life even *with* the spike!

I have gotten to this place previously, while doing my therapy notes for insurance claims. This activity was so boring to me, and large parts of it don't take much skill or intelligence, so I started watching YouTube while doing it. Bad idea! I had to reset my relationship with this activity completely and do it without any spikes for an extended period, until the pleasure–pain balance was restored and this process no longer felt like wading through quicksand.

It's much easier to not get to this bad place in the first place than it is to get out of it. So, be sure to "spike" randomly and intermittently. Commit to sometimes just feeling the water on your skin while you're doing dishes, or folding clothes Zen style. I really leaned into this practice during COVID, and I was very pleased to find that I could, as strange as it may seem, truly enjoy doing chores—I mean, opportunities. (Wink, wink.)

One of the slogans we have in our family to remind us of this is "discipline is delicious." By saying "no" to ourselves and embracing the discomfort of "just" doing the dishes, folding the laundry, or not having dessert, we can activate the innate pleasure of our own aliveness and appreciate and enjoy just about everything.

If thinking about going for a walk, doing a workout, or getting laundry done without headphones or YouTube brings feelings of dread for you ("OMG, you mean sit alone with my own thoughts and terrible boredom?!"), then you might consider doing a detox period before you get back to random, infrequent spiking. Dr. Lembke suggests in *Dopamine Nation* that we probably need a full thirty days to reset[34] from major imbalances, but even a weekend or a full day without any artifcial stimulation can be really wonderful. The more you might dread that, the more you probably need it!

I know, I know. It feels hard. I've been there. But oh, the joy—the bliss, even—of rediscovering your natural appetites! Thirty days of folding clothes with me, myself, and I. One week of going on walks without headphones. Twenty-four hours of chosen discomfort to create a lifetime of recalibrated pleasure.

You got this.

---

[34] Lembke, A. (2021): Dopamine Nation: Finding Balance in the Age of Indulgence, p. 76, Dutton Books.

What are We Stealing from Our Kids?

Consider what we are stealing from our kids and ourselves with all our super-stimulating treats, rewards, and distractions.

Oftentimes, we think we are doing our kids or ourselves a favor by giving a reward; that we are making life easier by offering them a distraction. Indeed, flexibility and participation in certain norms certainly have their place, especially where kids are concerned. My kids have video game systems and junk food (occasionally) for the simple reason that it's truly important to feel that we belong. But (and this is a big "but") when it comes to stimulation, such as screens, "dopamine," sugar, and so on, this leads to a slippery slope where ultimately, nothing in life is enjoyable anymore.

Before I continue, let me just say that this is not about parent bashing or blaming. This is tricky stuff. Here's an example of what I mean when I talk about this, though:

There is a certain innate pleasure we get from eating good food. We are motivated (through "dopamine") to seek and eat nutritious foods to further our survival and thriving. So, doing this feels good ("dopamine"), and we are programmed to do it again and again. However, when a kid (or an adult!) gets a hit of an artificially high amount of "dopamine" while they're eating food (such as via a show on Netflix, or intense amounts of sugar), their brain will register "regular" food, by comparison, as bland and boring. If this is done regularly, they may even lose the capacity to enjoy food by itself altogether and will require the "spike" to go with it always. Or, if kids become accustomed to eating carb-based foods that are on every kids' menu because it's "easier" than teaching them to enjoy a wide range of tastes, spices, textures and flavor this is how picky eaters are made and is why you see so many kids glued to their devices at restaurants, and demanding nothing but chicken fingers at home nowadays. They literally *can't enjoy themselves* without the device, and food without artificial spikes tastes "boring." If the parents try to take away the spike, the kid has what we have normalized as a "meltdown," which is really them going into withdrawal and screaming for a fix. The parents, who are often overwhelmed themselves, understandably say in response to this, "You know, we just want to have a nice dinner together. Nothing wrong with that," so they give the kid the device back, or serve the same meal and add a dollop of ketchup to spike it off, and everyone gets "rewarded" (and the cycle is reinforced).

Because the reward (e.g., the TV show the kid is watching while they eat) is as artificial as the frozen "food" and has no intrinsic value, they build a tolerance to it, and thus need more and more of it to feel the same amount of "pleasure," until ultimately, they get into a game of diminishing returns where neither the food nor the spike nor the show nor anything at all produces pleasure and motivation, and the whole world becomes flat and apathetic.

Have you noticed this?

Trust me, I know how much discipline it takes to train kids to have a healthy palate and undo the conditioning when the other well-meaning adults in their lives give them a "treat" every time, or they have to sit next to peers at lunch eating oh so enticing Takis (or whatever the fad snack of the day is) while they stare at their rice, meat and veggies. It gets even tougher to preserve their brains from screen damage when all their peers play Call of Duty until too late, screwing up not only their reward systems but also their circadian rhythms. Trust me, it also pains me to have hard conversations with my kids about the suffering they experience feeling "left out" from the "normal" stuff their peers are doing.

I've worked with too many teenagers—good, smart, previously vivacious kids—who've become flat as a pancake, for no other reason than the fact that they have gotten in over their heads in the seemingly innocuous "spike." After all, they were just gaming to connect with friends. Wasn't that a good thing? Or they were just getting a refreshing drink at a restaurant before their dinner (which usually contains as much as thirty or forty grams of sugar—seven to ten spoonsful).

Have your kids now come to expect, or even demand, a drink other than water every time you go to a restaurant, and if you say no, you are now some sort of control monster? Well, this is an unfair fight for both parties. By giving them that drink before, you have stolen their ability to just enjoy that dinner, because without that spike, it's like eating the cardboard menu, and now, they feel deprived. Frankly, it pisses me off the stuff is even available and we, as parents, need to be the ones to protect our kids from these seemingly innocuous spikes. They often even come from very well-intentioned places!

I remember once, my mom went to put sugar on my kids' strawberries, and I was like, "Mom, what are you doing?!" She was extremely well-intentioned and is a totally awesome grandma all around, but she was about to (unknowingly) rob them of their capacity to enjoy strawberries. Of course, she was just "giving them a treat. Relax, Mike!" and she's right. Grandma's prerogative. I can now relax more about this stuff than when my older boys were younger. Still, I also don't think we realize that it's these little things, day in and day out, over time, that add up to big problems.

I teach my kids, "If you have it every day or every time you are in that situation, that's not a treat. It's a compulsion." The best practice is random, intermittent, infrequent rewards. These same principles apply to when someone is watching a sunset, and they pull out their phone to post it on social media (and get all sorts of spikes in the process). In this situation, that simple universally beautiful moment in nature becomes lame, stupid, and boring without the share and like buttons.

I fear that most people are telling themselves they are doing this stuff "in moderation," but really, "spiking" comes in so many forms that in one way or another, it's ubiquitous and problematic, and most of us are seriously overdoing it (and suffering accordingly). With time, we find we can't just enjoy the sunset, or the concert, or the car ride, by itself, without the spike. And how about those boring, "intermission" moments of life when we are just waiting? Bring in the demand for the spike. We now hate those moments or feel terribly anxious in them without a spike—so we reach back for it. During long car rides, we can no longer just stare aimlessly out the window and wonder about the stars without feeling like we are being tortured by that longing for the artificial spike. Forget long car rides, most people can't walk from room to room in their house without checking their phones.

The medicine we are using is actually the poison we are trying to medicate ourselves against.

So, I ask again, what are we stealing from our kids? What are we stealing from ourselves? Are we really doing them (or us) a favor? Are we really making life easier or more fun? Are we even (actually) enjoying ourselves? Or are we robbing ourselves of the capacity to experience *real* joy?

Saying No

To combat everything we have spoken about in this chapter, get into the habit of saying no to the "more" button. Make it a discipline to say no to thirds, dessert, seconds on dessert, checking your feed every time you walk from room to room, one more episode, and one more refresh. Discipline is delicious, and (please sear this in your brain) *there is no amount of "more" that will ever satisfy you anyway.* In fact, the more you have the kind of "more" we are talking about here, the more you guarantee that your brain will produce more *pain* to balance things out. So:

1. Stop.
2. Feel and lean into the craving of wanting more.
3. Wait. Do nothing.
4. Allow homeostasis to return.
5. Feel the satisfaction that ensues.

If you give yourself a chance, your pleasure–pain balance will return to center, you will feel satisfied, and the craving will dissipate naturally. Most cravings don't last more than ninety seconds if you don't keep fueling the fire with fantasies of having more. Surf the wave and wait for the spike to subside all by itself. Soon, you will feel *truly* satisfied.

As an exercise, try saying no to tiny comforts and dopamine hits twenty-five times a day. About to check your email? Say no. About to grab a cookie? Say no. Do it now or do it later? Do it now (slay the beast and do what you like least first). Tempted to refresh your FB feed? Don't. In tiny moments throughout the day, choose the harder thing. Choose the thing you don't want to do. Say no to the easy, familiar, habitual thing.

Discipline is delicious.

Big Highs

A final guideline: keep big "highs" deliberately infrequent. If you are going to jump out of a plane, don't do it often. And whenever you do get a "high" out of life (even for something positive, like a big win at work), remember to allow for a reset by sitting with the boredom, pain, and crash of the comedown. And by the way, stop telling yourself "awfulizing" stories about those feelings of comedown after a success. As we have covered, they are normal, natural, and part of our intelligent evolutionary design.... if we "sit with it" the real reward of authentic satisfaction will come once the pleasure–pain balance returns. This is not a dreary life-negative suggestion! This is learning to discover joy for no reason, beyond circumstances, this is cultivating the capacity savor the simple moments of life and to be free from the need for life to be a roller coaster destined to crash and burn.

The Pleasure–Pain Balance is Everything: A Case Study

Dan came to me at the behest of his wife. He was struggling with "drinking too much" as a chief concern, and his marriage and family life was a mess, as the most pressing symptom.

Instead of working harder and not smarter, I suggested he join me in the "twenty-five 'no's' a day" challenge, but only with "little things." We didn't even talk about applying this to alcohol. We just worked with the grace and ease question: "What's the next, easiest thing I am willing to say no to today?"

Dan followed my guidance by starting small. Saying no to checking his email made him realize he had been spiking dopamine about fifty times a day (hour?) unnecessarily. Saying no to scrolling through social media, helped by deleting the apps, saved him not only a bunch of time, but also lots of endogenous pain his brain was making while trying to get him back in balance. With these little no's, he stopped spiking "dopamine" as much, which meant he was not forcing his brain to make more pain. But, he also found it was uncomfortable to exercise this discipline—which, ironically, means his brain started making more pleasure. (He started to get a taste for the fact that discipline is delicious.)

Nothing is better for sustainable motivation than successful results, so Dan quickly felt confident enough to take on some bigger challenges after this. I didn't have to prompt him to do so; he *wanted* to, on his own volition. In fact, he hadn't even told me he had previously been watching a bunch of porn, which he decided to start saying no to also. This, as it turns out, was activating tons of artificially stimulating pleasure and (no surprise) huge doses of the pain known as shame. The porn habit was also a secret energetic barrier coming between him and his wife, resulting in a lack of real intimacy—a hole which he was attempting to fill with alcohol!

With that pleasure–pain rebalanced, Dan felt less inclined to fill the hole artificially, and his natural desire for intimacy urged him to reconnect with his wife. This produced a bunch of "oxytocin" (feelgood chemicals that help us to feel safe and heal and thrive). With this boost in oxytocin, Dan felt less angry and anxious and therefore had less desire to drink or avoid the stresses and strains of life around the house and kids. His kids started warming up to him more and he started rediscovering his goofy, playful side.

When he realized he literally had an extra hour in his day that he used to spend spiking dopamine, he started to dedicate thirty minutes of that to playing with his kids and the other thirty minutes to exercise. This exercise produced some healthy pain, which stimulated endogenous pleasure, which led to some direct benefits in the bedroom.

For the first time in a long time, Dan felt that spending time with his kids was truly fulfilling and not just a duty or obligation – he was able to *feel this* because he had adequate stores of "oxytocin" coursing through his veins instead of artificial pleasure. His relationship with alcohol came to be "take it or leave it" (and he naturally wanted to leave it more than take it). After all, discipline is delicious, and Dan knew, through his direct experience, that it feels better to feel better!

The Pleasure–pain Balance is Everything: Recap and Reflection

- "Dopamine," as a useful generalization, is the neurotransmitter of desire and anticipation of a reward. It is not the reward itself, or at least not a truly satisfying one.
- When our "dopamine" surges (which, in the present day, are readily available to us at all times) are triggered by stimuli that do not lead to intrinsically satisfying and beneficial rewards, we can get stuck in a loop of "seeking." In this loop, desire only begets desire, and since there is no fulfilment in the equation, we get tricked into wanting more and more, without any beneficial payoff.
- Pushing the "more dopamine" button too frequently to alleviate discomfort, boredom, anxiety, frustration, numbness, lethargy, and "depression" is what is likely causing said discomfort, boredom, anxiety, frustration, numbness, lethargy, and "depression" in the first place, in the form of tiny withdrawals throughout the day that urge us to "take another hit."
- There is never an amount of "more" that will be satisfying, because we are designed for our pleasure–pain balance to remain in equilibrium. The more we seek pleasure, the more we activate pain. This pleasure–pain balance is something all modern humans must master, lest we, too, become a part of the zombie apocalypse.
- Safely and moderately pushing the "pain" button activates pleasure, so my goal is for you to do challenging things in the short-term so that life gets easier in the long-term. Regularly choose the easy, comfortable way in the short term, and life will get harder in the long-term.
- Train your brain to enjoy effort and simple pleasure for its own sake.
- Rewards work best if they are random and intermittent. Rewards every time a certain behavior or context occurs are counterproductive and harmful.
- Be careful with dopamine stacking. Sometimes just do the thing without anything extra.
- Discipline is delicious. By saying no to ourselves and embracing the discomfort of just doing the dishes, folding the laundry, or not having dessert, we activate the innate pleasure of our own aliveness and appreciate and enjoy just about everything.

- Complete the badass challenge: say no to tiny cravings for "more" twenty-five times a day. I wonder how the natural trajectory of this practice could benefit you, like it did Dan?
- Safely and moderately step on the "pain" side of the pleasure–pain balance to produce endogenous pleasure and inoculate yourself to distress. Tried-and-true approaches for this include exercising, intermittent fasting, cold exposure, and embracing the daily grind with grace and ease, recognizing life as a challenging opportunity (and not as an overwhelming threat)!

12
MOVEMENT IS EVERYTHING

WE HAVE DEDICATED SOME TIME TO exploring the fact that stillness (sleep, rest, and relaxation) is everything. Now, I'm going to tell you that movement is everything. That doesn't mean I was lying when I said that SRR is everything; both statements are true. Now, let's move it or lose it!

Eighty-five percent of the suffering related to the normal stresses and strains of life can be alleviated through appropriate movement (in my opinion). Dr. Peter Attia, who is perhaps the biggest name in "biohacking" and longevity science at the time of my writing this draft, says there's no reason to even consider dietary plans and supplements if you aren't already getting adequate exercise[35].

When I get back to exercising after a hiatus, I joke to my wife, "It should be illegal for me to not exercise," to which she responds, "You don't need to tell me!" with a bit more sass than I sometimes think is funny. As much as I like to think that I have enough mind control to supersede what's going on in my body, I am simply a better person when I have moved my body with as much vigor as possible that day.

There's a small caveat to this, though: I've worked with a lot of clients, usually those with PTSD or "anxiety," who overexercise in a compulsory, need-based way that overstimulates the nervous system, so they can exhaust themselves enough to experience a sort of false relaxation. Is this you?

The body is a beautiful place to live, but (like many of you) I have experienced times when it didn't feel good to be in my own skin. Rekindling

---

[35] Huberman, Andrew. "Dr. Peter Attia: Supplements for Longevity & Their Efficacy." Huberman Lab, Feb 13, 2023.

a kind and loving relationship with one's own body exactly as it is, is the essence of the moving "everything." Your body is the only one you've got, and it has hung in there despite you and others beating it up, bruising it, neglecting it, chastising it, complaining about it, and disrespecting it. Imagine, then, how it might thrive when you start deliberately showing it the love and appreciation it deserves!

You've learned about the impact the stories you tell yourself—your mental chatter—have on your experience of life. So, it should come as no surprise to you that moving with grace and ease begins with you cultivating a kind attitude toward your body. You may be quick to say, "My back is killing me," but when was the last time you thanked your body for the near-infinite miracles that allow it—and you—to exist and function right now? When was the last time you said, "Thanks for beating, heart. Thanks for breathing, diaphragm and lungs?" When I walk from inside to outside and the temperature drops 50 degrees in one second, "Thanks for staying 98.6 degrees, body!"

I challenge us all to begin cherishing our bodies with consistent, daily, deliberate appreciation, not only in our minds, but through our actions – even if, aside from, and especially because we are facing a health challenge. Everyone is facing a health challenge (which is not to minimize that some are facing harder challenges than others). We are all dying from the primal cause of being born. Most of us, however, will have taken about two hundred and sixty million steps in our lives by the time we pass, so it might be a good idea for us to start saying thank you to our feet and having a better relationship with the only companion we have for life: our body.

Starting the Day on the Right Foot

Starting the day "on the right foot," so to speak, can be a literal practice.

1. When you wake up, see if you can become conscious of this and notice, "I am awake," before you begin your day in a deliberate way. The point here is to start your day creatively as who you are, Aware-Will, instead of reactively, "I am so tired, I am sore" as your identities scan the day for all the problems you need to face, "There's so much to do, and not enough time."

2. While you are still lying down, consider invoking love and gratitude for your life and your body's ability to move to whatever degree it is currently able to. Focusing on what you can do (versus what you can't) will enable you to move toward doing more.

3. Invite yourself to pandiculate while still in bed. I often joke (kind of not jokingly) that pandiculating is the only yoga posture you will ever need. Pandiculating is stretching, twisting, yawning, flexing, and shaking all at once, basically like a dog or cat does. The key here is to be spontaneous and organic and to allow your body to move however it wants to. Listen to your body and go with its flow. When you get it, you will notice that this feels pleasurable, and your body will subtly tremor, perhaps right at the apex of a movement. Animals in the wild do this to "shake off" tension and trauma. You can do that, too. I've included a video about "The Only Yoga Posture You Need" in your book resources (Module 7) at www.alltogether.academy/joy-bucket-tools.

4. After pandiculating, lie still again for a few moments and just feel alive.

5. Sit up, put your feet flat on the floor, bring your hands together in the prayer position at your heart, and say internally or aloud, "I greet this day with love and gratitude. I value this day and choose to make it the best day ever!" It's important to develop the habit of saying something like this even if you don't believe it every time. Let the momentum of this exercise work its magic. The reason why it works is called "priming" and, you guessed it, I've included a video about it in lesson 7.2 "Priming Your Day" which you can find in your https://www.alltogether.academy/joy-bucket-tools. In this video you will also learn about "whole brain change."

6. Make your bed. I'm serious. And no, I'm not your mom or drill sergeant. Starting the day with a sense of accomplishment makes a huge difference, and a tidy room makes for a tidy mind. This is an easy way to get a win under your belt.

Exercise Snacks

The most effective exercise principle I've incorporated in my life is what I call "exercise snacks." Whether or not this was a wholly original name or idea upon my inception of it I cannot confirm, but it was certainly new to me when the "A-ha!" moment dawned. Either way, it works and is now popular among the biohacking gurus.

If you are not training to be an athlete, you want to be in good shape, and you enjoy the psychospiritual benefits of feeling alive and well in your body, then a great approach to the movement "everything" is to "drip feed" yourself hormones and chemicals that have you feeling good and that decrease distress all day long. How? Via short bursts of exercise spread throughout the day.

Sedentary lifestyles and long periods of stagnation are killers, and the idea of devoting specific time to exercise (such as by going to the gym) is a pretty modern phenomenon. For most of our evolutionary history, we just moved most of the time as our standard lifestyle. So, I have found that a handful of one- to five-minute bursts of exercise throughout the day is effective, more realistic, and less daunting than going to the gym and thinking, *I need to work out for an hour*. My routine of this, plus one to two walks or hikes in nature per week, plus one to two fun physical activities (like skiing, biking, dancing, swimming, and playing a game) per week, has resulted in me being in the best shape of my life, body and mind. This, along with choosing to walk whenever possible, always parking my car as far away as possible, and taking the stairs whenever there's the option, can be the difference that makes a difference in a life that is well-integrated with movement. It also turns out that I feel *dramatically* better when I exercise the discipline to get in the recommended ten thousand steps per day.

To get you started with this lifestyle change:

- Make a list of as many one- to five-minute exercise snacks as you can think of or research. I Google searched "office exercises" and found snacknation.com/blog/office-exercises while I was writing this, which is a great resource (no affiliation and total coincidence on the "snack" nation URL for exercise "snacks"). There are also many other options.
- Whenever you have a moment and an impulse to move, try this cognitive trick to blast through inertia and analysis paralysis: count down from five to one while picturing a rocket ship, and when you get to zero, "blast off" and just start moving. Randomly pick an item from your list if you need to, but don't stop and think about it. Just move. What you do matters far less than the fact that you do it. I learned this lesson reading Mel Robbins' *The 5 Second Rule*[36], but I just saved you a few hours and 15 bucks by giving you the gist of it here. Do whatever is easiest for you to do that you are willing to do. Objects at rest tend to stay at rest. Objects in motion tend to stay in motion. So: five... four... three... two... one... move! Move it or lose it. Moving is living. Ask, "What's the next, easiest thing I am willing to do?" It doesn't have to be hard! In fact, if it is hard, you will quit.

---

[36] Robbins, M. (2017): The 5 Second Rule: Transform Your Life, Work, and Confidence with Everyday Courage. Savio Republic.

If you move and feel better for it, you will want to move more. You won't have to force yourself. Force doesn't work, or at least, it doesn't last.

- When in doubt, pandiculate!
- Move in a way that gets you short of breath and your heart pounding as much as possible (though check with your doctor first, if need be). This means endorphins are on the way!
- However, or whenever possible, make the effort to get outside and get sun on your skin. As a friend's mom is known for saying, "Put yourself in the way of beauty." How wonderful is that? Words to live by! Nature heals.
- Smile! When you are exercising, you are circulating chemicals more efficiently throughout your body. The "no pain, no gain," "grin and bear it" chemicals are not your friend, despite the non-sense we hear from machismo men and women who brand themselves as exercise gurus. No thanks, David Goggins. (There, I said it.) Instead, enjoying your body moving through space with grace and ease.

For those of you who want to take your movement up a notch, I have also tried out two fantastic exercise models from two books. My research supports the utility of the ideas conveyed in these books. I will summarize what they teach here, so that you can decide whether you'd like to investigate them more in depth, or to just borrow the principles and apply them more generally to your moving and living. (Again, I have zero affiliation whatsoever with these authors, books, and programs.)

The Quick and the Dead *by Pavel Tsatsouline*[37]

The gist of this book (and others by the same author) is, predators are relaxed, and prey are stressed, so you should endeavor to exercise (and live) like a predator (in a neurochemical sense).

Predators lounge around and relax when they're not doing quick, ballistic movements in very short bursts (exercise snacks, anyone?). If they don't catch their prey during those "exercise snacks," they peel off, rest, and do it again later.

---

[37] Tsatsouline, P. (2019): *The Quick and the Dead: Total Training for the Advanced Minimalist.* Strongfirst, Inc.

This author has done tons of research and trials on getting the exact timing and sequence for only two exercises—kettlebell swings and pushups—to imitate the hormone and chemical production that takes place in predators. (Don't worry, it won't make you mean; quite the opposite!) He claims (with validated research) that typical exercise, where you build up lactic acid and "tear" muscle to grow it, produces distress and is counterproductive. He reports that instead, one should "peel off" their workout at the climax of mitochondrial production (aka, energy-plus!), right before degenerative stress takes place. In this way, one can grow stronger, faster, and healthier without ever getting sore (i.e. without producing lactic acid).

This author, by the way, is credited for bringing kettlebells to the USA and trains Olympic and professional athletes, so this is no joke even for the highest performing athletes in the world.

I love this approach. It is a total "work smarter, not harder" method that plays chemical and biological realities to your advantage. What's more, the workouts are surprisingly short and easy (twelve to thirty minutes each) and incredibly effective, because they are research driven and dialed in.

Convict Conditioning *by Paul Wade*[38]

This guy learned and developed this bodyweight-only, six-exercise method for achieving incredible strength and flexibility *while locked up in jail*. Yes, it can all be done in a jail cell, and apparently there is a practical mentor to disciple, generation to generation, exercise tradition being passed on in the jail system. As an aside, I find that fascinating!

I love how methodical it is. There are ten steps to each exercise, and you simply cannot cheat. Step 10 leads to marvels of the human body, and Wade gives you a real method to get there.

Paul was locked up for a long time, so this is a realistic and patient approach. It could literally take years to reach Step 10. As I write, I am on Step 3 of Week 17's exercises. You progress in each exercise at your own rate based on actual results instead of artificial ideas. You simply don't move on until you hit the numbers. Even if you can "skip ahead," you lose the profound benefits that come with strengthening your small muscle fibers, tendons, ligaments, and nervous system. Do so at your own peril (i.e., failure

[38] Wade, P. (2010): Convict Conditioning: How to Bust Free of All Weakness Using the Lost Secrets of Supreme Survival Strength. Dragon Door Publications.

or injury). Alternatively, follow the steps, and gain ridiculous strength, slowly and surely, over time.

Paul Wade presents an incredible combination of badassery and a philosophy centered on being very gentle and kind to yourself. His approach focuses on getting you to build your body up in a truly sustainable way.

Again, the workouts are short (fifteen minutes, twice a week) and no equipment is needed, so it fits perfectly into my busy life.

Brilliant.

With exercise snacks and either of these approaches to movement, you will be in the best shape of your life, too!

At times in my life when I've felt my best, I've done exercise snacks in combination with Tsatsouline's and Wade's approach, but I've been at this for a while, right? Love yourself enough to do the next, easiest thing you are willing to do right now, and keep it moving.

Bodyfulness

I'd like to introduce a new concept: bodyfulness. This (I believe) also started as an original thought of mine, though at this point, you may have heard it elsewhere, too! Sometimes, different people in different places have realized similar things at similar times. I sometimes think of things my mentor has been planning to teach in his next class, before he teaches them—which is wild! All of this is really cool and mysterious, but a different topic, granted. Back to my point:

You've all heard of "mindfulness," right? Well, that term is a poor translation of the original Buddhist teachings on mindfulness. Even Buddhists use the term "mindfulness," but what they really mean when they use this is a word I am making up: "bodyfulness." In my opinion, "mindfulness" suggests a *mental* experience, but it is actually (originally) far from that. What the term "mindfulness" is trying to get at is a very direct visceral experience of the *physical sensations of aliveness* in the body. This is more than just "mindfully" paying attention (only) to what you are doing as you are doing. Attentiveness is a waning skill for many, and a great thing worth cultivating, but it's the very tip of the meditation iceberg.

Bodyfulness is the essence of "extra attention" (again, we'll cover this in more detail later), and it is very important to integrate this concept into your daily living. For example, when you're in the shower, feel the sensations of the water on your skin instead of thinking of your to-do list. When you check out and start going off into mental movies about things that aren't happening right now, notice this and return to the feeling of the water on your skin. The same goes for doing dishes, changing diapers, eating, drinking water, driving, and hiking. Put your mind in your body. Get out of your head and direct your attention to the actual living sensations of your body. Feel the flow that surrounds you (which is ever-present and always waiting to be rediscovered, no matter how many times you forget about it). Life is always living you. Feel this and allow it to enliven you!

As you get good this you will be able to maintain "extra" attention on the sensations of aliveness in your body, while you are also paying attention to whatever you are doing. *This* is the true meaning of "mindfulness."

Moving is Everything: A Case Study

PH was hit hard by the isolation that came with the COVID-19 pandemic. As an older single woman living in a rural area, she depended on the day-to-day interactions she had when she was out and about to satisfy her need for human connection. So, as the quarantine dragged on, she became more "depressed."

Depression, as you will learn later, is what we call it when the brain is more or less in a "freeze" state. The part of the brain that activates in "freeze" is the same part that plays dead hoping a predator will move on, or that becomes immobile to avoid being seen, or that goes numb when it realizes impending doom is inevitable. In short, this state triggers a sense that it is literally unsafe to move. But move we must. If depression equals "freeze" and "freeze" means being "immobile" or "numb" then we can melt this "freeze" state (i.e., our depression) by moving, and feeling. We need to "feel to heal" and by that, I mean feel the sensations of aliveness in our body (extra attention) in the present moment, not the sensations driven by the thinking-feeling loop you learned about earlier.

That said, if we've been "frozen", we don't want to move with too much intensity (a common mistake). If we get sore, exhausted, or overstimulated after not moving for a while, this can also trigger our "fear" or "overwhelm" state, and we may end up back in "freeze." Instead, when emerging from "freeze," it's great to go on walks or do things like restorative yoga, tai-chi, gentle stretching, and anything outside in nature, to provide a smooth transition out of the "freeze" state.

When PH came to me for help, I understood this was what was going on with her. So, I introduced her to the simple but profound practice my clients have come to call "the morning miracle walk." I suggested she make it a keystone habit and not concern herself with doing anything else but this one thing: going for a twenty- to thirty-minute walk every morning, within the first twenty to thirty minutes of waking up (and within the first two hours after her local sunrise).

That's it. Simple. Miraculous, even.

Sure enough, this movement got her out of "freeze" and literally activated a part of her brain that told her that she was moving through or away from danger. This means she became able to process anything that was bothering her in a much more efficient way. The low-angle sunlight she was getting in her eyes also reset her circadian rhythm (see Chapter 10 on SRR), and this gave PH the boost she needed. She was now out and about, connecting with mother nature in a way that enabled her to feel mobile and motivated enough to start doing other things that would bring her meaning, joy, and satisfaction.

Soon enough, PH started to get ideas and notice opportunities for human connection. Instead of walking in her isolated rural neighborhood, she started walking along a track in the middle of town, so she could be around people. It was still safe as far as COVID went (she had a compromised immune system), and just those little smiles and nods from other people walking around the track lifted her spirits.

From there, she had momentum back on her side, and she got motivated to grocery shop, cook, and eat healthily. In other words, she literally put herself on track for a positive upward spiral, and by doing so, she put "depression" in her rearview mirror. All through moving in quite simple and easy ways.

Moving is Everything: Recap and Reflection

- Eighty-five percent of the ailments many of us struggle with everyday can be alleviated via appropriate movement.
- Rekindling a kind and loving relationship with one's own body exactly as it is, is the essence of the moving "everything."
- Sedentary lifestyles and prolonged periods of stagnation are killers, and the idea of devoting specific time to exercise is a pretty modern phenomenon. Try "exercise snacks" (one- to five-minute bursts of activity spread throughout the day) instead.
- If you are already doing longer workouts and love those, no need to drop them! Still, be on the lookout for long periods of stagnation, perhaps at work, and add in an extra snack or two.

- Embrace bodyfulness. What you focus on grows, right? So, focus on your tangible aliveness, and you will grow more vital.
- Begin cherishing your body with consistent, daily, deliberate appreciation, not only in your mind, but through your actions.
- Pandiculate! Learn how in this throwback video in Module 7.1 of your book resources at www.alltogether.academy/joy-bucket-tools. This may just be the only yoga posture you will ever need!
- Start your day off with discipline and success by Priming Your Brain for What You Value and Choose (lesson 7.2 in Joy Bucket Tools). Then, make your bed for an easy win!
- Five... four... three... two... one... move! Move it or lose it. Moving is living. Follow the grace and ease question: "What's the next, easiest thing I am willing to do?"

13
HYDRATION IS EVERYTHING

MANY ADULTS ARE LIVING IN A state of chronic (albeit subtle) dehydration. Could this be you? Let's examine your daily routine to find out:

After losing about a liter (approximately 2.2 lbs. or 1 kg) of water weight every night, you wake up and stumble to the coffee machine first thing in the morning and drink something that further dehydrates you. Then, you proceed to drink a few glasses of water (maybe) throughout the day. And you've been doing this for, what? Decades? You probably don't need me to tell you your body requires a lot more than that.

You are thirsty. So thirsty, perhaps, that you don't even know it. Your brain is parched. And it will work a lot better if you give it what it needs. And, don't worry, you don't need to join the brigade of people attached to their water bottles all day long – that's not the best way to stay hydrated anyway, more on that shortly.

Before I wax philosophically, please allow me to share one of the easiest, simplest, most effective things you can do to dramatically improve your health: every day for the rest of your life, drink sixteen to twenty ounces of room temperature to warm water within the first fifteen minutes of waking up, and wait one to two hours before you have coffee. I know the "waiting on coffee" part might be the hardest of this process, so if needed, wait twenty to thirty minutes instead. The one- to two-hour guideline has to do with "adenosine," improving your energy levels throughout the day, and getting better sleep, but if you have to start with a shorter wait, there is no shame in that. Still, be sure to give your body enough time to assimilate the water. A squirt of lemon or lime and a pinch of salt can really help with that.

We'll continue talking about literal hydration shortly. For now, let's talk about the most important kind of hydration: spiritual hydration.

Water as an Element

Water is life. When we're born, we come in juicy and snotty, full of rolls, fluids, flexibility, resilience, and joy. When we die, we dry up—brittle and frail.

Real talk.

Have you ever met an aging person who has retained their "juiciness?" I aim to be one of them! My kids often marvel and gently poke fun at the fact that my mentor (who is in his late seventies) looks younger than I do. (Kudos to him. I clearly still have some relaxing to do!)

By now, you know I am all about cultivating a love for life that "juices things up" and not waiting for outer circumstances to "make stuff happen." This way, I can feel the pleasure and good feelings I seek *now*. I choose to *create what I seek* as much as possible. After all, we are always either waiting or creating, and if we are waiting, that's what we will be creating: more waiting.

I have had the good fortune of witnessing three healthy babies up close and in intimate detail, and one thing is for certain: it is natural to feel good! Pleasure in one's skin (a quality of the "water element," as understood by holistic Asian medicinal systems) is a birthright. If we have lost this pleasure because of the aches and pains of life, we can still get back to our Creative-IAM (our most evolved self) with some effortful ease.

What I'm getting at is, I want to share more than just information about physical hydration. In this section, I will draw upon the wellspring of India's science of life (also known as Ayurveda) to elaborate on the water element.

Traditional medicinal systems around the world, from India and China to Japan, Greece, Egypt, and Native America, are all based on the five elements that combine, in infinite variety, to produce our seen and unseen reality: earth, water, fire, wind, and space[39]. These elements (and the medicinal systems based on them) are related to (but not the same as) the actual tangible earth, water, and so on. For our purposes, we need to understand these elements as qualities, energies, or forces. Something can be "earthy" or "watery" or "fiery," and we can cultivate and enhance these qualities through specific attitudes, foods, exercises, herbs, breathing exercises, meditation practices, chants, rituals, yoga postures, and daily

---

[39] For a very enjoyable and informative look at the elements, check out the cartoon *Avatar: The Last Airbender*. Your kids will love it and learn, too!

routines. The training I have received about this type of truly holistic health cultivation inspires a great deal of how I live my life and work with clients.

"Watery" qualities (which we are covering here) are about connection, cohesion, pleasure, joy, satisfaction, nourishment, taste, love, contentment, flow, ease, and relaxation. When the water element is imbalanced, you may experience a general sense of "lack," as well as neediness, attachment, craving, disconnection, dis-ease, and malcontent. On the other hand, when the water element is balanced and replete, you will feel a sense of peace and connection that boosts your immune system and prolongs your life quite profoundly.

I view something as "watery" if it makes me go, "Ahh." When was the last time you deliberately did something that made you go, "Ahh, that's nice"? From now on, I want you to do something like that every day, at least once a day. Don't make this a burden or difficult. That's not "watery." Make it easy, graceful, sensual, and consistent. Enjoy, relish, taste, and feel... life. If you don't do something—at least one thing—that you enjoy every single day, how can you expect to be happy?

What are you waiting for? Forever?

You have to do it, on purpose, every day, more and more. Even if, aside from, and especially if other hard stuff is happening!

The purpose of life is to live it to the fullest, so join me in filling your cup and letting it overflow.

The key to a "watery" life is sensuality. Note that I didn't say sexuality (though that can be a part of it). Sensuality entails enjoying and enhancing the senses. It means really feeling the air on your skin and enjoying that feeling[40]. It means listening deeply to the sacred sound of rain falling, or, more profoundly, to the sound of silence. It means really indulging in the explosion of flavor from that orange—that watery feeling (which you might be feeling right now by thought alone!). It means staying stuck in awe at the sight of that beautiful sunset—that watery feeling. It means feeling and savoring the water on your skin in the shower, or the soap suds on your hands while you do the dishes—that watery feeling. It means chewing every morsel of your favorite food with relish—that watery feeling. It means closing your eyes and disappearing into the symphony of sounds around you—that watery feeling. The water element is about enjoying life on

---

[40] Those more "in the know" about the elements might say that touch is about the "wind" element and listening is a function of the "space" element, and I concur, but the *enjoyment* itself—the savoring and relishing of the beauty—is the watery feeling I'm talking about.

purpose and by design and feeling connected in a beautiful, harmonious way to the natural and nourishing world around us.

This is true hydration.

Water Consumption

Now for some practical tips on literal water consumption. Being well-hydrated is one of those things that can be a total gamechanger, so here are some rules I live by:

- Every morning, without fail, I drink sixteen to twenty ounces of room temperature or warm water within the first ten to twenty minutes of waking up. I then wait at least thirty minutes before having anything else to eat or drink (ideally, one to two hours before caffeine). I find cold water at this time to be shocking to my system and harder to digest (more on that in a sec). Therefore, if I drink ice cold water at this time, I am not boosting the "watery" feeling of, "Ahh, that's nice and nourishing." However, in the afternoon heat, iced water is just what I need to go, "Ahh."
- Sometime thereafter, I fill a large mason jar (sixty-four ounces/half a gallon) with good quality water and I keep it within my line of vision, to remind me to finish that sucker before the day is done. I've already had twenty ounces by this point, and I will usually have another drink of tea or something else in addition to this jar, too. This gets me to my ninety ounces of water per day, or thereabouts.
- I am not rigid about this (because that would not be "watery"), but I am aware that a good rule of thumb is that half my body weight (one hundred and eighty pounds) in ounces is about what I need to drink in order to be properly hydrated. Whatever other liquids I have (such as high quality coffee and tea) take me beyond these ninety ounces of H_2O, which I can definitely benefit from [41].
- I often add a pinch of good quality salt (pink, normally) and a squeeze of lemon or lime into my water.
- When I'm in ketosis, I am much more deliberate about replacing electrolytes. I make my own homemade version of "LMNT" with

---

[41] Yes, I know some people say tea and coffee are diuretics, but remember, being "watery" is about being a bit more chill. Plus, I really like coffee and tea, and that's "watery!"

salt, potassium, and magnesium, and none of the other crap or cost. I add a squirt of lemon or lime for flavour. Replacing electrolytes when in ketosis is vital, and depletion in this regard is one of the main reasons why people experience the "keto flu." Ketosis feels great when it is done intelligently, and you dial it in.

- I space my water out and drink large quantities at once. I do not sip water all day long – which is why I don't need to attach my water bottle to my hip. Water, like anything else, needs to be digested, and digestion needs time and space with no new input, so that what is needed can be extracted and disseminated. Sipping water all day long interrupts digestive cycles and starts new ones repeatedly, and also puts a burden on the kidneys over time. Think of water like you do eating food, and give the space to digest (and if you don't do this with eating food, please start! "Picking" here and there is a sure way to crush your metabolism.)

- Soup of life! I drink a little water with food to make whatever I eat more "stew-like" in my belly, which aids the digestion of my food, and then, I wait an hour or two after I eat before I drink some more. Then, an hour or two before I eat again, I drink sixteen to twenty ounces of water in a few big gulps.

- The kidneys are more efficient at processing water earlier in the day, so it is ideal to frontload your water consumption and drink less later in the day. This will also bring sounder sleep because you will not need to get up to pee too often.

As far as literal hydration goes, this is what works for me. I drank a gallon a day for some time, and I must say, it felt pretty darn good, but it wasn't sustainable for me. I can do ninety ounces in a "watery" way (i.e., with ease and flow), and that's a difference that makes a difference. If you like, you can figure out what works for you by applying these principles and adjusting as you see fit. Considering most people are chronically dehydrated and hydration can be an easy fix for lots of problems you had no idea even existed, these steps may unlock a whole new "normal" for you.

How do you know that part of the reason why you don't feel so great isn't that you are chronically dehydrated? Why not systematically rule it out? This is an easy box to check off. See what happens after a few months of following these principles in a way that works for you. As always, though, please consult your doctor before starting if you have any circumstances going on that are out of the ordinary.

14

FOOD IS EVERYTHING

B EFORE WE MOVE ON TO OUR supreme state of being, let's address eating.

I guess I am, in a way, saying that eating is the least important "everything" on the hierarchy. This is a radical thing to say. It doesn't mean eating is not important, though, or that I think you are likely to thrive if you are eating McDonald's three times a day, or even "healthy" cereal every morning. The "standard American diet" is truly "SAD."

Plus, if you think about eating in the esoteric sense, it could jump right back up the scale of everythings to the tippy top: if food is anything you can digest and poison is anything you can't, then when it comes down to it, you are always digesting (or not digesting) experience. After all, digestion is the process of breaking something down and nourishing something else so that it can become better, healthier, stronger, and happier. To be in love with life—to have it ALL—is to be able to turn hard times into optimal health and happiness, not by denying or avoiding the shit that's inevitably thrown on your plate, but by embracing it (or digesting it) as rocket fuel for the best possible outcome: Awareness Loving Life.

Getting back to literal food, though (and yes, having stronger physical digestion will help with esoteric digestion), I'd like to share my experience over the years of watching so many people (and I was once one of these people) try to "get healthy" with a rigid, dogmatic approach to diet that lacks the most important ingredients: enjoyment and love.

As you read this chapter, you might find yourself scratching your head at what seem to be contradictions to this philosophy of enjoyment and love: there is a lot of technical information we will cover here that is easy to get rigid about. I'm telling you upfront that that kind of approach—one of rigidity—won't work. If you are coming from a place of fear, self-hatred, self-rejection, self-abnegation, duty, or obligation, your efforts will be sabotaged from the start, because your approach would be missing the water element. They would be too dry and inflexible. You can't thrive from a survival orientation, and you can't get to a positive place by being negative. So, if you follow these principles because you are scared shitless about "getting worse," you won't "get better" (what you focus on grows). You also won't "get better" if you take the opposite approach of completely having your head in the sand and eating junk just because you want it or because your body has grown so insensitive that you think it's not harming you.

What *does* work is loving yourself, your life, and your future enough to choose the relaxed discipline of eating for the sake of health, vitality, and enjoyment.

I'm also telling you upfront what may seem to be another contradiction: enjoyment of food is vital, but if what you "enjoy" is junk food, I would like to challenge you to really examine the difference between your enjoyment of truly nourishing, satisfying, delicious foods, and your enjoyment of the stuff you are *addicted* to and *think* you are enjoying but really are not, in the beneficial sense. Hiding by the cupboard eating cookies is not enjoyment; it's addiction. Having dessert every day is not enjoyment; it's compulsion. If you can't easily say, "No, thanks," then "Yes, please," is not a free choice; it's compulsion. Need I say more?

Unfortunately, the reality of the current food paradigm in our world means that we must be deliberate, discriminating, and disciplined about what we eat if we are to thrive. Our grocery stores and restaurants are loaded with "foods" that are bioengineered to be both addictive and deadly. Why the hell this is permitted by the FDA is another sociopolitical topic completely, but I guess it's not a coincidence that it's called the Food and *Drug* Administration. So much of what is approved as "food" is really as harmful as illicit drugs, in terms of its impact over time. The manufacturers and vendors of much of the "food" we eat today are no better than drug dealers—meaning, these "foods" are an unfair fight. If you eat them enough, you will get addicted, and when you are addicted, "real" food pales in comparison and seems "boring" (see the "dopamine spike" content in Chapter 11). Until, that is, you go through withdrawal, your natural tastebuds come back online, and you recognize that carrots are actually super-sweet and satisfying all on their lonesome[42]. To make matters even

---

[42] I know because my son Finn eats carrots after dinner when some might have "dessert." Granted, he does add hot sauce, but still, he relishes his sweet, crunchy, and delicious carrot with exuberance!

more complicated, even the grocery store's "healthy" stuff, like veggies, are depleted of the nutrients and minerals they once abounded with thanks to modern GMO and monocrop farming practices. This is why most of us "need" to supplement.

Here's a thought of mine I'd had percolating for a while before I saw Tim Ferriss had put it into words (with research to back it!) in his book *Tools of Titans*:

> *If you are over 40 and don't smoke, there's about a 70%–80% chance you will die from one of four diseases: heart disease, cerebrovascular disease [i.e., stroke], cancer, or neurodegenerative disease [i.e., Alzheimer's, etc.].* [43]

He goes on to elucidate that *these are all largely preventable.*

Would you like to eliminate seventy-five percent of the most common causes for premature death?! Holy smokes! I want *that* life insurance plan!

A big part of this life insurance plan lies in the way you eat. I do not refer to this as your "diet" because if you create solutions instead of trying to fix problems, your problems will dissipate more effectively. Focus on adding nutritious and delicious foods instead of eliminating "bad" stuff. Simply eat well and move appropriately and you will lose weight, if need be. As you eat more healthful food, you will "crowd out" the ability and desire to eat junk. We change better by feeling better.

Eating Principles

This is how I, personally, live my life, which is really the only approach I can share with you if I am to authentically present something that might be useful to you. However, this is not (thankfully) the "Religion of Mike", so I implore you not to follow these principles like dogmatic rules. Instead, hypothesize, experiment, assess, adjust, and discover what works for you and your family.

- Eat more nutritious food and exercise appropriately, and you will lose weight sustainably over time, if you need to.

---

[43] Ferriss, T. (2016): *Tools of Titans: The Tactics, Routines, and Habits of Billionaires, Icons, and World- Class Performers*, p. 28, Houghton Mifflin Harcourt.

- There's no need to "diet" in the vast majority of cases, but you may need to restrict junk food and over-eating as an emotional numbing mechanism that always makes you feel worse.
- There is no such thing as "junk food." There is food and there is junk.
- There is very little reason to walk down the middle aisles in the grocery store. The outer walls are where the food (vegetables, fruit, meat and dairy) lives.
- Food is anything you can digest. Poison is anything you cannot digest. In other words, "healthy" food is only healthy if your body can digest it and make use of it. A lot of the food we think of as "healthy" becomes toxic as it ferments inside us.
- Inflammation lies beneath Tim Ferris' four causes of dying, not to mention a host of other illnesses. Inflammation (not fat, or meat, or whatever else) is the silent killer and is largely incited, first and foremost, by survival mode being activated (this is, again, why the food "everything" is on the bottom of the list). I repeat: distress, upset, rushing around, overwhelm, frustration, anxiety, etc.— dripping through your veins practically 24/7 cause more "inflammation" than your "diet."
- Fat is not your enemy. Eating "bad fats" or combining fat with lots of processed carbs and sugar is what kills. Your brain loves fat! Remember the water element we spoke about in the previous chapter? Well, fat is "watery," and I want you to stay juicy. The weight gain and health complications normally associated with "fat" do not come from fat *per se*; they come from "bad fat" and fat combined with processed carbs and sugar. Sure, if you keep eating lots of carbs and then start adding "good fats" because I've convinced you that butter is your new best friend, you will gain weight if you're not moving enough to use those calories. High-fat power nutrition needs to go hand in hand with low carbs, and appropriate moving—and that takes discipline. Please consult your doctor if you want to try this (but you may need to find a doctor that is steeped not just in regular "medical" knowledge but actually embodies *wisdom*).
- Eat for enjoyment some of the time, but most often for your actual energy related needs. It is remarkable how many people are accustomed to eating more calories than they need as fuel for their specific lifestyle every day and then they wonder why they are overweight. Are your appetites based on actual hunger? Or are they more similar to Gollum's quest for the "One Ring?" If your body is

used to overconsuming, you will *feel* hungry, that doesn't mean you are hungry physiologically.
- Continuing the last point, "emotional eating" is probably most people's biggest challenge, but when you learn to tolerate and "digest" the discomfort associated with the emotions you are avoiding via food compulsions, you will have a rocket fuel far more potent than the most nutritious meal!

Being Glucose Adapted versus Fat Adapted

A note about the role sugar plays in our diets:

Your brain loves sugar, and I don't just mean sweets. Pasta is sugar. Rice is sugar. Potato is sugar. "Healthy" cereal is sugar. Alcohol is *lots* of sugar. Why is this a bad thing? Because your brain's love for sugar is a biological maladaptation that leads to short-term pleasures and long-term distress and disease. Allow me to explain:

For millions of years, our ancestors came across sweet stuff very rarely. Our system was originally designed to be "fat adaptive," not "glucose adaptive," meaning that for most of our evolution, we burned fat, not sugar, as our primary fuel. As hunters and gatherers, our ancestors ate veggies, nuts, and roots—mostly bitter foods. Even berries are not that sweet (well, they weren't, until farming and intentional processes to sweeten them came into the picture). The mineral composition of live wild honey is amazing, and if our ancestors could eat the whole hive the one time they came across it in a year, they were stoked.

The problems came when we began to have easy access to sweet things all day, every day, on every shelf of our stores and pantries. Ouch. Add the engineered sweetness and artificial fats that are injected into this food on top of that, and we can't help but become addicted. It is *engineered* to get you hooked. Hence my suggestion to stay out of the grocery store aisles and abstain from processed food most of the time!

Nowadays, unless we are engaged in a very deliberate process to burn fat as our primary fuel, we are sugar (glucose) adapted. If this is you, you'll know it from your energy spiking and waning and you experiencing food compulsions, chronic inflammation, lack of energy, "brain fog," indigestion, aches and pains, bad quality sleep, fluctuating moods, and getting "hangry" or shaky if you go too long without food (sugar). Most people have come to think "its normal" to get "hangry", which perhaps, it is. But that doesn't mean it's the only possibility. Normal is not the limit to what is natural, and most people can get to a point where not eating a meal or two here and there can actually feel quite wonderful.

Perhaps the major magic bullet to kill the four causes of death mentioned by Mr. Ferris (in addition to movement, hydration, and meditation) is becoming fat adapted. This is not easy, and I am not necessarily recommending that you undertake this practice and discipline. Consult a doctor (as mentioned previously, hopefully one that is open-minded and progressive) if you would like to do so. Different things work for different people. It may just be that being fat adapted is *your* magic bullet. Personally, I've been there and done that, and full "keto" doesn't work for me as a permanent lifestyle, and I prefer to go back and forth between that and what I will explain below so that I can enjoy metabolic flexibility and, occasionally, pasta!

If you are interested in gearing up for the advanced science of ketogenesis, you need to study more. A book that should tell you all you need to know is (ironically) called *The Carb Nite Solution*, because part of the program involves pigging out on carbs for one day a week[44]. This proves to be imperative not only for maximizing the efficiency of this powerful biological capacity of ours, but also for our mental health. After a 1-night-a-week guilt-free blowout, this practice of "carb cycling" I've found works best after a 4–6-week period of full discipline keto. These days, it can be very useful to use AI prompts to create a very dialed-in plan and approach for your specific needs and goals.

Eating Guidelines

Now for some less extreme guidelines if you don't want to do hardcore ketogenesis:
- Intermittent fasting can be done as part of the ketogenic lifestyle, and it can also provide similar (albeit less dramatic) benefits when done on its own. This involves only eating in a six- to eight-hour window. This means consuming nothing that will activate your blood sugar during the remaining sixteen to eighteen hours per day. Example: I eat my first meal of the day at noon and then my last meal before seven. Between 7PM and noon the next day, I have nothing but water and coffee. I sometimes make my coffee

---

[44] Kiefer, J. (2005): *The Carb Nite Solution*. Kiefer Productions, LLC.

"bulletproof" (by adding MCT oil and/or grassfed cows' butter), which can assist the ketosis process and doesn't spike blood sugar. Otherwise, my coffee is black. Even a little morsel of anything other than full quality fat—even milk or half and half—will disturb the chemistry. Heavy cream might not, however; the fattier the better. Obviously, sugar in your coffee is out of the question.

- Good fats come from grassfed or free-range meats[45], MCT oil, coconut oil, olive oil, grassfed butter, grassfed ghee, red palm oil, fish oil[46], avocados, lard from grassfed, well-raised animals, nuts[47], sunflower seeds, chia seeds, flax seeds, sesame seeds, and olives.

- Vegetable oils are toxic and often rancid. Throw them out. It's all too much to explain here, so feel free to look it up. *Brain-Building Nutrition* by Dr. Michael A. Schmidt is a comprehensive book on the topic[48].

- A good simple rule of thumb is to have lots of colors in your meals (I'm sure I don't need to say that I mean natural colors here, not food coloring. Why "yellow #5" is allowed in our "food" is perplexing to me). A wide range of natural colors means a wide range of vitamins and minerals!

- High temperature oils and fats also go rancid and make even healthy fats toxic. I only cook with coconut oil, avocado oil, butter, red palm oil, lard, and occasionally olive oil when I am doing lower temp stuff (but olive is really best when used raw, like in salad, due to it becoming toxic at higher temps). I'm Italian, so I make some exceptions with olive oil because life is too short not to; just not too many exceptions, or life can be made shorter than it already is!

- The 80/20 rule is a great place to start. Eighty percent of the time, eat according to the plan of your choosing. Twenty percent of the time, let it go. Flexibility is vital (unless you lie to yourself and use flexibility as an excuse to abandon your eighty percent discipline and are more like 20/80!). Remember from your pleasure–pain

---

[45] I know they're expensive. I don't always choose to pay these costs myself. I do my best.

[46] Boosting omega-3 is pretty vital (not omega-6 and—9, which we already likely get more than enough of). I supplement to boost omega-3.

[47] Eat a variety and alternate so you don't become sensitive and so you gain a variety of minerals. I rotate almonds, pecans, Brazils, macadamias, and walnuts.

[48] Schmidt, M. A. (2001): *Brain-Building Nutrition: How Dietary Fats and Oils Affect Mental, Physical, and Emotional Intelligence.* Frog Books.

education that discipline is delicious. Eat real food. If it walked, swam, breathed, or grew out of the ground, it is food. If it didn't, it is not. Again, this leaves very little reason to walk down the center aisles of grocery stores[49].

- Good water. If you can afford a Berkey water filter or a Clearly Filtered pitcher (gets rid of fluoride! Yay!—and no, I'm not a conspiracy theorist coming out of the closet as seems to be happening in America at the time of this writing, I just understand that proper nutrition and exercise naturally results in healthy teeth, sans unnecessary chemicals... that being said, if you or your kids are on the SAD, Standard American Diet, you might need fluoride), you can make good water great and bad water much better[50]. If you can't afford that, you can make all water better with gratitude.

- Learn to cook. Use spices. Try recipes. Get your hands involved. Smell stuff. Savor it. Explore tastes. The water element is heightened when you enjoy the full sensory experience food offers and this will also stoke your digestive fire for enhanced metabolism!

- Don't snack or "pick." Digestive processes are... well, processes. Give your body enough time to finish one process before starting another. Each part of the process has its own chemistry, so if you are two-thirds of the way through one digestive process and you have "just a taste" of something else, then your body has to kickstart another involving completely different chemistry. *No bueno.*

- Stay hungry. You are designed to thrive that way. Then, enjoy the heck out of your food when you do eat.

- Give your body time to adjust. If you have been eating engineered food, it's been an unfair fight. Very smart people have paid a lot of money to make most of what's at the grocery story addictive so that you buy more of it, regardless of the health consequences. F them! Eating good food and being healthy is activism! If you give your body time to adjust, you will recover your natural taste buds and remember the delight of real food.

---

[49] Clearly, I am not a vegetarian, and I will respectfully decline to argue with you about my belief that there are moral, spiritual, physical, mental, and emotional merits to eating animals. Vegans don't own the moral high ground. This is not to say I am opposed to "their" morality; I am just also comfortable with mine.

[50] We don't use fluoride in our toothpaste, and we filter it out of all our water. Zero cavities.

My Current Eating Routine

I've never had my diet so dialed in. I've tried pretty much every approach out there, and this one is just too good not to share.

The overall gist of the plan that works for me (yes, we are all different, so mix-and-match as you see fit) is as follows.

- I eat no food from 7PM until noon the next day. That's a seventeen-hour fast and a seven-hour eating window. Even when I do eat during the day (during my "eating" window), I typically undereat, and I only eat densely nutritious foods like Brazil nuts, macadamias, heavy cream or grassfed butter (in my coffee), grassfed raw cheese, or a grassfed burger patty by itself, perhaps with an egg on top and avocado. This keeps my neurochemistry sharp, focused, and energized. Think of a tiger on the hunt: you are relaxed, poised, calm, clear, focused, and ready.

- Unless it is a rare occasion, I don't eat carbs or sugar during the day, and I don't graze (i.e., snack here and there). "Just a taste" throws the entire chemistry off. Grazing animals are destined for slaughter and disease. "Carbed" and sugared animals (humans) are numb and dumb.

- I have learned to enjoy the taste of nothing; of discipline; of restraint. As in, I really like it. I'm not faking or forcing it. Discipline is truly delicious! However, I am flexible and sometimes eat a bigger lunch. Today, for example, I ate bacon and 4 eggs, because I lifted weights yesterday and will again today. So, my body needs the extra fuel. Principles, unlike rules, are flexible.

- At night, I "overeat." I don't hurt myself, but I do let it rip! I throw the rules to the wind and enjoy the heck out of whatever I want. Because I've been fasting, then undereating, then exercising (not to mention stoking the fire with small fat- and protein-based snacks) throughout the day, my metabolism is super-high and I burn my big dinners quickly, don't feel bloated, have regular bowel movements, even though I'm in my mid-forties. I also eat carbs (still not junk, though) at night. This promotes good sleep (think of a tiger, having hunted and gorged, crashing out without a care in the world) because of the "dopamine" and "serotonin" it creates. I have three hours of no food before I sleep, though, so it has digested completely by the time I sleep. This is key for not building up toxins and for promoting deeper sleep.

- On weekends, I am a bit more flexible and am not afraid to enjoy pancakes with my kids if that's what's going on that day. I think it's vital when living in the world we live in to not be "too clean." If your system is too fragile to deal with French fries and a burger every now and then (at a real restaurant, though, not fast food, which I avoid completely without any ounce of feeling like I'm missing out), then your system may be too fragile.

Overall, this combo of fasting, undereating, overeating, gorging, no carbs, carb loading, rules and no rules, and so on, is a perfect physiological, hormonal, and psychological balance for me. My energy levels are high and focused when I want that, and I sleep deeply at night. Plus, I don't at all mind—in fact, I quite enjoy—the discipline of the undereating phase, in part because of the kickass neurochemistry involved and in part because I always have a "gorge meal" to look forward to every evening, when I let loose and enjoy family time. This reminds me that enjoyment is key, not only for its own sake but also for its chemistry (i.e., "serotonin" and "dopamine" for pleasure, motivation, and satisfaction). Enjoying it all with family or good company boosts "oxytocin" (love, trust, connection, and healing) and the water element you learned about in the previous chapter.

And there you have it! That's how I roll, having tried pretty much every approach (including a long stint with vegetarianism that almost killed me and one where I pricked my finger and tested my blood to make sure I was in ketosis every day, but I still felt "off"). This current, well-rounded approach is what is most useful to me these days, though as a human being who is in constant growth, this is subject to change.[51]

Food is Everything: Helpful Resources

This chapter's content has been rather information rich. I encourage you to explore each of these different ways of eating for some time, until you find what works for you. As you do, know that all of it is worth the effort, if it works for you. If you want your body to run smoothly for a long time, you

---

[51] Perfect example, as I write this, now the eighth draft of this book, I am in a "Phase 1" 4–6-week strict ketosis mode where I am, again, pricking my finger every day to test my glucose and ketones level, and this time, I feel great!

need to fuel it wisely. Follow the grace and ease question—"What's the next, easiest change I am willing to make?"—do it, celebrate, and build on that.

The key to long-term success with eating, regardless of what approach you adopt, is to adjust your mindset to enjoy the discipline for as long as it takes to adjust your chemistry, so that you really feel the benefits. Doing it and hating it won't work. Focus on adding good stuff in and enjoy the natural result of no longer wanting some of the stuff that is not as healthy.

You don't get there without doing the work; and getting "there" is no place worth getting without effortful ease and enjoyment along the way. By asking yourself the grace and ease question and acting accordingly, you can feel better today, easily, without any gimmicks, in a totally sustainable way that makes perfect sense. Along the way, you will experience tremendous gains, heal huge losses, and traverse the curriculum of your life, from suffering to ALL: Awareness Loving Life.

Return to these pages any time you are ready to add more to your plate. Not struggling with, avoiding, or resisting work is how you transition to a place of more play and beauty.

To supplement everything I've taught you so far in this chapter, I would love to share with you a recap of a bunch of books about "ways of eating" (which I have no affiliation with whatsoever) that I think are immensely valuable. There's no need to reinvent the wheel, and I think you can benefit from these approaches, depending on your needs.

The Virgin Diet *by J.J. Virgin* [52]

In *The Virgin Diet*, you learn about the seven foods that many people are allergic to.

One of the tricky things about the "inflammation" concept is that oftentimes, you are so accustomed to feeling like crap that you don't feel or notice overt symptoms of intolerance. All the while, your body is fighting a chronic allergic reaction to certain foods that you have made staples in your diet. Inability to lose weight, fatigue, brain fog, muscle pain, depression, anxiety, attention deficit, and more can all result from this endless cycle. Accordingly, this book provides a user-friendly approach to eliminating these seven foods and then reintroducing them to your diet one at a time, to ascertain whether you have an allergic response to them. The idea is,

---

[52] Virgin, J.J. (2012): *The Virgin Diet: Drop 7 Foods, Lose 7 Pounds, Just 7 Days.* Harlequin.

when these foods are eliminated for long enough and then reintroduced, the body *noticeably* reacts if there is an allergy or "food sensitivity." When I first eliminated gluten from my diet and then reintroduced it, for example, my tongue got very swollen, and I got a rash all over my inner thighs. I had eaten gluten my whole life "without symptoms," but then again, I had been tired and depressed for most of my life, too! Now, I have rebuilt my gut flora and can tolerate gluten in moderation without a problem, but I abstained from it for a long time (with great results) after assessing myself through the J.J. Virgin Diet.

Nourishing Traditions *by Sally Fallon*

Get to know and love food, yourself, your body, and life with this absolutely essential cookbook!

The Every Other Day Diet *by Krista Varady*[53]

This approach surprised me with its effectiveness. It is geared specifically toward sustainable and enjoyable weight loss. The gist is, don't restrict any foods. Eat whatever you want (again, not junk, but that's my addition!) and as much as you want for one day. But then, only eat five hundred calories the next day. Repeat—and lose weight!

On this diet, I found I didn't mind restricting myself to five hundred calories (which definitely is not a lot of food) for the one day, because I always had tomorrow to look forward to.

As simple as this approach sounds, it's worth reading the book if you are going to do it.

For straight up weight loss, this approach rocks. As always, though, please consult with your doctor first.

The Warrior Diet *by Ori Hofmekler*[54]

Don't be alarmed by the title of this one. This book is based on the premise that for most of our human evolution, we hunted and gathered and endured long periods of hunger, food restriction, and even borderline starvation,

[53] Varaday, K. (2013): *The Every Other Day Diet: The Diet That Lets You Eat All You Want (Half the Time) and Keep the Weight Off*. Hachette Books.
[54] Hofmekler, O. (2001): *The Warrior Diet*. Dragon Door Publications.

followed by gorging and excess. Therefore, our system operates better when we sometimes go hungry. We are designed that way.

Most modern disease comes from consistent excess. I emphasize "consistent" here because Hofmekler's book recommends *intermittent* excess. The same way our ancestors would have gorged on an entire animal after a successful hunt, or eaten a whole beehive if they found one, this approach recommends that we purposefully undereat throughout the day (imitating how we used to snack on berries, nuts, and tubers while looking for bigger game) before purposefully "overeating" in the evening, as if we've hunted a pizza!

The author shares important specifics in the book, so if you are enticed, read it. I like this approach because I feel lean during the day and then get full at night, which leads to deep sleep (just like an animal passing out after a gorge).

The Slow Down Diet *by Marc David*[55]

This is the "water element" approach to eating. In this one, there are no dietary changes suggested or required in terms of what or when you eat. This book is instead about *how* you eat, and your relationship with food. It provides the gentlest and perhaps most important and effective approach. I believe the sentiments in this book should be the foundation of all more "extreme" approaches, lest they be counterproductively rigid and reactively fear- and vanity-based.

If you have struggled with your relationship with food and your body, this book is healing and amazing.

It Starts with Food *by Dallas & Melissa Hartwig*[56]

This book revolutionized the way I think about food. It has all the science, in friendly terms, for what you need to know about real food, from the "paleo" movement perspective. It recommends the "Whole30," which is a thirty-day program of eliminating foods (similar to J.J. Virgin's approach).

---

[55] David, M. (2005): *The Slow Down Diet: Eating for Pleasure, Energy, and Weight Loss*. Healing Arts Press.
[56] Hartwig, D. & Hartwig, M. (2012): *It Starts with Food: Discover the Whole30 and Change Your Life in Unexpected Ways*. Victory Belt Publishing.

It provides the foundation for solid, modern science around nutrition for optimal performance.

Brain-Building Nutrition *by Michael Schmidt* [57]

I referred to this one earlier, when we were talking about vegetable oils. It's a little headier to read (pun intended), but, lest you think I made up the stuff above about fat and oils, it's all in this book.

Cure Tooth Decay *by Ramiel Negel* [58]

See my description in the next section about Rudi's teeth and the many, many underlying health conditions that would have arisen if we had treated his situation as "just cavities." I have this book to thank for the fact that we managed to avoid that. Just because cavities are "normal" doesn't mean that they are natural!

Food is Everything: A Case Study

When our eldest son was a toddler, his teeth literally started rotting out of his head, and we were totally perplexed. My wife and I had been studying Ayurveda for years, we were living in the Bay Area (the home of conscious food movements and healthy options on every block), we ate mostly organic food, and I have to tell you, we were probably more on top of our diets than most. So, we were pretty shocked to learn that our son had twelve cavities during one visit to the dentist! He was developing abscesses and had to have teeth pulled, and the dentists told us we would have to just keep filling the cavities and removing the teeth as needed and that we were basically on track for our kid having a mouthful of lead within a mere few years.

It was a nightmare.

I wasn't just concerned about Rudi's teeth or appearance, or him (and us) being judged. All those concerns were there, of course, but what I also knew from my Ayurveda training was that teeth are a product of bone

---

[57] Schmidt, M. A. (2001): *Brain-Building Nutrition: How Dietary Fats and Oils Affect Mental, Physical, and Emotional Intelligence.* Frog Books.
[58] Nagel, R. (2007): *Cure Tooth Decay: Heal and Prevent Cavities with Nutrition.* CreateSpace.

tissue, which is deeply hooked into the nervous system. In other words, healthy teeth are like flowers blossoming from a tree with great roots. Unhealthy teeth, by the same logic, are an indication of serious underlying problems that will absolutely wreak havoc in much more detrimental ways further down the line than the inconvenient, painful cosmetic issues we were currently dealing with. Of course, though, the dentists around us had absolutely zero answers for how we could reverse this situation. Oblivious to the underlying health implications, they tried to comfort us with, "Don't worry, this is pretty normal. Lots of kids have fillings in every tooth." Argh! They didn't know me at all! None of these placations made me feel better. They just made my heart ache for all those kids, and they made my head shake for the lack of wisdom in the medical profession.

Frustration aside, I could only work with what was in my sphere of influence. So, I got back into action. I studied inside and outside the box about how I could help my son. I was not going to accept the prognostic fate that had been laid out before us by so-called experts.

Finally, we settled on a plan and knew what we had to do. [59]

We knew it would be too hard for a four-year-old to radically change the way he ate while watching others eat the foods he wanted to (we're talking fruit and crackers here, mind you, not candy). Plus, "Together, we thrive," is not just a business slogan; it's the way we live our life. So, the whole family went basically zero-carb and zero-sugar and started consuming a very large amount of very good quality fats and proteins. We also refused medical treatment and stopped with all the fillings. I was a bit worried our urban Oakland dentist office might make a Child Protective Services report on us for medical neglect, so we got out of there and found a guy in the North Bay who understood "old school" dentistry, back when it was a truly holistic, scientific art. He was still a licensed medical provider, but he was willing to give us one month to show results. After that, he told us he would also insist that Rudi have his twelve fillings (he had already had four). He was also willing to monitor the abscess with us, because that was an acute medical condition that we could not delay improving.

Within twenty-four hours of us using our new approach, the abscess was showing signs of improvement. We sent pics to the dentist, and he said we could keep going. Within seventy-two hours, the abscess was gone. And the magic didn't stop there.

---

[59] FYI, much of our plan was based on the book *Cure Tooth Decay* by Ramiel Nagel. (I have no affiliation with Ramiel or his book.)

We had been explicitly told (even by this more holistic dentist) that we would not be able to reverse the cavities. The "mainstream dentists" wouldn't even entertain this conversation in the first place. At one point, I'd had to excuse myself from their office because my lecturing on their lack of wisdom and intelligence was getting mean and unproductive. Even the holistic dentist said, "You can stop the cavities from progressing, but you won't be able to reverse them, and Rudi will likely still need small fillings. But that's better than the prognosis you were previously given, which would likely require many root canals."

Well, you probably know where this is going. After one month, the cavities stopped progressing. The dentist was impressed and willing to give us more and more leeway. We were out of the "tooth pulling and root canal" woods, though not the "fillings" woods. Still, we insisted, "No fillings. We're going to reverse the cavities." The dentist shook his head and smirked a bit but didn't say anything.

For the record, from a medical lens, Rudi was totally safe and clearly in good hands, so he didn't object to us delaying the fillings. And this paid off, big time. Within three months, one hundred percent of the cavities were completely gone, and his teeth were healthy and hard as rock. The dentist was blown away, and we were so grateful, not to mention pretty damn proud as parents! We knew our family discipline had just saved not only our kid's teeth, but a lifetime of deeper, more concerning health complications.

But that's not all! We had no idea this would happen, but: both Rudi and Finn also stopped having tantrums of any kind during this period. I mean zero. They almost never got upset at all. Rudi was four and Finn was two. Don't those "terrible twos" happen to everyone?! Clearly not, because I'm telling you, those kids were totally equanimous and vivacious. This is nothing short of a miracle when you consider the fact that this was otherwise not an easy time in our life. Remember that story about my head injuries, living in one room infested with fleas, and all that? Well, this dental nightmare was all around the same time!

Who says we can't act according to our values in spite of anything?

Those who know me personally know my kids and are aware they aren't "normal"; they are extra-ordinary. They also aren't robotic automatons, though. As they started going to school and being exposed to other kids, birthday parties, and so on, we knew we couldn't keep up the way were eating without them being "the weirdos" who always felt left out. Some level of emotional dysregulation returned as our family transitioned to the 80/20 principle (following the low-carb/-sugar, high-fat/-protein plan eighty percent of the time and letting loose twenty percent of the time). Still, there were zero cavities in our home. Just Dad left wondering why we have to adjust to unhealthy norms in order our kids to feel "normal" and why most people wouldn't rather copy what we were doing!

As I write this, that was nine years ago, and since then, we've had a third child. Rudi took one for the team and taught us that even the most privileged diet that is offered to first- world people with access to great resources was *no bueno*. As I write, Finn and Sofia have never had a single cavity. Finn is eleven and Sofia is five.[60]

---

[60] Poignant update! Now in draft eight, almost 1.5 years later, living back in the USA after a stint in Mexico, with our kids wanting to participate more in their "norms" of the "SAD (standard American diet) and us as parents trying to find the balance between empowering choices, letting them make mistakes, and enforcing the rules, Finn and Sofia have since had their first cavities! Wah! Life is a journey. LOL.

PART III
THE STATE OF BEING

15
YOUR STATE OF BEING IS *EVERYTHING*

You can never change things by fighting the existing reality. To change something, build a new model that makes the existing model obsolete.
—Buckminster Fuller[61]

If you bring forth what is in you, what you bring forth will save you. If you do not bring forth what is within you, what you do not bring forth will destroy you.
—Gospel of Thomas[62]

You are not your thoughts and feelings. You are your values and your choices to express those values aside from what you think or feel, and aside from the arising conditions.
—Michael Boyle, inspired by Lar Short

RECALL THE BRIEF CONTEMPLATION WE DID at the end of Chapter 2. What is your "why" behind your desires? Why do you want

---

[61] According to most reliable sources, the quote "You can never change things by fighting the existing reality. To change something, build a new model that makes the existing model obsolete" is attributed to Buckminster Fuller; however, there is no single definitive source for this exact wording, as it is often paraphrased across different contexts, with the most likely origin being from his various writings and interviews throughout his career.

[62] Gospel of Thomas. (c. 140 AD). Saying 70. In *The Nag Hammadi Library*.

more money? Why do you want better health? Why do you want a better marriage?

The end desire of all our efforts in life is "happiness," however one might define it. Isn't our drive for enjoyment what lays beneath everything we do? Even the depraved among us only do messed up things because we enjoy them.

Many of us set goals and pursue achievements, possessions, relationships, jobs, wealth, and fame so we can "get" happiness. In other words, we try to "get" happiness *inside of us* from "everything else" *outside of us*. We want that perfect relationship with someone *outside of us* so that we can "get" the feeling of love *inside of us*. But why, even, do we want to get that feeling of love inside of us? Well, of course, so that we can be happy. Yet haven't you noticed that despite your best efforts—your many external successes, accomplishments, relationships, orgasms, desserts, possessions acquired, and goods consumed—you still feel largely dissatisfied, and often distressed?

What we are missing here is the understanding that you can't "get" a state of being. By definition, you can only *be* a state of being. And happiness is a state of being. Your state of being is the filter through which you experience everything and so if you are trying to "get" happiness from an unhappy state, you will keep getting what you've already got. The quality of your state of consciousness is the single determinant of your quality of life. It is the make-or-break factor. Accordingly, I am often perplexed over why people don't prioritize the cultivation of their state of being—the direct source and literal experience of "happiness" itself—upfront. Why not cultivate the result we want first and foremost? Why not learn how to *come from* that place regardless of anything and everything else? Why not cultivate the only skill that improves all others? Why not raise the real bottom line beyond the ceilings of our wildest dreams?

I contend that we need to get better at the skill of being happy and living life in a way that actually works.

A lot of people don't consider happiness to be a skill. Yet, it is a skill that not only *can* be cultivated, but that *has* to be cultivated. It won't just "happen." In fact, you will soon learn that if left to live out the demands of the automatic, default mode we were all born with, we are designed to be unhappy! Even if we get most of the things we want—jobs, money, cars, relationships—"happiness" still eludes us if we don't *cultivate it on purpose*.

Consumerism = "Me"-Consciousness = Survival Mode = Unhappiness

You may have heard people say that we are living in a consumerist society, but what does that mean, beyond the obvious fact that we regularly buy, sell, and consume stuff? It means that (not only from a materialistic perspective, but also from a consciousness perspective) we are constantly attempting to "get" from life. However, should we want to actually be happy, we need to *discover* happiness inside of us and *express* it into life. "Happiness" is a state of being, so we can't *get* it, but we can *be* it. We can't *take* it, but we can *give* it. According to renowned psychiatrist Phil Stutz (whose star has risen, for good reason, with Jonah Hill and a recent Netflix documentary named *Stutz*):

> *In our consumer culture, we look outside ourselves for everything... This fixation on things outside of us makes change impossible. If you want to open the door to a future with real potential, you'll need to access the inner power of the lifeforce.* [63]

Furthermore, Phil Stutz reminds us in *Coming Alive*:

> *You must choose to inspire yourself. Making this choice in your head isn't enough. You register your choice through action. Living a life filled with unstoppable passion doesn't happen by itself; it requires a heightened lifeforce, and that takes work.* [64]

Why does it take so much work? Because what Stutz calls X (or ego or vanity) is similar to the "force" of entropy, atrophy, and negativity I have referred to in this book so far as the Reactive-iWAS.

> *Its presence doesn't mean there is anything wrong with you. It's not an illness or a punishment. But it's always there, and every commitment you don't keep, every challenge you avoid facing, every impulse you give in to, is the work of this force. When you wake up at 4AM worried about*

---

[63] Hill, J., 2022, *Stutz* [Film]. Netflix.
[64] Michels, B. & Stutz, P., 2017, *Coming Alive: 4 Tools to Defeat Your Inner Enemy, Ignite Creative Expression, and Unleash Your Soul's Potential*, p. 12, Random House Canada.

paying your mortgage, when you hate someone so much you can't concentrate on your own work, when you've been publicly humiliated and think the whole world is laughing at you, you are seeing the world through the eyes of this force. [65]

In other words, you are perceiving through the filter of your conditioned identity (your Reactive-iWAS).

There is an alternative to this, though. Instead, we can look inside ourselves, find that "identity" is a malleable recipe, discover what matters most to us, and align our identity with those values and express them to the best of our ability, so we can Do → Become → Be what we value and choose with, through, and as Awareness Loving Life.

The cool thing about cultivating our state of being directly is that it works in the opposite way that consumerism does: the more joy, love, appreciation, and gratitude we give to life, the more we receive. The more we give it away, the more we feel it and bring it inside. Values are anything we are happy to have in endless supply, and the more we embody our values and "give them away" by expressing them, the more we actually "get them back."

You may have heard the term "objectification" before. In the most profound sense, objectification is when we perceive ourselves as a limited object - a separate sense of self that feels discrete, incomplete, disconnected, and insecure. In other words, it is when we view ourselves as a separate "me," or as "Me + Everything Else = All." From or as this objectified, separate sense of self, we objectify and commodify the various aspects of life and experience, so that we can "consume" them, in a vain attempt to fulfil our sense of "lack." From this limited self-sense, we are essentially in a codependent relationship with everything. This frame of consciousness (which, in survival mode, is as "normal" and taken for granted as the air we breathe and the nose on our face) is also how we can come to "objectify" a partner, for example. We experience them or their love as an "object" we can "consume" to make us feel fulfilled.

Our appetite to fulfil this feeling of "lack" in these ways, while totally the norm, is insatiable, and our attempts usually end in us blaming our partners, relationships, jobs, or "lack of stuff we want" for the fact that we don't feel satisfied. We operate under the false assumption that we need to "get" *more*, or a new, better "me", partner, job, relationship, vacation, or car to be truly happy.

---

[65] Ibid, p. 14.

All of this may sound really shallow and egocentric when you read about it so plainly, and this may trigger the thought, *That's not me. I don't really expect my happiness to come from all those things.* But if I was a betting guy, I'd wager you're operating from this place. How can I be so sure? Because I am also operating from this place every single second I spend not being consciously aware of my state of being as Awareness Loving Life.

Hang with me a bit more as I lay the philosophical foundations here. We will ground it out with some practical tools soon:

When we perceive ourselves as a discrete object that is separate from everything else, this "me" interacts with everything else in a vain attempt to feel secure, whole, and perhaps even happy. But really, as we have seen, this separate sense of self doesn't actually care about wholeness and happiness. It cares about survival alone, and to that end, it will always default to what is familiar (even if it is awful).

This sense of "Me + Everything Else = ALL" is what philosophers are getting at when they explain "duality" or "dualism." "Me + Everything Else" = dualistic consciousness. And this dualistic, objectified "me" can never and will never feel whole or "happy." By its very construction, the limited self feels walled off, separate, and isolated (which is why we can feel alone even when we are surrounded by people).

"Me"-consciousness is rampant—the most pressing pandemic of all— and it arises as a result of survival mode. Survival mode demands that we preserve ourselves at all costs. It's all about "me." When we are stuck living in this reactive state, we don't realize that in thriving mode, we can perceive ourselves as part of an interconnected "we" that is free to exchange value as part of a interconnected "whole" in an ongoing dynamic of giving and receiving, based on a sincere desire for everyone to benefit. In this interconnected heart- space, life is innately fulfilling and characterized by a sense of worth, meaning, importance, contribution, aim, participation, safety, love, trust, connection, and joy.

If you're still not convinced, recall that there is no amount of "more" (go back to Chapter 11 for the mechanical explanation of these esoteric ideas) that will ever satisfy the story- based, limited, separate sense of self (the Reactive-iWAS) that you are about to learn about in detail. The very form and function of the Reactive-iWAS is dissatisfaction. From this basic sense of "lack" (recall the 3 poisons), we objectify and consume, looking for love in all the wrong places and finding suffering as an inevitable result.

I often tell my clients, "We cannot paste wings on a caterpillar and expect it to fly." If we do expect it to fly, we are sure to be disappointed.

The Reactive-iWAS, which is a product of survival mode, will never be happy in a lasting way. When operating as this limited, conditioned, reactive self, we can certainly still experience pleasure, but a truly happy life embraces both pleasure and pain in a balanced way. Feeling whole, connected, "together," and "at one" is the antithesis of the story-based, reactive version of who we think we are; of the person who craves pleasure, fears pain, and hopes that one day, we will finally "get" happy.

One of the Reactive-iWAS's most pervasive sticking points is the fact that it demands for us to continually seek and consume if we are to feel satisfied; for us to constantly think, *I still haven't found what I am looking for...* We erroneously consider (albeit unconsciously) that we just haven't improved our "me" enough or gotten the right amount and kind of stuff yet in order to be happy, instead of questioning our entire approach. It's not working, not because we aren't good enough, need to try harder, or get more. It's not working because it's designed that way. Only through conscious work can we break free from this prison for emotional drunks.

Doing the Work

To discover what is beyond the Reactive-iWAS—to wipe the slate clean through meditative insight, activate thriving mode, and live through the expression of your values—is to die as who you were (a caterpillar) and become a different species altogether (a butterfly); to be "born again" as a human who is no longer ensnared by their reactive, animal-brain-dominant, limited, dualistic, separate sense of self. It means shedding your Reactive-iWAS and embodying your C-IAM.

When you go through this transformation, qualities that are characteristic of thriving mode effortlessly start to come forward. These are joy, openness, love, kindness, awareness, gratitude, presence, and surrender—the JOLKA-GPS.

Doing the work so you can experience and express your virtuous self is to simultaneously lay to rest your limited, suffering, reactive self. This work (which is continual) means cultivating the ends we all want, upfront, in every moment, so we can truly have it ALL: Awareness Loving Life.

Why just cope with suffering when you can end it?

Your state of being is everything, and it permeates all the different dimensions of life. As Jon Kabat-Zinn said, "Wherever you go, there you are."[66] You can, then, consider it useful to cultivate your state of being directly, and to support your developing state of being by cultivating the other facets of your being (the hierarchy of everythings), which *all* occur within your state of being! There is no better investment of your time and resources. This is your bottom line—the only skill that matters most. This is putting the ends upfront. It is "first things first." From this place, everything else is better.

You are in a state of being twenty-four hours a day, seven days a week, three hundred and sixty-five days a year, forever. Your state of being—your mind, emotions, spirit, and consciousness—is the number one influence on your quality of life, because it *is* your quality of life. Everything is embodied in your experience. There really is no separation between the "mind," the "emotions," the "body", and your experience of circumstances. Everything you know arises within Awareness. Thoughts about arising conditions ("internal" or "external") produce emotions (which are chemicals that are and become the body). Every cell of your being, every instant, is immersed in a neurochemical cocktail of your state of being. If I feel anxious, that is a stew of hormones, neurotransmitters, blood chemistry, posture, PH levels, muscle tone, heart rate, blood pressure, organ activity, thought-words, images, electricity, brain activity, facial expression, tone of voice, type of focus, and so much more. Optimal health and happiness are therefore an inside job, whereby I recognize all these components of life as ingredients that I, as an Aware-Will, can intentionally put together in a way that tastes fantastic!

I must add in here, in the interest of presenting the whole picture, that there is even a State of Being, of Aware-Will, that is beyond identification with this body and its neurochemistry, with all its identifications, thoughts, emotions, and sensations. State of Being is simultaneously aware that "our" Awareness often gravitates to "my body, thoughts, emotions, and sensations," while also being fully aware that the apparent, separate self/other is a mental construct, a projection of consensus belief we call truth, or reality. In essence, there is only Awareness. We come to know in a far deeper, more profound way than we've ever known anything, that we are neither the body, nor not the body, neither the self, nor not the self, neither caught up in the limitations we are talking about in this book, nor not caught up in the traps of suffering. I will wrap it up here, lest I wax on,

---

[66] Kabat-Zinn, J. (1994): Wherever You Go, There You Are: Mindfulness Meditation in Everyday Life. Hachette Books.

because it really can't be described in words, and even if it could be, this would be more a topic of book three, Energy of Mind: Secular Spiritual Work for Practical People. It will have to be more sufficient to say that, when we loosen up our reactive identity with our bodies, thoughts, emotions, memories, experiences, and we realize this body–mind vehicle is neither me nor not me—that is, both me and not me—and that who I am is more like a consciousness-energy field of unlimited potential that appears to be bound to its gravitational pull around this body and its habits, we literally open up new dimensions of experience that seem like the stuff of hallucinations or drug trips—only both of those are the counterfeit versions of this absolutely authentic reality I am pointing to here. When you touch into this Space of Aware-Will, far from feeling trippy, it feels like the most real "thing" you've ever experienced, and while completely novel, fresh, and spontaneous, it feels totally familiar, completely safe, and like you've finally come home after a million-years journey. A note of warning, however: a lot of people out there understand the *concepts* of what I am mentioning here. They *think* they are in this "non-dual" state—and who am I to say they are not? Well, there's a good chance some of them (a lot of them) are not. After a couple of decades of consistent, dedicated spiritual work, I am confident I can say I've tasted what I'm talking about here, and well aware that, most of the time, I am not living in such an unfettered state. Now, back to our more practical "realities"!

To make these complex ideas a bit more digestible, we can say that "the work" might look like this (I credit my mentor for sharing with me just last week, as I write the third draft of this book!):

1. Self-awareness.
2. Self-acceptance.
3. Self-compassion.
4. Self-love (i.e., really wanting to flourish and thrive).
5. Self-cultivation.
6. Self-actualization.
7. Self-transcendence.

If you "do the work," not only will you embark on this journey from self-awareness to self-transcendence, but your experience and expression of life will also develop naturally, on a path from work to play to beauty.

What do we say when we see a master at their craft in action? We say, "They make it look easy!" Similarly, when you put in the work, you get to a point of "effortful ease" where you and your expression are one, in a union where your presence alone is both beneficial and satisfying. In this state, it feels good to be alive! Why not master the art of living life well? Of being "happy?"

But no master of their craft gets to that place without lots of practice. We become what we practice, and in the process, we can discover what my mentor calls "joyful diligence." We realize, *through* discipline, that discipline is delicious! Whenever we get stuck in the "working harder," "struggling" mindset of survival mode, we need to remember the purpose is to play. By doing so, we can open back up to the beauty of ALL.

Your design is such that you require a deliberate, skillful, dedicated approach to life if you want to really thrive. That's what you are learning here. If you are left to your own devices without this deliberate work, then entropy, atrophy, apathy, fear, and anger (survival mode) will rule the day. So, putting first things first, you need to develop the "change state" muscles that, for many of us, have atrophied for lack of use. Use it or lose it.

If I want to impart one thing to my kids, it is for them to know that it is possible for them (and for them to know how) to be in charge of their own state of being, aside from anything and everything else that may be going on. This capacity is important, and because the love in me wants for you what I want for my children (to thrive), I've included a "Checking and Changing State" video in Module 8 of your book resources. Head to www.alltogether.academy/joy-bucket-tools for access.

"Together"

Our motto at ATA ("Together, we thrive") doesn't only refer to our connectedness to others and ALL, or how we help and support each other.

You are already familiar with the sayings, "I've got it together," or "I need to get it together." You intuitively know what it feels like to be "together"; to feel a sense of union in the various aspects of your life; to be clicking on all cylinders, with a sense of cohesiveness between you, your environment, and the people around you—or, more subtly, a sense of coherence in your body, mind, spirit, thoughts, feelings, and actions.

What follows from this is, if you know what this feels like and what it does not feel like (i.e., when you feel "off"), then you can cultivate this state of "togetherness" on purpose. You can know, "This is not 'it,'" and, more importantly, you can recall what "it" is and then invoke, stoke, cultivate, and create "it." You can directly cultivate your state of being (that feeling of being "together") and also dial in and "up" on the states of everything else. This creates a sense of cohesiveness, congruence, and coherence in and around you. You can "get it together" and organize your life for the best possible outcomes—for the benefit of yourself, others, and ALL.

Together, we thrive.

The Essence of Freedom is Choice

You get to choose how you think, feel, and act. The more you own and exercise the power to choose, the more powerful you get and the more able to affect your choices you become, even when tough stuff is going on all around you.

Nothing except your prior conditioning demands you to think or feel one way or another. If life has taught you to re-act in a certain way to its demands, you can learn to respond differently, now and in the future. You get to choose. And this begins with you using the types of tools that will get you the results you want (happiness, freedom, healing, health, love, joy, and peace). There is no magic pill to motivate you to do the work, and nothing does more to build confidence than results.

You can choose for this moment, this book, this part of this book, this journey of a thousand miles, starting with this step, to be a turning point that will dramatically alter your life forever, for the better. No moment need be mundane. Any moment can be the moment you've been waiting for.

In this work, contrary to the cultural trance that says you must struggle to succeed, you can start by asking, "What is the next, easiest thing I am willing to do to move in the direction I value and choose to?" You can feel better today, and everyday forward, easily, without any gimmicks, in a totally sustainable way that makes perfect sense. That said, it takes energy to make energy, so if you are waiting until you "feel like it," you're going to be waiting forever. Objects at rest tend to stay at rest. Objects in motion tend to stay in motion. When you make the choice to use the tools you are learning in this book in an ongoing and consistent manner, even though, aside from, and especially because you don't feel like it, you reach a tipping point where you *do* feel like it. I call this mojomentum! When or how this "tipping point" (i.e., when you start really "feeling like it") occurs is something of a mystery. If I could make it happen for you, I would—and I'd be in line for the Nobel Peace Prize, at that—but I've seen it enough times in myself and clients to know it happens. Isn't that marvelous? Isn't that worth working for?

Like planting seeds, your job is not to make the seeds of action sprout and blossom. That's up to nature. Your job is to plant the seeds and cultivate the soil so that the conditions are optimal for your true nature to flourish and thrive. Your job is to choose.

We have all experienced times in our life when we simply chose, "I am going to be happy. I am going to get up off the couch, stop feeling sorry for myself, and get my act together. I am going to let this go once and for all." Sometimes, we do this with such conviction that the choice itself affects the change. We choose to come from a place inside ourselves that we were passively waiting around and hoping for moments before. Such choices are powerful, and the more we exercise our ability to make powerful choices *by* making powerful choices, the more impactful and effective our powerful choices become. Just don't wait! Start making powerful choices *now*. And don't stop!

Here is a trick: take something that you are certain of, like, "I am certain I am drinking this glass of water." Feel the certainty of this; that feeling of no doubt. It's okay if this seems obvious or elementary for now; we are attempting to activate the way you organize yourself when you are absolutely certain of something. We are cultivating that sense of clarity, because clarity is power.

Feel the sensations of certainty and clarity, which become confidence. "I am absolutely certain I am drinking water." Focus on how certain you are that you are drinking water and feel the sensations of the cool, wet liquid in your mouth. Get out of your head and into your sensations. Feel your muscles swallowing. Savor the sense of, "Ahh." Feel how that certainty organizes your posture; your breath; your state of being.

Now, merge that sense of clarity with some things you want more of, but stay out of "wanting" and get into the state of being clear and sincere. Blend clarity into some powerful questions: "I wonder what it would be like to be truly happy? I wonder what it would be like to feel really free? I wonder what the best possible outcomes might be?"

This instruction might seem to be contradictory. Merge a feeling of certainty and clarity with *questions*? What I mean here is, lean into being certain—being clear—about the fact that you do not know exactly how or when what you value and choose will come to be, but that you are curious, sincere, and clear-headed. You are sincere about what you value and choose, you are honest about "not yet knowing", and you are willing to "do the work."

What's the relevance of this exercise to "the work?" Simply, when you are in survival mode, you fear the unknown. In thriving mode, you understand that the unknown is the source of all possibility; that anything new must, by definition, arise from the unknown. Therefore, you can open yourself up to opportunity by asking questions about the unknown with sincerity and clarity. This is "prayer."

These types of questions work better than saying affirmations that you know are actually bullshit. Wondering about the solution instead of focusing on fixing the problem puts your mind, body, and spirit on "search mode" to explore, discover, learn, grow, and create more of what you value and choose.

We are just playing with this for now. Explore it. See what happens. Maybe it really resonates. Maybe it doesn't right now. You might hear a little voice inside saying, "Bullshit! You're unworthy and are going to be miserable forever!" That's okay. You will learn in a bit that that is not who you are. It is who your survival mode—your Reactive- iWAS—has learned to think you are.

16
TURNING SHIT INTO FERTILIZER

BEFORE YOU CULTIVATE A MORE BENEFICIAL state of being, you need to make space for growth, and you need to turn your shit into fertilizer. Put it this way: if your life is full of weeds, how can you expect fruits and flowers to grow? In other words, how can you expect anything new to show up in your life if you're too busy doing what you've always done, thinking what you've always thought, feeling what you've always felt and choking on weed (pun intended)? In this setup, there's no space for anything new.

Once you've cleared some space by not doing what you were doing, you can then take all that old garbage, compost it, and turn it into turbo fuel.

More on that later.

The crux of change is thinking, feeling, and acting differently today than you would have in the face of the same stimulus yesterday. You may look at the wasteland of your life and think, *I'd like to grow a garden here. I'd like life to be more nourishing and beautiful and to feel the simple joy and connectedness of a lifestyle that truly feeds my soul.* This is a beautiful vision and is a necessary first step, but it's really easy to become so temporarily satisfied with your *plans* for a better future (or a more bountiful garden) that you never actually go about doing the work that will make it happen. You can obtain the best maps, tools, and instructions, but the bottom line is, there comes a time when you have to roll up your sleeves and get dirty. You have to move rocks and pull weeds. And even though it's tiring and you may resist some parts of the work, there's a deeper part of you that feels good because it's wholesome and refreshing to do this work.

You might be tempted to use a weedwhacker—to seek quick fixes—but if you don't get to the roots, they will just grow back. By working smarter and not harder, you can recondition the soil so that it will be more fertile for your new seeds. Instead of just "weedwhacking," you can pull weeds from the roots, throw them in a compost pile, and plant nourishing speeds in their place.

While working to create a beautiful garden (life), you may discover that your septic tank has been leaking, and that the only plot of land you had (which you were planning to build your beautiful garden on) is full of shit (literally). Fear not: because you have some awesome maps, tools, and instructions from a person who's been cultivating a garden for twenty years (me!), and I learned those from generations of master gardeners that reach back before time. You can discover (here and now) that *shit is useful*. In fact, it can turbocharge your garden's growth, if you know how to use it.

Importantly, you can't deny the fact that shit exists in this life. Nor can you misuse it and expect a good outcome. Shit can't be avoided or denied. If you plant your seeds in a toxic leech field, they are going to either die or become toxic themselves. But it also wouldn't make any sense (and would actually be really gross) if you were to dig up your shit and start massaging yourself with it, or throwing it around at your friends, partners, kids, colleagues, bosses, or the people in line at the grocery store. No, that would make everything in your life a lot... well... shittier.[67] Instead, we can ask, "What is useful about shit?" Well, it can be used as fertilizer. If I purposefully shovel my shit into my weed pile and leave it alone, it will soak into the pile and turn it into a furnace of potent fertilized soil that I can plant my wonderful new seeds in. These seeds can then be nurtured and nourished in such a way where they will become super-delicious and nutritious fruits and vegetables and beautiful flowers. If, on the other hand, I throw the shit at my spouse, or drown in it by wallowing, or keep digging it up to "understand where it came from," the compost pile will lose its potency, and my mind and life will become a whole lot shittier.

Continued Cultivation

An important note: when you start seeing sprouts, shoots, buds, and flowers, it is not time to stop cultivating your garden. Thankfully, life will continue to produce plenty of weeds to feed into your compost pile, and occasionally, you will receive another dose of shit that you can mix in there for turbo fuel. Furthermore, you must continue watering and nurturing the

---

[67] That's kind of what it's like when we grovel in our upset stories and "project" our "issues" all over everyone and everything in our life. It's pretty shitty.

seeds you have planted. You must also continue to trim the bushes, get sunlight for some plants and shade for others, alter the temperature, bring in complimentary plants, encourage bees to pollinate, and deal with fungi, predators, and other beings that want to eat your fruits and veggies before you are ready to share. In fact, there will never be a time when you can stop cultivating your garden (i.e., living life in a way that nourishes you). But there most certainly can and will come a time (if you follow the maps, tools, and instructions) when your garden takes on a life of its own and offers you fruit and flowers (i.e., wisdom, joy, peace, and satisfaction) in a way you never could have imagined it could have when you started doing the work.

Tending your garden is an ongoing responsibility, not because you are doing it wrong or because you haven't yet found Shangri-La, but because that's the way it is. Gardening *is* Shangri-La. The purpose is the path! Life is for *living*—and how you live it is up to you. Entropy and atrophy will win the day if you choose to stop doing the work. The master gardener realizes that what he has always been looking for lies in the gardening itself; that happiness resides in cultivation for its own sake; that delicious fruits and vegetables and beautiful flowers are simply the *ornaments* of a well- loved life, and that goals are good for giving us direction but not as satisfying as the joyful diligence of doing the work to better one's best.

Sprouting and Pruning

Everyone is seeking the "meaning of life," but in our search for meaning, we often miss the point: we are the meaning-makers. One of our greatest superpowers (and our Achilles heel) is our power to grant significance and make meaning. Whether we know it or not, we are the cause and the effect of this power, always. There is enough evidence in our history, lives, world, and universe to prove anything, and what we choose to focus on, we grant significance to. In other words, what we focus on grows, for better or worse.

I make this point to lay the foundations for the neuroscience concept of "sprouting and pruning":

Whenever we think a thought, it generates all kinds of activity throughout the body. This activity has associated infrastructure in the brain. After some time, when there is repeated similar neurochemical activity, a neural "groove" is created. I liken these to drops of water in dirt: at first, they create just a trickle, but with more drops of water, eventually, there is a creak, and then a stream, and then a river that has power, direction, and a life of its own. From this groove, similar neural activity starts "branching out" and latching onto other areas of the brain.

This means that if I have an "anxiety" branch that gets activated for the first time when I go to the dentist, it can start branching out and becoming associated with white dentist coats, and then doctors who also wear medical garb, and then hospitals where there are doctors, and then ambulances, and then the street where I saw an accident one time, and then the time when I was young and heard a siren, and then the time I fell and my heartrate was the same as when I heard the siren, and then the color white (regardless of whether it's on a dentist's coat).

This neural groove is now a neural network. It has "sprouted," and it has a life of its own—*until* I take the power back and starve the "problem" of my attention, heartbeats, and breaths.

That's not all: by nature, when one network is "sprouting," other networks (due to inactivity) are "pruning." This also aligns with the "for better or worse" principle.

If I am focusing on how much I hate anxiety and want to get rid of it, or if I am going to therapy to "fix" the reasons why I am anxious, or if I am praying to God to take away my anxiety, or if I am wishing I never had the trauma that led to all this anxiety, or if I am doing breathing exercises to calm my anxiety, I am expanding the anxiety "web"—my anxiety neural network—and thereby strengthening (not diminishing) my anxiety. At the same time, I am inadvertently "pruning" my capacity to experience joy and freedom from anxiety!

This is what the founder of Acceptance and Commitment Therapy (a relatively new, exciting, evidence-backed psychotherapy modality), Steven Hayes, is getting at when he says, "To put it bluntly, human beings are playing a rigged game in which the human mind itself, a wonderful tool for mastering the environment, has been turned on its host."[68] If, however, I focus on what I value and choose and therefore "sprout" neural grooves and networks of what I choose to experience more of (e.g., calmness), I will, by default, "prune" the networks that I no longer wish to activate in my life (e.g., anxiety). There is even a mechanism in the brain that comes in and sweeps away old unused neurochemical material ("unused" being the keyword here). Focus on what you value and watch as what you are sick and tired of fades into the distant past. Focus on what you don't like, don't want, hate, or want to get rid of, and you will strengthen the very patterns you wish to release.

---

[68] Hayes, S. C. (2005): *Get Out of Your Mind And Into Your Life: The New Acceptance and Commitment Therapy*. New Harbinger Publications. (p. 1)

I am not saying this is easy work or that pain and discomfort won't arise along the way, but I am saying it is *simple* work. Focusing on what you want more of leads to the sprouting of what you want more of, thereby automatically pruning what you want less of. (This is why I use the gardening analogy.) But recall from the previous section, it also doesn't work to be in denial of the shit... it's all about how we are *using* the arising conditions. Do we stay stuck, drowning in shit? Or do we throw it in the compost pile, pull weeds, and plant seeds?

The tricky part is that survival mode narrows your focus to lock on to anything it perceives as a threat, thereby sprouting more of it. It is up to you to recognize that this mostly happens when there is no actual threat and to use the tools we are about to cover so you can "pivot" to a more optimal state.

Again, I am not suggesting that you deny, repress, or "gaslight" yourself or others. What I am suggesting is truly the opposite of denial. Survival mode tells you that the stick you can see from the corner of your eye is a snake, when in actuality, it is a stick. Anxiety is a liar and a thief! The more afraid you get that it could be a stick, the more you perceive it as such. You may even get mad when someone walks by and casually points out, "Hey, that's a stick." *They don't know how I feel. I'm really scared of snakes. I was once bitten by a snake.*[69] *How dare they deny my experience!* Instead, I suggest you look at life through a larger and more inclusive lens; that you acknowledge the reality of the situation without staying stuck in toxic emotions (even if they are "valid" and "true"). More often than not, *the stick is a stick*. Not to mention, thoughts and feelings are so malleable, and "truth" is so relative that a better question than, "Is it true?" is, "Is it useful?" You can choose to accept the shit that's been thrown on your plate, activate a more useful state, pivot toward your values, turn your shit into fertilizer, and cultivate the fruits of joy, openness, love, kindness, awareness, gratitude, presence, and surrender. If you want to be happy, that is! If you'd rather keep suffering, then feel free to do what is easy, automatic, convenient, and familiar.

---

[69] True story. I was bitten by a Malayan pit viper in Thailand. Yikes!

To Conclude

The skill of managing your attention is the bottom line of the work we are doing here. What you focus on grows, and what you grow, you become. Therefore, it's a good idea for you to learn how to train yourself to focus on what you value and choose to have in your life, lest you continue to become everything you'd rather not because your attention is reactively grabbed by the fierce economy of confusion and distraction.

If you are lost in the woods (as many of us feel we are in life), paralyzed with fear of snakes, it is very useful to have maps, tools, and instructions for how to get home. The map is not the territory itself (it's a depiction of it), but it certainly helps along the way. You will still encounter obstacles, bad weather, fears, doubts, challenges, triumphs, and perhaps even real snakes along your journey, but still, to have a compass and a map is priceless, and to know how to orient yourself so that you can use these maps and tools is even more invaluable. Lucky for you, the Creative-IAM (C-IAM), which we will create in Chapter 22, is how you orient yourself to get back home to who you are. The Neurochemical Roadmap to the Future You Value and Choose (your NRF), which we will create in Chapter 23, is the easiest route there.

17
ALL THE REASONS "WHY"

IN THE UPCOMING CHAPTERS, YOU WILL discover your Creative-IAM and create a Neurochemical Roadmap to the Future You Value and Choose (NRF). As you do so, you will realize that it is when you make choices that align with what matters most to you, even when you don't feel like it, that you experience the "ego death" of your reactive self. This sounds like an esoteric concept, but it can actually be made very practical. Here's an example:

Intrinsically, I value feeling fit and healthy. I *want* to feel good. Still, I sometimes think or feel that I don't want to get up and exercise (recall the "thoughts and feelings" everything). I may even identify with the thought-feeling construct that "I'm a piece of shit" or "I'm not worthy," and therefore, it feels more appropriate for me to stay in bed and justify feeling bad. But wait! I can recognize those thoughts and feelings as not "me" or "mine," but just as passing thoughts and feelings that anyone who's been in survival mode might experience, or that anyone who's watched commercials might experience, or that anyone who's eaten too much pizza the night before might experience (just as a few of the infinite examples of conditions that can disorient us). I know that my identity (which we will cover in more depth shortly) is merely a story of bundled, familiar thoughts and feelings that I have told myself about myself. This story inspires me to act in ways that "defend" this identity as "true" or justified. When I activate extra and open attention and come from my C-IAM, I can witness this whole thought-feeling- story mess and choose to instead express my values about health, fitness, and wellness by getting up and exercising anyway, despite whatever I think and feel.

My mentor, Lar Short, tells us in *Opening the Heart of Compassion*:

The "real cause" can never be determined. We are the way we are only partly because of our parents, who were somewhat the products of their parents, who grew up with their parents, and so on. Other factors may include the beliefs we formed from anomalous experiences, the influences of long-gone friends and acquaintances, and not getting enough sleep last night. It is much easier to stop the suffering now by interrupting the patterns than it is to find a real cause *(emphasis mine). We can take charge of now; we cannot do anything about the past. We can use our experience as the beginning of wisdom rather than as a continuation of ignorance.* [70]

With practice and time, reactive thoughts and feelings become less and less significant, to the point of *irrelevance*—which is a good thing, because they are totally unreliable and the ultimate source of misery. In their place, you develop an inherent willingness to embody your most cherished values (represented by your C-IAM) much of, most of, or all the time. This is also a good thing, because the C-IAM is the source of unlimited satisfaction and, ultimately, the great joy of being. Therefore, we can say that if we are to embody the great joy of being, we must first stop identifying with all the thoughts and feelings we have about why we think we are suffering. So, let's examine those.

X, Y, and Z

"X, Y, and Z" is the phrase I use to refer to all the "reasons" we think we are not truly happy and radiantly healthy. These "reasons" are usually mistaken as the *cause* for why we are not truly happy and radiantly healthy.

When we mistake effects for causes, we (understandably) misspend lots of energy and resources trying to fix what we think is broken. Like a game of whack-a-mole, more "causes" keep popping up despite our efforts to be happy, because we are "fixing" the wrong "problem." This means that no matter how hard we try, how good a person we try to become, how effectively we appear to have "solved the problem" at first glance, or how sincere our efforts are, something else will always come up, and we will

---

[70] Lowenthal, M. & Short, L. (1993): *Opening the Heart of Compassion: Transform Suffering Through Buddhist Psychology and Practice*, p. 68. Tuttle Publishing.

always find ourselves stuck in a futile (and unfun) game we didn't even ask to play.

Most people think their marriages and lives are unhappy, anxiety inducing, frustrating, depressing, or overwhelming because of the "reasons" they point to about their current realities, past experiences, or future worries. Yet as challenging as these circumstances may be, and as valid and justifiable as our reactions to them may seem, thousands of hours of professional experience and decades of radical personal growth have proven to me that these reasons are not, in fact, the real root cause of why we suffer. What if all those reasons are instead secondary effects?

I'm not saying that your problems are all in your mind, or that you are operating in a vacuum and have "manifested" all of them. Nor am I here to deny the fact that there are some circumstances that are much harder than others to deal with, and that largely lie outside of individual control. Quite the contrary. There definitely are forces and influences that are bigger than us and that can dramatically change our experience of life, unalterably and forever. You may be truly experiencing any of, many of, or all of the "problems" I will list shortly in very valid, legitimate, real, and impactful ways. Still, I bet if you really examine your inner experience, you'll find that you think there always has to be some degree of suffering in your life, because "that's what it is to be human." Right? To go with that, perhaps you think, *I can never be "happy" if I still have all these painful experiences to tend to.* Right?

I know I am asking a bold question here, but: why just cope with suffering when you can end it? What if, despite your painful experiences, you could feel better today, easily, without any gimmicks, in a totally sustainable way that makes perfect sense? What if I told you that life doesn't have to be a struggle, and you believed me? That in fact, life *can't* be a struggle, or you won't bring all its potential to the fore? What if struggle (resistance) is an important ingredient that *makes* your suffering, not an inevitability we all must face.

Before we get back to all the good stuff (like love, trust, connection, and joy), here is that list I was talking about before. This is a list of adjectives, feelings, and sentiments you may or may not currently use to describe your life. Does any of this sound familiar?

- Anxious.
- Stressed out.
- Overwhelmed.
- Flat.
- Numb.
- Depressed.

- Angry.
- Unable to sleep well.
- Indigestion.
- Frustrated.
- Often feeling criticized.
- Often giving criticism.
- Controlling.
- Lacking intimacy.
- Not having enough fun.
- Exhausted.
- Disconnected.
- Greedy.
- Needy.
- Overwhelmed.
- Righteous.
- Vengeful.
- Bitter.
- Not in love with life.
- Lacking a love life.
- Burdened.
- Impotent.
- Resentful.
- Worried.
- Lacking family harmony.
- Arguing too much.
- Lacking vitality.
- Not feeling the zest of life.
- Life looking good on socials, but not feeling the gratitude and joy that you think you "should."
- Traumatized.
- Compulsive and excessive screen use.
- Physical health red flags.
- Brain fog.
- Not having enough time.
- Addicted.
- Rushing around.
- Broken.
- "Damaged goods."
- Hopeless.
- Helpless.

- Possessive.
- Jealous.
- Fragile.
- Insecure.
- Hurt beyond repair.
- Distracted.
- Having a hard time focusing.
- Eating compulsively.
- Fear of death.
- Apathetic.
- No sense of meaning or purpose.
- Existential angst.
- Lonely and isolated.
- Arrogant.
- Condescending.
- Judgmental.
- Complaining a lot.
- Guilty.
- Ashamed.
- Not good enough.
- Pervasive sense of "lack."
- Never feeling satisfied, even with success.

How can this list so accurately describe your life when I don't even know you? Well, these experiences are predictable because they are the natural and logical consequences of you operating from the default mode of the brain we were all born with (survival mode) and then identifying with the stories you tell yourself *about* those feelings. Regardless of the specifics of our situations, this (non-exhaustive) list reflects what will happen to anyone who is in survival mode too often for too long.

Lar Short tells us:

We need to examine the nature of pain. What makes it so painful, aside from the fact that it hurts? What is the difference between pain and suffering? How does pain become suffering? Blood clots, and then stops flowing. Similarly, pain congeals into suffering. We prevent it from passing with our fear, hope, expectation, frustration, anxiety, blame, guilt, and shame. We become extra sensitive, thinking that every sensation might be the beginning of more pain, thereby painfully bracing ourselves against the pain that might happen. We split ourselves between our desire for control and our ignorance of what is coming. We try to be prepared, "pre-tensing" to the point that we cannot move. Each "what if," "why" "how bad can it get," and "you did this to me" keeps the pain from fading into the past. We extend the pain as suffering. [71]

Even if you don't identify with everything on this list, there are practical actions you can take to outgrow all of them. It's okay if you don't believe that, though; your default mode (SM) has a built-in negativity bias, and if that is active, you won't be able to experience happiness or believe that good things are coming, or that anything that great is possible. Instead, you will likely believe that I am just another schuckster selling snake oil. The default mode we are all born with is designed to assume a stick is a snake; to believe that what can go wrong will go wrong; that there's got to be a catch; that radiant health and true happiness is... well, impossible, "at least for me."

In fact, I bet some of the items on this list are not only familiar to you but are what you've come to perceive as the "normal" experience of modern day living. After all, everyone's feeling these things. Parenting is "stressful." Work is "stressful." In-laws are "stressful." Finances are "stressful." Marriage is "stressful." Going grocery shopping is "stressful." Doing the dishes is "stressful." In survival mode, *everything* is stressful, and complaining about it is the new black.

Here's the thing, though: just because this way of experiencing life has become "normal" does not mean it is the only possibility for you. Just because it is the default option for your brain and nervous system doesn't mean there isn't also a natural, practical, and logical upgrade available to you. Remember, it doesn't matter if you are on the proverbial beach in Hawaii; if your brain is in survival mode, you will find something to be stressed about.

This is not your fault. Everyone who has not yet deliberately learned how to consistently "turn off" survival mode and "turn on" thriving mode is continuously looking for love in all the wrong places and blaming anything and everything else for why they aren't finding it. Thankfully, though, you can do much more than talk about your problems; you can actually do something about them. In fact, the only way to thrive is to thrive *on purpose.* Your brain is hardwired so deeply for survival as a priority that you will

---

[71] Lowenthal, M. & Short, L. (1993): *Opening the Heart of Compassion: Transform Suffering Through Buddhist Psychology and Practice, p. 66.* Tuttle Publishing.

continue to default to being "stressed out" until you deliberately, consciously, consistently, purposefully, and skillfully change state.

Train your brain or remain the same. Well, not quite. In this case, it's train your brain or get worse. Entropy and atrophy will take over if you don't do resistance training (which sometimes means letting go of resistance!).

This brings me back to a powerful choice you can make, right now, as you are reading these words. Is today the day you turn your back on the past, let the dead be with the dead, and turn toward life? Is this the day you choose to stop suffering and start living?

Powerful choices can be made at any point, for better or worse. Then again, the ones that really mess us up aren't actually choices; they are reactions. Alternatively, when our choices are creative, deliberate, and based on our values, they can lead us to the sublime. When our reactions are dictated by survival mode, they can lead us down a pathway to hell. Speaking of...

Programming

I can trace my pathway to hell back to when I was five. I was sitting on my mother's lap and watching the evening news. Deep in the recesses of my childhood mind, I planted a seed in that moment that would take root, grow steadily, and alter my trajectory from that day going forward. At that moment, the intensity of the suffering I was witnessing on the evening news was too much for me to bear. I remember telling myself, "It's too much. I can't feel this, and I don't ever want to feel again." That clear intention, combined with the potent chemicals that were being unleashed while I was in survival mode, seared this message into my system so deeply that it became a way of being that would spiral out of control for decades before I was able to regain my creative choice. Suffice it to say, I didn't know then that decisions that are made when the brain is in a hypnotic state can form the entire basis of a person's perceived reality.

As a five-year-old, my brain was already primarily in alpha and theta brainwaves, which are both "sponge"-like states that receive experiences and convert them immediately into identity, or "reality." I was also sitting on my mom's lap while watching the TV, which means I was deeply relaxed. Finally, as the icing on the cake, evening news and commercials are purposefully designed to induce and strengthen hypnotic states (it's no wonder it came to be called TV "programming!"). In that highly programmable state (which was no one's fault, by the way), my nervous system became so overwhelmed that I unwittingly made a life-altering decision then and there.

Of course, I didn't become aware of this until decades later, while I was in a deep state of healing meditation. That decision to "never feel again" had, up until then, spiraled into decades of soul-numbing depression that had almost killed me.

A long time after that fateful day, I learned, as an adult, that I could, as a skill, enter these deeper brainwave states on purpose, to effectively choose to reprogram myself.

The strange truth of "posttraumatic growth" is this: I truly have no regrets about any of it. Look at the incredible journey that "unfortunate" decision has taken me on! When I look around at most of my peers who are suffering despite their "success," I am thankful I crashed hard and early and was forced to learn, over the last few decades, everything I am sharing with you in this book.

By the time you are done with this part of this book (and thus this book as a whole), you will not only know it is possible for "someone" to be truly happy and radiantly healthy, but that it is possible for *you*. By the time you are done reading this book—if you do the work—you will have a recognizable taste of this reality. You will be able to touch it, smell it, see it, and feel it in your life, and others will notice that you are different. By the time you are done reading this book, you will know how to cultivate the conditions in your life that will naturally result in ongoing healing, increased health, and robust happiness. You will not only have gained practical tools, but (if you have used them) you will also have some degree of proficiency at alleviating "X, Y, and Z," and many of your problems will very likely no longer be problems at all.

Why just cope with suffering when you can end it? Coping skills are great—truly—but outgrowing the problem so that it no longer needs to be coped with and unleashing the aliveness that was locked up within that problem leads to complete ecstasy.

By the time you are done reading this book, you will possess a map of the most important and impactful territory you could ever possibly navigate: your state of being. But only you can choose to follow the map and instructions and use the tools. If you "do the work," all is revealed. If you don't, all remains hidden, and you quickly default back to the familiar; the easy; the automatic; the habits of the past; suffering. While extra and open attention and "letting go" clears the canvas, it is up to you to proactively create what you value and choose to in the space of this awareness, lest the "same old, same old" sprouts again, and again, and again.

How to Find Joy
Even If You Have a Hole in Your Bucket

Get your paintbrush ready, because I am going to give you some fantastic colors to paint your future with in the upcoming chapters. Do you mind if we touch on the power of questions first, though?

18
WHY ASK WHY?

BEFORE WE PROCEED ANY FURTHER, PLEASE allow me to ask you a question: are you willing to feel better, today, easily, without any gimmicks, in a totally sustainable way that makes perfect sense?

I'm not just being a bit cheeky here; I am really asking, because some people actually don't want to feel better. They may or may not *say* they do, but their actions speak louder than their words. Many people come to therapy or self-help work on what they say is a quest to "get better," but really, they are (perhaps subconsciously) looking for proof they are unfixable and that their life circumstances are too much for anyone to bear. In short, they identify as victims and almost take pleasure in a doctor, therapist, or coach feeling stumped about why they are not improving. The more failed attempts to "fix" themselves they accrue, the more proof they have that they are truly "damaged goods."

In this vein, Lar Short explains:

> *By identifying with the role of the victim and relating to life as a problem, we betray life in many ways. Part of us knows how to be alive in the moment, but we betray that part [of ourselves] by putting all our attention on our story, our reconstruction of our life history. Our identity does not allow us to relate to the present as it really is. We stubbornly see ourselves as a victim, again, rather than as the author of our experience, now.* [72]

---

[72] Lowenthal, M. & Short, L. (1993): *Opening the Heart of Compassion: Transform Suffering Through Buddhist Psychology and Practice, p. 66.* Tuttle Publishing.

This in mind, let's come back to my question: are you willing to feel better, today, easily, without any gimmicks, in a totally sustainable way that makes perfect sense?

This question is meant to elicit more of a meditation than an intellectual exercise, so slow down, close your eyes, and ask, "Am I willing to feel better, today? Easily? Sustainably? Would that be okay?" If I could explain to you a path with maps, tools, and instructions to that end, in a way that makes perfect sense and without any gimmicks, would you be willing to feel better today?

This is a sincere question. Let it in and truly ask inside.

Questions are really brilliant, by the way, and, like many elements of nature, they are subject to the laws of "for better or worse," as your mind can't *not* answer a question. Don't you agree?

Do you see what I just did there? Got it?

Thanks for answering, even if only internally, and proving my point.

Okay, good.

By the way, even if you ask yourself a question and it evokes an answer you don't like or want, that's okay! Remember, what arises are thoughts and feelings, and you are not your thoughts and feelings. Questions are always great because they either evoke more of what you value and choose, or they smoke out your resistance! So, if a little voice inside says, "No, I am not willing to feel better," that's wonderful! You now have the opportunity to dis-identify with those thoughts and any concomitant feelings. You, as an Aware-Will, can notice those thoughts and feelings and affirm, "I am not those thoughts and feelings—those thoughts and feelings aren't me or mine—and I value and choose to feel better, today, easily, without any gimmicks, in a totally sustainable way that makes perfect sense."

I have lots of slogans hung up around my house, and we talk about them as a family regularly. One of them is, "I am not my thoughts and feelings. I am my values and my choices to express my values and choices, no matter what I think and feel."

In the heightened state of being that lies within, there are many more possibilities, and questions are a great way to access these resources. Life actually has the ability to feed back to you something greater than your current state of limitation could ever imagine. This is why open questions are even greater than closed questions—and by "open," I mean to possibilities; to receiving more than you even bargained for. Be careful what you ask for, though! You might not want to ask, "How could this get any worse?" because you just might find the answers. It was quite a shock when I realized that worry is literally the same thing as praying for what you don't want. I figured I better get good at this mind training stuff, because I worried a lot!

Okay, I digress. Back to questions. Mind if I ask you a few more? Which really means, are you willing to ask yourself a few more questions? (They will only work when you take the questions inside yourself and ask sincerely.)

1.   What would it be like to feel better today?
2.   How would you know that you feel better?
3.   What would you be doing differently if you were feeling better? How would *that feel*?
4.   Do you notice any images or flashes of brilliance when you close your eyes and lean into feeling better?

These questions are also a bit of a meditation. So, relax into it. This is not just an introductory exercise; these questions are gold. Ask them in a relaxed state where you are open to the unknown, and you will get great answers.

5.   When you are feeling better, what do others notice about you?
6.   What does it feel like in your body when others notice you are feeling better? (Think in terms of actual, raw, physical sensations.)

The answers you receive may not come in the form of words, as such, that might be part of it; but more optimally these questions will evoke *images* and *sensations* of what you value and choose and with these, you are cooking with gas.

Okay, great questions. Great answers. Great work. Like I said, this is easy, and you can do it. You *are* doing it. *We* are doing this together.

Whatever you discover is less important than the very fact that you are discovering, non-stop, step by step. Even though you are where you are and I am where I am, we are together, and so we are not alone. We can feel together. Together, we thrive. You can feel better, today, easily, without any gimmicks and in a totally sustainable way that makes perfect sense.

Four Open Secrets

I would like to share with you four open secrets that will turn any "change work" you've ever tried on its head and position you for thriving and healing. This is foundational and unique stuff, so read closely.

Secret #1

Most of you think that truly changing and feeling better will be really hard. Some of you even think it will be impossible. Many of you think that at the very least, it will take a long time and that you will have to do a ton of things you don't want to do and stop doing a ton of things you don't want to stop doing to get there. But none of this is necessarily true—unless, of course, you believe them to be true. In that case, it's also "true" what Henry Ford said: "Whether you think you can or you can't, you're right." Remember, the things we think of as "truths" are usually beliefs, and beliefs are not "true" or "untrue" *per se*; they are thoughts and feelings we have thought and felt so many times that they *seem* to be true. Beliefs filter our perception, and our perception generates our experience.

BELIEF → PERCEPTION → EXPERIENCE

You will sometimes hear me refer to this as "B-P-E." (I credit Lar Short for this terminology.)

"Beliefs" formed under the influence of the default survival mode of the brain are re- active and much likelier to be "untrue" than thriving mode beliefs. In all likelihood, the stick is not a snake. But your brain is designed to "believe" it is a snake and to feel this with such intensity that you act as if it is "true."

> *Suppose we are walking around in the world afraid of snakes (that are actually sticks). As we journey through snake country at dusk every long thin shadow triggers our snake "radar" and places us on alert. In fact, our fear and caution would make us run or strike out, rather than examine the evidence. This type of misperception creates a body response, in which the reality of the body's reaction overwhelms whatever is actually occurring at the time. The reaction becomes a reality unto itself.* [73]

This mental process, when magnified and amplified over time via SM-driven interactions with others, is one of the main roots of all suffering, and is an origin point of all dis-ease.

---

[73] Lowenthal, M. & Short, L. (1993): *Opening the Heart of Compassion: Transform Suffering Through Buddhist Psychology and Practice*, p.65. Tuttle Publishing.

I can't go further into B-P-E now. It's a huge concept, with many layers and implications. It's also not what I am trying to explain to you right now. Rather, it's what lies beneath our first secret, which is:

It's not hard to feel better; it's easy.

This does not mean that the shit going on in your life is necessarily easy, or that the shit you've had to deal with in the past has necessarily been easy. It means that *it's easy to feel better*. It also means that if you're currently feeling like it's *hard* to feel better, this is because you are going about it the wrong way.

Got it? Okay. I am now going to move on to secret two. Is that okay?

Secret #2

Many of you think it will take "forever" to feel better, or at least a really long time. Maybe you think you "never" will feel in love with your life ("never" is a really, really long time). Well, remember what I said about beliefs? They are not "truths." It is certainly *possible* that it could take "forever" for you to feel better, or that it will never happen, but secret two is:

It is possible for you to feel better today.

This is not just a trick of words. This is actually how it works. Seemingly small actions performed consistently over time yield staggering results. No matter what your past and no matter what your present, you can feel better easily (secret one), today (secret two). In fact, if you are waiting for something in the future to happen to "make" you feel better, you are going to be waiting forever (meaning you will be right about that belief, in that it will be true for you).

Lest this message be confused for the kind of bullshit that asshole, gaslighting, new age, victim-shaming conspiracy theorists spread in the form of condescending criticisms, I can assure you that what I am attempting to convey here is full of loving kindness (not to mention skillful means).

Now, do you mind if I share secret three?

Michael Boyle

Secret #3

Most of you think that you "must"; that you "should"; that you "ought to." This, in effect, boils down to you "whipping yourself into shape." You think that if you feel bad enough about yourself and your circumstances, you will finally have the motivation to do better; to *be* better.

Fear and punishment are often effective motivators, but they are not *good* motivators, and they most definitely aren't *sustainable*. Eventually, this approach leads to healthy rebellion—rebellion you beat yourself up for, calling it "self-sabotage." This is backward: it is healthy to rebel against things that are motivated by fear, anger, and control (even if you are the one wielding these threats against yourself).

Has anyone here whipped themselves into a frenzy to do what they "ought" to do? What they "should" do? What they "must" do?

How has that worked out?

If you are also like most of us, the results of that change strategy have been "do it for three days, then quit." Maybe you even got to two weeks before quitting. Maybe a month. Or perhaps you just had a "never mind, what's the point?" attitude from the start because you already knew it wouldn't work or last.

Your belief in this lie—the lie that you "should," "ought to," and "must" make change a miserable process of doing a bunch of stuff you don't want to do and not doing a bunch of stuff you don't want to stop doing—is the primary reason why your prior sincere and well intentioned efforts to change for the better have not been sustainable.

To put all three of our secrets so far together, I am here to say:

You can feel better easily, today, and sustainably.

This leads me to secret four.

Are you ready? Are you excited? I'm excited about this, because it not only works, but is also easy and totally sustainable, there are no gimmicks, and it makes perfect sense. It is simple and beautiful, really. Above all, secret four brings it all together.

Secret #4

The key to easily, sustainably, practically feeling better today (and every day forward for the rest of your life) lies in you following the simplicity that is revealed by the grace and ease question:
"What is the next, easiest thing I am willing to do, right now?"

I repeat: "What is the next, easiest thing I am willing to do, right now?"

Let's break down the components of this question, because it's a thing of beauty, and I don't want the profundity to get lost in the simplicity.

1. It's a question, and your brain can't not answer a question. Can you not answer this question? See what I mean? Input good questions and you will get great answers. Ask yourself, "How much worse can life get?" and duck for cover, because you might just find out. It is more useful to ask questions that automatically illicit thoughts, images, and sensations that amount to thriving!

2. "Next" means it's available and doable, here and now. It is present and actionable.

3. "Easiest" means it's... well, easy. It doesn't have to be hard. In fact, it *can't* be hard, or you won't feel better. So, make it easy! Actually, no, don't just make it easy; make it the easiest it could be!

4. "Willing" means that you are willing to do it. There is no resistance—and because there is no resistance, there is no suffering and no need to rebel against it and "self-sabotage."

5. "Right now" means you are dealing with the only possible portion of life you can work with and change: reality!

Because it's what's next, because it's easy, because you are willing, and because it's now and always, it becomes totally sustainable. As a result, you change better by feeling better.

What happened the last time someone told you you "had to," "must," "ought to," or "should" change in a way that seemed critical, judgmental, controlling, or shaming? Did this not activate an inner sort of "F you, I am going to do exactly what you think I ought not to do" within you? Well, this is exactly what you are doing to yourself. Because you are "whipping yourself into shape," because you are believing lies, and because you are "shoulding" and shaming yourself into being better, you are setting up dynamics that you must actually rebel against to preserve your dignity (albeit in a sort of self-defeating and counterfeit way). No one wants to be controlled, even if by the petty tyrant inside their own head, so you buck and kick and assert what turns out to be a kind of false freedom (because you do it in a way that is counterproductive to your true aims).

We change better by feeling better.

Here's an example of this: have you ever experienced that feeling of being "in shape" and *wanting* a salad? You genuinely *wanted* healthy food. There was no "should," "must," or "ought to" about it. You were willing and it was easy. And not only did you genuinely desire what was good for you, but you also had no interest in what was not. You didn't need to force yourself to resist the donut, because you sincerely didn't want it. It was easy and you were willing.

By continually orienting to the grace and ease question ("What is the next, easiest thing I am willing to do, right now?"), you can feel better today, easily. This is sustainable, because when you ask this question tomorrow, or in the next moment (having already acted on its wisdom in the previous moment), you genuinely desire to do more; to feel "more better". When you do something—anything—that makes you feel better, you easily and sustainably want to do something more, and something more, and something more—unlike the counterfeit dopamine hits we talked about in the pleasure–pain chapter, this kind of "more" truly satisfies and is sustainable. When you eliminate the "ought tos," "shoulds," and shame from the equation, you release any need to quit, because there is nothing to rebel against.

We change better by feeling better.

Of course, "shoulds," "musts," and "ought tos" are going to come up sometimes, whether from inside you or from well-meaning friends and family. It's most definitely going to come up on your Instagram feed. But don't believe the hype! All you can really do is what is next anyway. There is only this moment. And when you do what is easy and what you are willing to do now (and you feel better), it becomes easy to do something that previously would have been hard, next. Because you have grown stronger by focusing on what you *can* do, you become not only willing to, but able to, do more! Plus, you stop wasting so much energy, because you have been freed from the lies (shoulds, ought tos, musts) that tricks you into doing less; into quitting; into stopping; into hiding; into staying stuck in a downward spiral of shame about your unfulfilled potential; in your "woe is me"; in your "I've tried everything, but nothing works."

The way you were going about feeling better was unsustainable. This new approach isn't. Does this make sense to you the same way it does to me?

I'm using clever language here, but it's not a trick. It's the way it actually works!

They say the devil's greatest trick is to make us believe lies and think that un-truths are truths; to think that that which causes us harm is the very thing we should do or ought to do, in the "name of goodness, amen!" But you don't need to whip yourself into shape, you don't need to be made "worthy" by some external force or result. You can feel better today, easily, without any gimmicks, in a totally sustainable way that makes perfect sense. It all starts here.

19
SURVIVAL MODE

I N A VERY LITERAL SENSE, THE deepest addiction we all have is our addiction to who we were. This means becoming someone new—a butterfly instead of a "better" caterpillar—can be as challenging as putting down the pipe (even if we truly want to and know it's better for us).

Don't believe me? Put it this way: "stress" chemicals are potent. This is the stuff that enables moms to lift cars off kids and firefighters to feel invincible to flames. Stress is designed to save our lives when everything is on the line. The problem is, most people are activating these survival chemicals when they are merely commuting to work, trying to get their kids out the door on time, or arguing with their spouse. As a result, they are constantly drunk on a neurochemical cocktail that tricks them into constantly re-acting the same patterns, dramas, and problems, just so they can "get their fix." They try to fix and change everything outside of them by "getting," to no avail.

It's important to know that survival mode is our default mode. It's like the software we were all born with. Evolution's priority is survival at all costs, so SM is easy and automatic. Unlike the parts of us that embody the JOLKA-GPS, survival mode (and its various expressions of "upset") happens "by itself." SM is governed by the same parts of our being that control our heartrate, keep us breathing, and keep our body at 98.6 degrees when we shift from a seventy-degree room to a twenty-degree winter day within a second. In other words, survival mode does not require deliberate, dedicated work to keep it going. Upgrading your software so it hangs out more and more in thriving mode (TM), however, does.

For such a long time, I blamed and shamed myself for not being where I wanted to be. I felt like I had no right to be depressed. And why the fuck was I so anxious all the time? Had something happened to me that I couldn't remember? None of it made sense. Until, that is, I learned about the mechanics of the nervous system. Then, it all made perfect sense. I was my own emotional abuser (which is not to say bad, wrong, or unfair shit hadn't happened to me), and the worst kind, at that. "I" (or, more accurately, the Reactive-iWAS I *thought* was me) was cursing myself for being a pathetic piece of shit, and, more often than I would like to admit, I was contemplating whether I should just make everyone's life easier by ending it all. It was when I finally understood why I constantly found myself coming back to those "same old, same old" patterns that I was able to take my first step toward true change. This understanding was just the beginning, sure, but it allowed awareness to "awaken" within me, and it was what gave me the motivation to use the tools to really thrive in life.

Here's what I needed to understand: survival mode wants us to re-act the same horrible dramas over and over again in a sort of deluded, "the devil you know is better than the one you don't" kind of way. This is because our brain records and evaluates everything on a "can I move toward this or should I move away from this?" continuum, and this mechanism can be quite literal in its interpretation of things. Everything we have survived up until now has been deemed "safe" by survival mode, simply because if we are alive today, that means we have (quite literally and by definition) survived everything that is past; which is everything that is "known" or familiar. Therefore, everything that we have not yet survived (anything new/unknown) is deemed "unsafe" by the survival part of our nervous system. Because of this, we will continue to re-act what is familiar and will seek out whatever is deemed "safe" (i.e., whatever we did before), even if it sucked and even if we truly desire something (new) and better for ourselves, which must, by definition of something being new, arise from the "unknown".

Why "Doing" Trumps "Understanding"

There are entire fields of therapy dedicated to trying to get you to "understand" more about your past. There's a reason why these modalities are long-term therapy (besides the business convenience of lifelong clients!): there is no amount of "knowing" that will ever result in you outgrowing your problems altogether.

It is easy to get stuck in "knowing" and "understanding" and trying to "figure things out," when really, if you want to experience something new, you can only do so by exploring, discovering, learning, growing, and *creating* something new, in the field of the unknown. If you aren't willing to move beyond what you know—to think, feel, act and experience differently today than you would have in the face of the same stimulus yesterday—then you can't grow, and your efforts to understand "why" will become a stop instead of a step.

Alternatively, you can exit survival mode (suffering) entirely and learn to "come from" your C-IAM, traversing your Neurological Roadmap to the Future you value and choose. You can start using your body, mind, and energy to feel better today, easily, without any gimmicks, in a totally sustainable way that makes perfect sense.

When we know how to do better (and *be* better), we become better. And when we become better, we realize we *are* better.

KNOWING → DOING → BECOMING → BEING

The good news is, you don't need to wait until you "get better" to be happy. As already mentioned, true happiness is not found in results, but in the very process of sincere engagement in cultivation, which includes trial and error. This takes the structure of:

HYPOTHESIS → EXPERIMENT → EVALUATE THE RESULTS→ MODIFY THE HYPOTHESIS → RUN A NEW EXPERIMENT → REPEAT...

I still have triggers that come up daily. My wife and I still occasionally argue, my kids and I still have spats about chores and responsibilities, and yes, though it happens very rarely at this point, I do sometimes cave into old depressive patterns and anxious worries. The main difference been now and then is that my response time for recuperating from these kinds of upsets is so much faster than it ever has been. At one point in my life, I spiraled into a major depressive disorder for two years after a moderate heartache. Now, I lick my wounds for two hours. I now know to "get to work and use the tools," even though, aside from, and especially because I don't feel like it.

I have taught a lot of people how to use these tools, and every single time one of them reaches back out to me because they are in a funk, I say, "So, when did you stop using the tools?" We both usually chuckle when I ask this (a sense of humor and kindness are essential on this path). We all lose our way sometimes, and, as my dad would say (from his AA wisdom), "Sometimes, we need to do more research in the suffering lab before we get back to what works."

Still, I don't know about you, but I am tired of learning in the laboratory of crisis. Sure, pain in life is inevitable, but suffering is optional, and I know that if I keep using my tools, I can stay in a "challenge" mindset, turn stops into steps, and rise over the ground on which I once stumbled. I know that if I use the maps, tools, and instructions, they will always work. The usefulness is *in me*. The work works if I work it (and working it means coming from my conscious, deliberate Aware-Will that purposefully identifies with the C-IAM as "who I am," and acts according to my NRF).

A hammer can build or destroy a house, depending on how I use it. Neither of those results are intrinsically right or wrong; it's about whether the result is what I value and choose to create. When I return to who I value and choose to be and I come from that place, it is natural and inevitable that I will experience and express more joy, openness, love, kindness, awareness, gratitude, presence, and surrender (JOLKA-GPS). When I enter this space, others view me as the loving, sensitive, joyful, and playful person I am, and when I shine this way, it tends to benefit not only myself, but also others, and ALL. So, my friend, I am glad you're here. Because now, the real work begins. I wholeheartedly congratulate you on taking charge and becoming a DIY happiness expert, too, so you can be the greatest possible benefit to yourself, others, and ALL.

It's Not Your Fault

Before we go further, you need to know none of this suffering crap is your fault. Really. I know I've said this before, but it bears repeating. That *Good Will Hunting* scene is legit. You didn't know your brain was designed to be unhappy. You didn't ask for a built-in default survival mode that would make you feel stressed, angry, anxious, and depressed when left to its own devices. You didn't know that this default survival mode would make you hurt yourself and shut out the people you love over and over. None of this is your fault... but it is your responsibility. Nothing and no one can make you shift from surviving to thriving other than you.

If you break down the word "responsible," you get "response-able." So, to be responsible means to respond in a more effective and creative way. And the only way you grow more "able" at anything is through practice. So, you can practice becoming more "able" at responding to anything and everything with more and more grace and ease.

If you break down the word "react," you get "re-act," and indeed, survival mode will have you re-acting the same thoughts, feelings, and actions over and over and over again. Haven't you noticed the merry-go-round nature of your life and relationships? Does the "same old, same old" sound familiar?

Unlike SM (which is re-active), thriving mode is creative. When you activate thriving mode, not only do you get to create a new and better future, but you also simultaneously heal the past (by "sprouting" solutions, we "prune" the problems).

What I'm explaining to you here is not exactly easy to achieve, but it's also not as hard to accomplish as you may think it will be. Your body, mind, and spirit are miraculous in their capacity to heal and thrive. In this very moment, your heart is beating without you needing to instruct it to or understand why or how it's happening—and, if desired, you can influence whether it slows down or speeds up. Similarly, *you* digest your food, after which it becomes flesh via millions of complex processes that you have nothing to do with, yet you can hinder or help the processes. You somehow wake up every morning, even though in sleep "you" are not there in your conscious awareness (where did you go?). The cuts on your fingers heal and your body doesn't care if they're a papercut or a deliberate knife wound inflicted with malicious intent; they heal just the same. We take all of this for granted, but for some reason, most of us don't trust that our memory, psyche, soul, spirit, mind, brain, thoughts, emotions, and relationships also have the same capacity to thrive and heal. I'm here to tell you 1) radical healing is possible and 2) you have a part to play in it. This is the dynamic relationship between your Aware-Will and the life that is living through you, as you. The same way your body knows how to heal your cut or beat your heart, your mind and soul know how to heal and thrive—easily, naturally, and automatically—provided you give them the right conditions to do so. True, I am not in charge of whether my heart beats, but I can influence it. True, I am not in charge of whether my food is digested, but I can make it likelier to be. True, I am not in charge of whether my cut heals or gets infected, but I can clean it and care for it.

For any cut to heal, however, we need to first stop the bleeding. And in the realm of the psyche, the gaping wound in question is that reactive part of us that makes everything all about "me... me... me... me... me!"

Survival Mode as "Me"-Consciousness

I already introduced the idea of "me"-consciousness in Chapter 9, and we revisited it in Chapter 15. I'd recommend that you skim back over those chapters if you feel you need a bit of a recap before we expand further here.

Did you look? Okay, great. Now you're all caught up, let's expand on the implications of "me"-consciousness, now you have a little more context to work with.

It makes perfect evolutionary sense that you have been wired to feel a sense of safety, joy, satisfaction, and pride when you do something that advances your tribe. Contrary to these feelings of safety, joy, purpose, and meaning is the sense of self-isolation you feel when you are in survival mode. The survival mode, even if triggered by perceived threats only, demands that the body-mind focus on self-preservation at all costs. In other words (and as hard as this may be to hear for those who have spent a lot of time in "mental illness"), all suffering is a type of self-absorption. Think about it: last time you were depressed or anxious, who and what were you thinking and obsessing about? Me! (Well, not me, but you, as me... You know what I mean!)

Note: there's no judgment here. I've made things about me and suffered a whole lot, too. That's what everyone with an "ego" does. We become closed in a self-sealing bubble that defends the *story* of our life at the expense of the *quality* of our life.

This does not only apply to those with diagnosable mental illness. This applies to *everyone* who is in survival mode.

Have you noticed how often you (and everyone around you) complain? Underneath all of that, if you look, is everyone making everything all about "me."

"I can't believe it's raining again." (Subtext: it is so inconvenient for me.)

"This traffic is the worst." (Again, Mr. Me, it might be a lot worse for the person in the accident ahead.)

Modern attempts to alleviate suffering (including talk therapy and everything on your Instagram feed) attempt to create a better, faster, stronger, more functional, and happier "me," but most of these approaches, like I've said before, are like pasting wings on a caterpillar and hoping it will fly, or putting icing on a shit cake and expecting it to be delicious.

The true "happiness" we all innately desire cannot be found in "me"-consciousness. It is discovered in "we"-consciousness. It is discovered when we find a way to fit into the grand scheme of things and when we participate and contribute to the "win-win" scenario, thereby benefiting not only ourselves, but others and ALL.

When we talk about this, please remember three things:

1. *This does not mean martyrdom and self-abnegation*

Martyrdom is a "lose-win" mindset. "We"-consciousness is a "win-win" mindset. That's why we are about to embark on a process of developing your C-IAM and your NRF: they will provide the best maps, tools, and instructions for how you thrive (which no doubt includes how you contribute to others thriving). "We"-consciousness requires you to have a strong C-IAM.

2. This does not mean that you need to specifically get involved in some type of "helping" or "service" profession

The type of contribution and participation I am talking about here comes down to your presence and how you show up moment to moment. "Helping" professions are great, but they can also be performed from or as "me," and they can also not result in any sort of life worth loving. Human consciousness works like a mirror (it reflects, immediately, how you show up), so in order to give love, love needs to already be coursing through your veins. You can only give what you already have—or, in this case, you can only express what you already are. What you give, you receive immediately (or, actually, simultaneously). If you are in a state of trying to "get," you are, ironically, "giving" a feeling of "lack" to life (since you are always "giving" something). Similarly, if you are "giving" anger or fear, you are immediately getting it back, in the form of anger or fear coursing through your veins. You are always contributing to the world, irrespective of what the state of your being is. It is only the quality of what you're giving that changes, in accordance with the quality of your state of being. You're always "getting" exactly what you are "giving."

The type of participation and contribution you are projecting makes all the difference. The state of being you are operating from makes all the difference.

Ask yourself: are you polluting your environment (inner and outer) with the toxic chemicals of fear, anger, and hopelessness? Or are you giving the love and joy that you wish to receive and experience?

3. This does not mean you should stay in shitty situations to "learn from them," or for any other reason, for a second longer than you have to

Nor am I saying you should condone wrongdoing, take responsibility for others' wrongs and shame, gaslight yourself with "positive self-talk," or avoiding doing what needs to be done to get to higher ground. What I am saying is, most people are running around trying to fix up their "me," when real change and growth means actually becoming a butterfly that no longer *has* caterpillar problems. It means dying as who you were (your Reactive-iWAS) and then being "born again" as who you value and choose to be (your C-IAM).

Note that just because butterflies no longer have caterpillar problems doesn't mean they don't face butterfly challenges. They just know that these problems mean it's time to go back into the chrysalis to become a new butterfly again. This process of living and dying is ongoing and, as far as we know, infinite. That may seem scary and daunting if you are still coming from "me"-consciousness, but once you spend more time in thriving mode, you will understand that it's only through consciously choosing to play the greatest game of ALL that you discover this cycle's unending benefits.

20
SURVIVING TO THRIVING

The Nervous System as a Filter: An Introduction

L ET'S GET CLEAR ON THE FUNDAMENTAL mechanics of the
nervous system (NS) before we dive into anything else to do with
survival mode. Knowing what's under the hood enables us to optimize
the health and happiness of our NS, which is the make-or-break factor for
our entire experience of living.

Note: we have already briefly touched on some of this in Part I, but I
want to reiterate here, to make sure you really understand all of it before we
continue.

Here we go:

As we have covered, the NS filters your experience, such that you don't
experience reality as it is. Your perception of reality is colored by the filters
of your NS.

I'm not sure if most of us really grasp that—that our NS is the filter for
everything. This means a filter of joy, openness, and love leads to actual joy,
openness, and love. It also means a "stressed out" filter leads to actual stress.
It really is as simple as that. Focus on love, and love will grow. Focus on fear,
and you will panic sooner or later. There is enough evidence in your life, the
world, history, and your imagination to prove anything, so whatever you
focus on will be "proven" to be "true" (because you will experience it more
and more). This is an inescapable law of reality, like gravity, and you can
learn to use it in your favor by cultivating the ability to predictably and
consistently manage your attention and choose what you focus on (and
thereby choose what you want to grow more of in your life).

Again, this does not mean turning a blind eye to injustice, wrongdoing,
threats, and real problems. It means turning your (open) eyes to life, so you
can look at it and interpret it more skillfully and usefully. This will allow

you to be resilient, strong, healthy, and happy enough to create solutions that actually alleviate injustice and more effectively get you out of jams. Instead of simply being crushed by your problems, you can acknowledge them with kindness and honesty, activate your C-IAM, walk down your NRF, and deal with the challenges we all face more successfully. Einstein taught us, "You can't solve a problem from the same level of consciousness that created it." This is the wisdom we're leveraging here.

The NS's filters are powerful, immediate, and often unconscious, and they have evolved over millions of years to prioritize survival over happiness. But we want more out of life than to just survive. I, for one, do not want to just resign myself to the biological fate of running around like a chicken with its head cut off, "stressed out" until I die. Instead, I think of cultivating the great joy of being as a form of activism; as the only actual way to contribute to the greatest good. It fires me up! No fucking way should most people only know a few people that are actually happy. We know misery loves company, and it is sometimes nice to know that we aren't alone in our struggles, but because nervous systems are contagious and mental distress is the most pressing pandemic of our time, I want to create such a robust and grounded nervous system that my state of being is infectiously joyful, open, loving, kind, and aware, with gratitude, through presence and surrender (JOLKGA-GPS). Not only am I sick and tired of being controlled by survival mode, but I also no longer want to pollute those around me with "woe is me."

Happiness—true happiness—requires cultivation and work. It is a skill, and it doesn't come from all the things we think it should. It comes *from us*, and is only accessible when we learn how to upgrade from the default survival mode to the thriving mode that we all can unlock first by knowing, then by doing (in alignment with our C-IAM), and then by becoming, the very best versions of who we are capable of being.

KNOWING → DOING → BECOMING → BEING OF THE GREATEST POSSIBLE BENEFIT TO OURSELVES, OTHERS, AND ALL

The Nervous System as a Filter: The Nitty Gritty

As we've stated, the NS has two main modes: surviving and thriving. Survival mode is just what it sounds like: it enables us to "get by," sometimes barely, and is meant for life- or-death moments.

If your NS is in SM, it only has three gears: fighting, flighting (or fearing), and freezing.[74]

- Fight: Anger, frustration, impatience, criticism, judgment, complaint, force, controlling behavior.
- Flight: Fear, anxiety, nervousness, worry, doubt, insecurity, paranoia, hypochondria, panic.
- Freeze: Depression, numbness, isolation, dissociation, apathy, suicidal thinking, hopelessness, helplessness, worthlessness, lethargy, lack of motivation, overwhelm, mental shutdown.

Many people shift in and out of these gears throughout the day, which results in every manner, variety, and degree of suffering and disease. Practically, you cannot stop yourself from thinking, feeling, and acting from a place of anger, fear, and depression when your brain is in survival mode. But you definitely can become an expert at noticing what's going on and turning off the alarm switch that activates SM and turning on the unlimited benefits of TM. When you do this (and the more you do this), you free up the capacity of your most awesome potential in body, mind, and spirit, and you also develop a sense of confidence and empowerment. This is valuable, because happiness that is generated from you is *yours*. It is not dependent on circumstances or other people. This is true freedom.

If you are into sports, you may have heard the saying, "The best defense is a good offense." Similarly, learning how to access and flip "the SafeSwitch" puts you back on the offensive in life, moving forward and setting the conditions of the game. This results in more wins and is key to what we are learning here.

Something that depressed, unhappy people report is what researchers call a lack of "self- efficacy." Self-efficacy is the sense that one can influence their own life for the better; that one has agency and a healthy degree of control over how their life turns out. With the tools you will learn here, you will be able to build your capacity for the ultimate kind of self-efficacy: the ability to change state at will and enjoy the freedom of psychological and emotional independence. To do so takes practice, time, and consistent, deliberate, dedicated action.

---

[74] I am aware some people add a fourth "fawning" to this list, and I can see value in that distinction, even though I am choosing not to focus on it here.

Michael Boyle

The Surviving–Thriving Continuum

To wrap up your NS education, I'd like to share a list of characteristics that correspond with either the SM or the TM of the NS continuum. The items to the left of the arrow indicate an SM experience, and the items to the right of the arrow indicate the corresponding TM experience. Circle the item you currently relate to the most for each bullet point.

- Surviving ↔ Thriving
- Turning off healing and growth to "survive" ↔ Healing and growth
- Turning off digestion to "survive" ↔ Digestion
- Turning off social engagement systems (thereby sending signals of "don't approach") to "survive" ↔ Social engagement and connection
- Turning off creative, rational thinking capacities to "survive" ↔ Creative rational thought
- Past oriented ↔ Present and future oriented
- Reactive ↔ Creative
- Problem focused ↔ Solution focused
- Closed ↔ Open
- "No" ↔ "Yes"
- Negative bias ↔ Positive realism
- Negative expectations ↔ Positive expectations
- Unconscious ↔ Conscious
- Automatic reactions ↔ Deliberate choices
- Old ↔ New and fresh
- Frown ↔ Smile
- Tense ↔ Relaxed
- Dull ↔ Radiant
- Fundamentalist or "always right" ↔ Curious: exploring, discovering, learning, growing, and creating
- Win-lose/lose-win/lose-lose ↔ Win–win
- "Everyone is a competitor or predator" ↔ Love, trust, and cooperation
- "Me" ↔ "We"
- "Alone" ↔ "Together"
- Anger ↔ Patience, flow, and contribution
- Fear ↔ Participation, ease, and alert stillness
- Depressed ↔ Inspired
- Apathy ↔ Engaged
- Known ↔ Unknown or beyond the known

- Danger ↔ Safe
- Forcing ↔ Allowing
- Exclusive ↔ Inclusive
- Distress ↔ Eustress (good stress)
- Desperate and hoping ↔ Confident
- Seeking ↔ Finding
- Complaining ↔ Celebrating
- "Never enough" ↔ "Much more than enough"
- Criticism ↔ Acceptance and kindness
- Condemning ↔ Uplifting
- Self-absorbed ↔ Contributing and caring
- Lack ↔ Abundance
- Entitled ↔ Grateful
- Nihilistic ↔ Optimistic
- Counterproductive ↔ Efficient and effective
- Struggle or strain ↔ Effortful ease
- Lackluster ↔ Inspired
- Convinced ↔ Curious
- "Can't" ↔ "Will"
- Victim ↔ Hero
- "Quit" ↔ "Keep going"
- Hatred/fear ↔ Love
- Finite ↔ Infinite
- Matter only; no spirit ↔ Spirit is inclusive of matter
- Shallow, rapid, fast, labored breath ↔ Full, deep, slow, easy breath
- Neck forward, eyes down ↔ "Tall and proud", eyes up, neck long, chest open
- Against ↔ With
- "Mine" ↔ "Ours"
- Conceit ↔ Humility
- Codependence ↔ Independence and interdependence
- Broken ↔ Whole
- Would; should; could; want to; excuses ↔ Willing; doing
- Fear based ↔ Trust based
- Upset ↔ Joy, openness, love, kindness, and awareness
- Dis-ease ↔ Health (which *is* happiness, even if you're sick or injured)
- Suffering ↔ Freedom

How much time—how many heartbeats and how many breaths—do you spend on the TM end of the continuum? What's the next, easiest thing you are willing to do to move in that direction?

Tools for Changing State

Fog breath and the power switch (which we both explored in Part II) are among the best practices I've discovered in my twenty-plus years of doing the work for turning off the alarm switch and turning on thriving mode. You can also learn the power switch in Module 8.2 of your free book resources, "Changing State," at www.alltogether.academy/joy-bucket-tools.

I've also mentioned extra and open attention, which is (no matter what we refer to it as) the foundation of all meditation techniques and all state-change tools. Let's learn this in more depth next. It's also the subject of Module 3 of your book resources www.alltogether.academy/joy-bucket-tools.

Extra and Open Attention: The Portable Pause

Extra and open attention is the pith of all state-changing tools and techniques. Without it, they would not work. Instead, they would just be mental exercises that don't get deep enough into the mechanics of your being to create real and lasting change. [75]

I like to use my phone to create a recording of myself reading the instructions for extra and open attention aloud. This creates a sort of guided meditation in my own voice. Alternatively, if you want to follow along with some ten-minute guided meditations, I have made a playlist of ten on my YouTube channel (www.youtube.com/@ALLTogetherAcademy). I've also shared these with you in Module 3.2 of your book resources at www.alltogether.academy/joy-bucket-tools.

If you prefer to also read the meditation instructions, here is what you need to do:

---

[75] Thanks to my mentor for sharing this terminology with me and for instructing me in this practice. Any mistakes or shortcomings in the instructions that follow are mine, not his.

How to Find Joy
Even If You Have a Hole in Your Bucket

1.   Sit comfortably, preferably upright and erect, without leaning back. If you are on a chair, place both feet on the ground squarely and try to "line up" your toes, knees, hips, shoulders, and head.

2.   Place your tongue gently on the roof of your mouth and let it remain there for the duration of the session. (This is a less well known, vital instruction for almost any meditation practice, and is generally a good idea to do unless you are talking or eating.)

3.   Make any adjustments needed before inviting yourself to remain still. Ask inside, "How can I make myself five percent more comfortable?"

4.   Direct your attention to the sensations of aliveness in your hands.

5.   As you notice this aliveness in your hands, notice that you are noticing more sensations taking place in and around you.

6.   Noticing that noticing begets noticing, even more "aliveness" sensations.

7.   Notice that you can also notice that you are noticing.

8.   Allow your awareness of this aliveness to spread up your arms, into your neck and head, down through your chest, back, abdomen, and groin, and into your hips, legs, and feet.

9.   Notice the sense of "aliveness" bristling in your whole body. Notice that this "noticing" enhances this sense of aliveness and that more and more sensations arise as a result.

10. As you pay attention to this aliveness in your body, invite a sense of stillness. Envision this like a mountain with lots of activity and life (sensations) that maintains a sense of poise and stillness.

11. Notice more by internally repeating, *Stillness, stillness, stillness.*

12. Now, shift your "noticing" to the space around your body. Become aware of the space in front of your body, behind your body, to the left of your body, to the right of your body, above your body, and below your body.

13. Notice the space all around you, spherically, all at once, in every direction.

14. Allow your awareness to fill the room you are sitting in.

15. Allow your awareness to expand to the entire building this room is in—perhaps even to the neighborhood or area around where you are. Expand as far as you can imagine.

16. Return your focus to the space around your body, in the room where you are.

17. As you pay attention to the space around your body, invite a sense of "spaciousness" - vast like the open, cloudless sky.

18. Notice more by internally repeating, *Spacious, spacious, spacious.*

19. Play with the awareness of both: your still body and your spacious awareness.
20. Pulse back and forth between focusing on your body's aliveness and on the space all around your body, until you can maintain awareness of both simultaneously.
21. As you notice the alive stillness of your body (extra attention) and the spaciousness of your mind expanding (open attention), you will notice a growing sense of peace, ease, and calm; a place where you can pause, reset, and choose how to move forward in this next moment.
22. Dedicate this refreshed feeling to yourself, others, and ALL, recalling someone you specifically wish to benefit from this exercise.
23. Finish with your resolve to move forward with your life in a creative, resourceful, responsible, and beneficial way.

As you practice more and more, you will learn to "come from" this place of extra and open attention, and you will have a "portable pause" through which you are freer to make choices that align with your values.

Daily Meditation

Consider the benefits of cultivating a daily meditation practice (head back to Chapter 9 for a reminder, if needed). Entertain the prospect that daily meditation might not have to be as hard as you've perhaps experienced it to be before, or that you think it would be. You might also consider that while it may take some time and effort to prioritize this practice, it takes a lot more time and effort to deal with unnecessary suffering that could be prevented or alleviated through meditation.

It took me years of meditating before I *wanted* to meditate daily, but it needn't take you that long. I went about it the hard way, not the smart way! The best way to build a sustainable habit is to feel good about it, start small, and build on success with confidence. And nothing is better for confidence than positive results! Like we discussed in Chapter 9, start with thirty seconds of meditation a day until you are bursting at the seams to do a minute. Then, do that until you can't wait to do ninety seconds. And so on. If anything, the discipline here will lie in not skipping ahead. Really wait until you genuinely want to do more because doing the shorter session was so on point and magnificent that you didn't want it to end.

You may also find it useful to practice what you've learned so far in a certain order. To steer your energy into a state of serenity, first practice the power switch, followed by fog breath, and then end with extra and open attention. As you grow more familiar with the practice of extra and open attention, you can invite in the possibility of making it "portable." This means practicing maintaining your extra and open attention practice as a way of being, day to day, moment to moment, not just when you are formally "meditating".

Why just cope with suffering when you can end it?

Stop priming yourself for failure by saying "I can't meditate" or "I've tried that" or "it's too hard," and instead ask your grace and ease question: "What's the next, easiest amount of meditation I am willing to do right now?" How about just one breath? I mean it! That can be all it takes to tip you toward mojomentum. Celebrate your success and watch your desire for more grow naturally and sustainably, in a way that makes perfect sense.

A Check-In

If at this point you haven't been using this as a workbook or doing the work as much as you would like to, you probably haven't been getting the results you want, either. This is not a shame or "should" game, but this is also not a world where everyone gets a medal (at least, not one worth getting). The Catch-22 is that you can't wait until you feel like doing it. Waiting for certain inner or outer circumstances to occur before you use the tools or do the work is a sure bet that you will be waiting forever.

As we round out your PhD level nervous system education, I will leave you with this quote from a book I recommend, *The Power of Decision* by Raymond Charles Barker:

There are people everywhere who have decided to expand their lives. They have decided to be well and not sick. They have decided to prosper and not continue in financial limitation. They have decided to give and receive love. They have decided to be themselves. As a result, they have the right ideas revealing themselves in their minds to accomplish their decisions. These people are willing to be temporarily uncomfortable in order to achieve expanded consciousness and reach new goals.

Such people make contributions to the world. They do not wait for others to create the new, the vital, and the futurative. They do it. They are willing to change consciousness. They consciously or unconsciously realize they are important to the grand scheme of Life. They may never acquire fame or fortune, but they have the sense of wellbeing which accompanies all creative activity. YOU BELONG IN THEIR RANKS. [76]

Survival Mode: Recap and Homework

- The fact that suffering has rippled through your life isn't your fault.
- If you want things to get better, it is your responsibility to *create*. You are the only one who can do the work on your behalf, which doesn't mean you need to do it alone or won't benefit from assistance. Together, we thrive.
- It is futile to expect to be anything other than upset if your alarm switch is flipped on and your brain is in survival mode.
- There will never be a time when you remain perpetually in thriving mode. Your survival mode is hardwired as your default. You will always need to cultivate the skill of changing state if you want to thrive.
- You are not your thoughts and feelings, nor the stories (beliefs) of who you think you are. Your ego wants you to identify with who you *were*, because the survival part of the brain posits that whatever is past is safe (if you are alive now, that means you survived whatever once was).
- The ego (the Reactive-iWAS) loves your war wounds. When you identify with your limited past as the "cause" of who you are in the present, survival mode defends the past version of you by sounding the alarm, activating fight-flight-freeze, and getting you to think, feel, and act in the way you used to.
- We are actually, literally addicted to the neurochemical cocktail of who we have been. A plan, discipline, follow-through, persistence, and dedication are all needed if you are to create a new and better future.
- The neurochemical, biological, and chemical compounds of thriving mode are not just the absence of suffering; they are the presence of sincere joy, openness, love, kindness, awareness, gratitude, presence, and surrender (the JOLKA-GPS). If you were able to reclaim your biological overreactions and upgrade them to

---

[76] Barker, R. C. (1968): *The Power of Decision*, p. 55. Devorss & Co.

a *thriving* chemical cocktail for your body, mind, and energy, how much better do you think you would feel?

To optimize the upcoming teachings, please assign yourself this homework:

- Practice fog breathing five times a day. Leave yourself a reminder or Post-It note while you're getting into the habit, or tack it onto something you already do regularly, like going to the bathroom. Sounds silly, but it works! All you have to do is be willing to not check your email or Facebook while sitting on the can. And yes, fellas, you can pee sitting down without compromising your masculinity. Take a load off, fog breathe, and let go!
- Practice the power switch at least once every day. Initially, do this when everything is going well. Once you've practiced it a bit, you get bonus points if you try it when you feel survival mode is engaged. Follow each session with a "Yes!"
- Check in with yourself daily using the surviving-thriving continuum. Purposefully cultivate, explore, and invoke more thriving. Notice when you are in survival mode and ask, "What's the next, easiest thing I am willing to do to move in the direction of thriving mode?"
- Use the tools in succession for a complete practice every day (Power Switch → Fog Breathing→ Extra and Open Attention). This will allow you to go from being "ramped up" to chilled. Remember, it doesn't have to take long! Do whatever feels easy and doable. This could be thirty seconds, a minute, or a ten-minute guided recording, like the ones I've shared on my YouTube channel.

21

THE REACTIVE I-WAS

ALLOW ME TO TELL YOU A story about a chick in an egg.

There is a chick still in its shell on a beautiful, spacious, luscious farm, with kind caregivers and happy animals all about. Inside the shell, the chick has everything it needs to thrive. It is immersed in yummy golden nutritious yolk, and every day, it eats to its heart's content without a care in the world. As a natural result, it grows.

As it gets bigger and stronger and continues to enjoy the yolk's flavor, the chick notices that the yolk is starting to diminish. Not only that, but the shell is starting to get a little stuffy. There's not much elbow room in there anymore. Soon enough, it's downright claustrophobic. Whenever the chick thinks about its cramped conditions and increasing lack of food, it starts to panic.

One day, the chick notices that it has grown a sharp horn on its beak. Curious, the chick decides to explore and experiment with it. It pokes the horn here and there, learning that it hurts to peck its own body, but it doesn't hurt at all to peck the shell. In fact, doing so feels good, instinctive, and productive. However, the chick notices that doing so impacts the shell's integrity. This is exciting, but also scary. *Is this a good idea? Should I keep going? Is this destructive or productive? What would happen if I were to break this whole shell? I feel like I should keep going, but this is the only home I know. Am I crazy?*

The chick has no idea what is on the other side of the shell. Imagining from what it knows so far, it hopes for a bigger shell and another yummy yolk.

What the chick doesn't know is that what lies beyond the shell is the unknown.

Sometimes, the chick entertains disaster fantasies. What if there is no more yolk? What if there is something dangerous on the other side of the shell? What if breaking through means death? When the chick thinks about these things, it naturally becomes scared, which often results in it freezing—that is, it ceasing to peck, becoming depressed, and losing hope and motivation. At other times, it gets frustrated about its stinky, cramped shell, sometimes even getting downright mad and exhausting itself with its anger.

After getting upset, the chick feels kind of tired, and it slumps a bit. This makes the shell a little more spacious and comfortable, and for a while, the chick forgets about its excitement to discover what's lies beyond, and chooses to instead take solace in a numb, exhausted feeling of resignation.

One day, the chick wakes up feeling refreshed and decides to start pecking with vigor. When it pecks this time, it starts to hear a big, loud banging noise coming from above, as if something is responding to its pecking. The banging is so loud and powerful that it's scary, but this chick is a curious thing. *What is that?* it wants to know.

The chick's loving mother has noticed its pecking and is now pecking back, to accelerate the chick's progress. The chick doesn't know this, though. Instead, the chick gives into its fear stories and stops pecking, panicked. It sits around, waiting and wondering about that intense noise that rattles its shell every time it begins pecking.

The next day, the chick works up some more courage and decides, *What the heck,* and starts pecking more. Sure enough, Big Mama starts pecking back again. The chick still has no idea what that's about, nor does it know what lies beyond the shell, but today, curiosity, courage, willingness to explore, and excitement about the possibilities beyond the known outweigh the chick's hesitation, and the chick is going for it.

Finally, the chick breaks through!

What lies beyond is nothing like anything the chick could have ever imagined. There is no new and improved shell or yummier yolk, like the chick had hoped for. The reality is so much better and so much grander. It is a whole new world! Clear, open, blue sky; rich, green grass; fat, juicy worms; a loving mother; brothers and sisters and cousins all around; the amazing touch of wind on its skin; the ability to walk and run and even fly... It is amazing, and the chick is awestruck with wonder and filled with gratitude.

Perhaps you can tell that this story is about your life and what happens every time you grow to a new level of being. We often mistake the "symptoms" of change for proof that we are doing something wrong; that we need to quit. It will always require courage and willingness to "do it anyway"—to break through—and breakthroughs will often be preceded by tests. During these tests, we may feel scared, confused, upset, and as if it is dangerous to move forward, as if we're doing something wrong. However, when we learn to recognize that these are not signs of failure or indications to stop, but signs of progress, we break through our shells and enter ever-unfolding higher levels of being that become more and more characterized by joy, openness, love, kindness, awareness, gratitude, presence, and surrender (the JOLKA- GPS).

Even better, the universal loving mother will keep matching our willingness to "peck" with efforts that double, triple, quadruple, and exponentially enhance our efforts through grace, serendipity, and what we need.

When we start to break into higher levels of being, we learn to seek and trust that which makes us feel more alive, breaking free of our limitations. The more we learn to trust this process, the more we become who we are, the less we suffer, and the more we grow to embody beneficial forces.

Don't ask what the world needs. Ask what makes you come alive and go and do it. Because what the world needs is people who have come alive!

—HOWARD THURMAN

The symptoms of your suffering are often a result, a calling, a reminder, or a teacher of the fact that that you are stuck in and as the Reactive-iWAS—who you *were*. As you start to "become" more and more authentic, however, there comes a point where you no longer need to learn from suffering so much. Instead, grace, good fortune, and opportunity become your teachers and guides. There is still pain and discomfort, yes, but suffering, not so much. Remember, pain is part of life, but to suffer, we need to tell stories about our pain, which is entirely optional!

The grace, ease, and opportunities for thriving are only waiting for you to do your part: to create the future you value and choose to have by becoming the Creative-IAM and traveling on your NRF. All of this starts with you first shedding the Reactive-iWAS.

The difference between where you want to be (your future goals and values) and where you are (your exact current situation) represents the creative tension you need to use as fuel to get to where you want to be. Your problems, according to this view, are your opportunities. As you overcome a challenge, it becomes like a rung on a ladder as you turn stops into steps.

Even when we are upset, and even though it's inevitable and "natural" that "suffering stories" about our pain will arise, we can rest assured that it is usually safe to do what's appropriate and useful: to change our state from surviving to thriving.

Identity as a Generator of Experience

Do you remember when you learned about Beliefs → Perceptions → Experience? Well, the factor that drives the B-P-E train in whatever direction it's heading in, is identity.

As human beings, we can't help but have an identity to some degree. Some "enlightenment" perspectives report an experience of "self" beyond individuality. I'm not sure I even agree with that, or at least not in the way it's commonly conveyed, but that's more than we can dive into here. We will cover that in book three of this series, *Energy of Mind: Secular Spiritual Work for Practical People.* For now, and for truly practical intents and purposes, it is enough for you to know that you have a sense of self, and that you might as well make the best use of it.

"Selfing" is a function of being a human. I first learned about this concept in my dharma psychology studies, which I believe has a more sophisticated understanding of the subtle mechanics of mind than does the relatively immature "western" psychology. In Sanskrit, this "selfing" is referred to as the *ahamkara*, which basically means "the 'I am' maker." In simple terms, this means we can't help but have an "I am" experience, or an identity. What most people don't know is that we don't have to have a passive, unconscious, not-chosen "I am" that has been formed as a re-action to everything that has happened to us. This automatic, reactive sense of self is what I am calling, the Reactive-iWAS.

It's no wonder we feel like frauds! Imposter syndrome happens because we are coming from our Reactive-iWAS. Then people try to feel "authentic" by making their Reactive-iWAS stronger, better, etc., which makes them feel more like a phony! The Reactive-iWAS is a tangled mess of "truth" and "proof," and in case you haven't noticed, it is not useful.

Why is the Reactive-iWAS like this? Well, remember, most of what we take for granted as "truths" are really beliefs that filter our perception and consequently generate our experience. Over time, these factoids culminate to create "my truth." It *feels* true, so it "must be" true, and what we believe to be "true" we identify as "reality." (This is called confirmation bias.) As you know, this mechanism (which narrows our focus on all the problems we need to fix), when left unchecked, means we miss out on all the joy, love, connection, safety, inspiration, resources, opportunities, wisdom, and beauty that we can't experience when we are always, subconsciously, day in and day out, focused on "snakes" that are actually sticks. It also means that as we gather more "proof" for our reactive beliefs, we form a reactive identity: "I am afraid." This identity gets in the driver's seat of the B-P-E mechanism and calls all the shots.

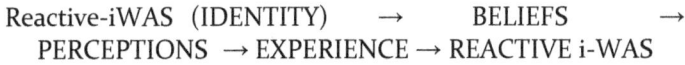

Reactive-iWAS (IDENTITY) → BELIEFS →
PERCEPTIONS → EXPERIENCE → REACTIVE i-WAS

"I am afraid," which is a sort of meta-belief of identity, spawns the multitude of thoughts, feelings, and sensations that will alter my perception across various settings—and not just in the woods, where there might logically be snakes. I will see through the lens of fear in the grocery store, when I have a gurgle in my belly, and when I wonder (worry) about my kids' future.

Many people go to their deathbeds defending their stories about who they've always thought they were and why they are right about all the reasons why they feel afraid (in the case of someone identified with anxiety). This is a tragedy. The importance of them being "right" about "their truth"— "No, you don't understand, open spaces really 'make' *me* anxious, so I can't go to work because *I am anxious*"—ruined their quality of life and likely even resulted in a shortened lifespan.

I know we have already covered all of this in dribs and drabs throughout this book so far, but I really want to make sure you understand the Reactive-iWAS's function as the driver of the B-P-E, so you can fully appreciate how radical a change you will experience in your life when you intentionally switch out a reactive identity with a creative identity. Your state of being (whether your Reactive-iWAS or C-IAM) quite literally determines whether you are an *occasional and accidental recipient* of happiness, or whether you are a *cultivator* of happiness. It determines your entire experience of your life here on earth.

I used to be a pretty legit hypochondriac. For a long time, I worked to change, and I realized (through lots of trial and error) that all my efforts were being thwarted by certain underlying principles (an identity) driving the train. Two moments during this journey of mine really stand out as examples of me being under the influence of the Reactive-iWAS "I am anxious":

1.   I told my mentor, "I am not so much afraid of dying as I am of not being there for my kids," to which he said, "Mike, every second you are worried about not being there for your kids, you are not being there for your kids." That hit hard.

2.   During a doctor's visit for my son, I took the opportunity to ask the practitioner an anxiety-driven side question about my own health while my

son's ankle was being examined for a sprain. The doctor read me like a book and said, "That most definitely is not going to kill you, but your fear about it might!" Ouch. She was right.

Remember Lar Short's words:

> *This type of misperception (snake, instead of stick) creates a body response, in which the reality of the body's reaction overwhelms whatever is actually occurring at the time.* The reaction becomes a reality unto itself.[77]
> (emphasis mine.)

To this day, and every day forward, I am working on coming from my C-IAM, even if, aside from, and especially when I notice that I feel sensations in my body that I used to identify with as "my anxiety."

Note that my freedom is not dependent on not feeling these sensations. My freedom is dependent on me acting according to my values, *even if* I feel these sensations. My commitment is to the practice of re-organizing my body, mind, energy and experience to align with my values and choices. My job is to tend to the garden. The blooming of fruits and flowers is in God's hands. My job is doing the work and getting better at the skills of doing the work. The outcomes, timelines, and external conditions are not in my control, but when I focus on what is my control, I do get better at influencing outcomes.

As I have said previously, typical therapy and even most popular models of self- improvement want us to solve the infinitely complex riddle of the Reactive-iWAS, thinking that if we can just understand why we think and feel the way we do, we will no longer think and feel the way we do; and/or that we can paste better wings on our caterpillar selves so we can finally fly free.

How's that working out? How many things do you understand you "shouldn't" do, but still do every day? How many times have you tried to fix yourself, only to default back to who you were before?

The truth is, there is no amount of "understanding" the Reactive-iWAS's unlimited stories, reasons, and justifications for pain that will free you from its complex web of lies and truths masquerading as one another. The only thing you need to know is that the Reactive-iWAS exists and is running amok, and that if you allow it to stay in charge, you will suffer. That, and

---

[77] Lowenthal, M. & Short, L. (1993): *Opening the Heart of Compassion: Transform Suffering Through Buddhist Psychology and Practice,* p.65. Tuttle Publishing.

that there is a better way that both keeps you safer and allows you to heal and thrive. You can choose to cultivate a Creative-IAM, a chosen identity based on your values that can govern the chain of Beliefs → Perceptions → Experience in a useful way. We will cover this in the next chapter. For now, remember you are not your thoughts and feelings. You are the Aware-Will that notices them; who can pause in extra and open attention and choose to do something different. The Reactive-iWAS will buck and kick and fight to stay alive, but only you can starve it of the fuel it needs to do so: your attention and unconscious participation in its nonsense.

The Reactive-iWAS: Homework

- Keep practicing extra and open attention. The brilliant thing about this tool is that it strengthens your ability to change state (through getting you to notice), and it is also a change state tool in itself. By consistently practicing "convergent" (extra) attention and "divergent" (open) attention, you can truly change your brain for the better.
- Do a daily check-in by practicing checking and changing state, as shared in Module 8.1 of your book resources at www.alltogether.academy/joy-bucket-tools. It's okay if you are not perfect at it or even do well at it. What is essential is that you practice and discover the authentic happiness that arises from doing the work, not from the results you get. The "Checking and Changing State" exercise will help you to notice and erase anything you don't value and replace it with what will get you back on track.

The Reactive-iWAS: Recap and Reflection

- We can't help but have some sort of identity, and by default, most people operate from their Reactive-iWAS, which has been formed through their reactions to everything that has ever happened in their past, survival mode's negativity bias, and the forces of entropy and atrophy.
- Over time, identity becomes the "driver" for the mechanism of Belief → Perception → Experience, and we "become" the Reactive-iWAS (Reactive-iWAS), reinforcing "my truth" through the "loop" of thinking what we feel and feeling what we think. We say to

ourselves, even if unconsciously, "It must be true because I feel it so strongly." (See Chapter 9's thinking-feeling loop.) To free ourselves from these chains, we can cultivate a creative identity—a C-IAM—based on what we value and choose to create. We can "sprout" the C-IAM, which automatically "prunes" the Reactive-iWAS.

- Our creative identity requires ongoing work to cultivate and a firm resolve to think, feel and act according these values even if, aside from, and especially when we don't feel like it. When we do this work, we can generate an entirely new filter for our future and yield the results we value and choose.
- The JOLKA-GPS is not dependent on circumstances, but on *how we choose to show up and engage with* whatever our circumstances happen to be.

22

THE CREATIVE-IAM (C-IAM)

CREATIVE-IAM → BELIEFS → PERCEPTIONS → EXPERIENCE →
CREATIVE-IAM

THIS IS USEFUL.
YOU CAN CREATE an identity that you place in the driver's seat of B-P-E, so that you can turn on your "lifeforce" engine and drive down the Neurochemical Roadmap to the Future You Value and Choose. This is something all of us can Do → Become → Be. Instead of everything and everyone else being the "cause" of your reactive identity, you can become the major dominant influence over your chosen, creative sense of self that naturally yields the beliefs, perceptions, and experiences you value and choose to have. You can die as your Reactive-iWAS and give birth to your C-IAM.

The path to freedom, wholeness, "self-realization," peace, and fulfilment cannot be found in trying to make the Reactive-iWAS better (remember "pasting wings on a caterpillar" or "icing on a shit cake"). It is discovered in the process of creating, expressing, and experiencing through, from, and as the Creative-IAM, aside from whatever conditions, thoughts, feelings, or sensations are arising.

Creating your C-IAM isn't where the work ends, though. Actually, establishing where you are coming from is the beginning of the adventure, and every moment is a fresh start. Once you are ready (coming from your values and choices), you are on your way. If you are no longer re-acting the past, known, familiar, you are now venturing into the unknown. If you get in the car to go somewhere you have never been before how will you get there without directions? (This is where the NRF comes in.) Similarly, if you have a map but you don't have a driver (C-IAM) who can make good choices in the face of obstacles, but instead an autopilot (Reactive-IWAS) setting programmed to only go where you've gone before, the map is useless and only leads to dead ends.

For your journey to the future you value and choose to create you need new maps and a new driver if you are going to arrive where you value and choose to be: in a state of Joy, Openness, Love, Kindness, and Awareness with Gratitude, Presence and Surrender (JOLKA-GPS).

When you set off on a journey, you can't foretell flat tires, when you'll need to take a break for gas, or when your kid will need to pee. So, you need a conscious, creative person at the steering wheel; a person who can adjust, ask for help, avoid potholes, fix flats, and fill the tank with gas. In other words, you need a C-IAM. You will also need a map that will give you a good enough idea of what to do next at any given moment (an NRF, which we will co-create in the next chapter).

When (not if) you hit a roadblock or need to take a detour, all you'll need to do is notice what has happened and then get back on the highway to where you want to go. You will not need to know *why* you took a wrong turn, or anything about the town you've found yourself in after getting off at the wrong exit, nor will you need to retrace your steps to understand your mistake better. (These are all common misperceptions in the therapeutic cultural trance that keep people in therapy or self-help programs for life!)

The difference between where you are now and where you want to be contains your opportunity for growth. I can't overstate this point. If you beat yourself up, shame or "should" yourself about where you are, or perceive the discrepancy between where you are and where you want to be as an overwhelming threat or proof of how awful you really are, then you are just choosing to suffer more and get further off course. You are still "coming from" survival mode and playing out your Reactive-iWAS. If, on the other hand, you perceive this discrepancy as creative tension—as an opportunity and challenge for you to cultivate your best life, regardless of the circumstances you're facing—then you are already activating thriving mode, coming from your C-IAM, and making new and better choices that align with your values.

I have mentioned the JOLKA-GPS numerous times. This is a term I have borrowed from my mentor. For millennia, wise beings from all around the world have observed and discovered that when a person is operating from their C-IAM and traveling on their NRF, they naturally experience and express joy, openness, love, kindness, awareness, gratitude, presence, and surrender. This isn't about what's going on in their life as much as *how they are showing up* in their life.

How to Find Joy
Even If You Have a Hole in Your Bucket

This is amazing to know. It means you can always ascertain whether you are "on the correct path" by asking yourself, "Is my state of being currently embodying any of the JOLKA-GPS qualities?" If it is, you'll know you are in thriving mode (even if you are in a difficult situation) and that you will do well to keep going as you are. If not, you'll know you are in survival mode and need to pivot.

I'm not saying you "should" be joyful if a loved one dies (nor am I saying that is not an authentic possibility), but couldn't you be open, loving, kind, present, and grateful for their life and the love you shared? Couldn't you surrender to the experience of what is? Clearly, one or more, and not other qualities of the JOLKA-GPS will be more apparent in certain situations. But they are always possibilities worth exploring, or more accurately you are a *source* of possibilities worth exploring.

Coming back to the more in-your-face declaration, if you are upset or feeling anything other than some or all of the JOLKA-GPS qualities, then you are in survival mode—and that's all you need to know! You don't need to "go back to the past" to get back on track or "figure out" why you are upset. It literally does not matter if you learned this pattern from your parents, or it's "because I have ADHD." That might sound harsh. I don't mean it that way. If you get what I'm presenting here, it's actually merciful to cut ourselves off from rabbit holes that only amount to more suffering, even if they "make sense" or are "valid." You can simply reinvoke the C-IAM, recalibrate to the NRF, and explore, discover, learn, grow, and create more of the JOLKA-GPS. You can:

1. Reset with extra and open attention.
2. Evoke the qualities associated with the C-IAM or the JOLKA-GPS.
3. Ask, "What's the next, easiest thing on my NRF I am willing to do right now?"

Importantly, the steps you take toward the future you value and choose must be chosen consciously and creatively, as an Aware-Will who no longer identifies with reactivity as "me." Re-acting is the opposite of creativity and is the domain of Reactive-iWAS automaticity. You can't choose freely if there isn't a pause in your reactivity; if you don't 1) notice and 2) change state when you are upset. (That's where the portable pause of extra and open attention comes in.) You can't be unconsciously creative. You can't unconsciously do something new. To explore, discover, learn, grow, and create, you must wake up, turn off the autopilot that re-acts old programs, and start driving forward as the person you value and choose to be, in a direction you value and choose to go in. Remember, it has to be a *choice*! Re-acting is bondage. Choosing is the essence of freedom.

Everyone, including you, can choose to create "happiness". If this choice isn't consciously made, survival mode (complete with all the suffering and violence it entails) will reign automatically, by default. And as we know, survival mode is dominated by negativity. Sustained "happiness" (which is different from fleeting pleasure), on the other hand, must be consciously created. It will not happen *to* you. Happiness is an inside job. It's about *the place you are coming from and the manner of your choosing*, rather than *what is happening to you*.

We tend to think we need to struggle to progress, but this is wrong. "Struggle" is just going faster in the wrong direction. Not a good idea! Instead, do whatever is easiest to get you back on track. Then, celebrate your success, roll your window down, turn up some good tunes, and keep the mojomentum driving forward!

At the beginning, remember that you are just breaking ground on this new highway to the future you value and choose. Your old (survival mode) habits are like smooth, paved superhighways: straight, with six lanes and no traffic. You can easily go ninety on cruise control toward the life you've already been living. Your new (thriving mode) road to the future you value and choose, however, is still a bumpy dirt road, and the going might be rough for a while. The more you traverse it, though, the more it will smoothen, widen, and get easier to travel on.

This analogy has literal neurochemical correspondences. As you think, feel, and act in new ways, you literally "sprout" new neurochemical wiring (as we explored earlier). At first, this takes a lot of effort, will, and determination, but the more you continue on the same pathways, the more associations get linked to the new neural wirings you have created, until eventually, you develop a thriving neural network. Once the brain gets the picture (literally) and realizes that you value and choose this new future (because you make it a priority and devote most of your heartbeats and breaths to it), then that neural network gets "myelinated."[78]

I like to think of this process as a waterslide. When you first start thinking, feeling, and acting in new ways, it's like going down a waterslide with no water: the ride is rough and sticky, and you need to shimmy your way down. You might even get some friction burns and a crazy wedgy! But once the water is turned on—*Whoosh! Weee!*—you find yourself on a thrill ride splashing into the cool pool below. That is "myelin" at work, and that

---

[78] Myelin is a mixture of proteins and phospholipids, forming a whitish insulating sheath around many nerve fibers. This increases the speed at which impulses are conducted. It's like the tubing on electrical wire that conducts electricity faster.

is what will eventually happen when you persist at thinking, feeling, and acting in alignment with the future you value and choose.

Sound good? Let's turn that into a reality, then. Before you learn how to create your C- IAM, though, we first need to bear in mind a few things.

Priming

As you read these words, notice the white page behind the words and the space between the letters (and notice that you are noticing this). You have now been "primed": you can't help but notice the white background and the space between the letters. You can't go back to noticing only the typeface, like you were just a few seconds ago, because I have primed your brain so that you see what I want you to see. (This is exactly why conglomerates like Amazon can "Prime" you into buying their goods. It's also why marketing, in general, works.) The space between the letters—the color of the page beneath the content of the words—was there before, but you didn't see it. Now, you can't not see it.

To illustrate the phenomenon of priming further, consider the fact that all the energy that ever was or will be is here right now (energy cannot be created or destroyed, it only changes form). However, you can't experience it all in your present body (it might be totally overwhelming if you did!) because of the filters on your nervous system. These filters are "primed" in one direction or another. They're like software programs that determine the functionality of a hard drive, and the master software program that generates your experience of life is your identity. So, when your identity is reactive (a Reactive-iWAS), you are constantly "primed" according to your brain's negativity bias. You don't notice this, though, because it's going on all the time, like the buzz of a refrigerator whose noise you only notice when it turns off. Still, it's true: you are filtering all your experience through the lens of the past and your "stressed out" feelings that tell you sticks are snakes. You are literally misperceiving reality in a way that has you generating potent, addictive chemicals that activate harmful thoughts and behaviors.

What does this have to do with the C-IAM?

The C-IAM is a creative and useful identity you can use to prime yourself *instead* of the being primed by Reactive-iWAS, which is the end result of being conditioned by everything and anything other than YOU. By priming yourself you gain the essence of autonomy, agency, choice, and freedom. You can become the dominant influence in your life, instead of your past, your traumas, commercials, the government, your parents, or the religion you were raised with. In other words, instead of priming being something that happens *to* you without your consent, you can *prime yourself* to notice, experience, and express more of what you value and choose to notice, experience, and express.

Wanting

Before we develop your C-IAM and NRF, it is important for you to learn that the mind interprets "wanting" as a confirmation of "lack." "I want to be rich," is experienced in your nervous system as, "I am poor," because wanting to be rich literally confirms that you are not currently rich.

As you have learned, whatever you focus on grows, for better or worse. This therefore means that when you focus on what you want (which is really confirming the belief "I don't have what I want"), it is the neural network of "not having" (or "lack") that gets stronger.

This doesn't mean you should lie to yourself. When you take the new age affirmation approach and say to yourself, "I am rich, I am rich, I am rich," even though you know are not, you trigger an inner rebellion, and all sorts of voices inside retort, "Bullshit! You're broke!"

Questions

All is not lost! There is a way to work with this conundrum.

As we've covered, the mind can't not answer a question.

The Solution

The way you work around the mind-trap of focusing on your lack when you have an authentic and healthy desire for more wealth and abundance, is by putting your mind in "search mode" with intelligent, evocative questions; by priming it to notice more of the result you value and choose to receive.

Let's illustrate with a fairly obvious example:

Next time you stub your toe, you may notice you give a habitual reaction of, "Dammit, how clumsy can I be?" If you pay attention, you may also notice that after you ask yourself this, your mind starts scanning for memories to answer that question, pulling up all sorts of "proof" about just how clumsy you can be or perhaps "flashing" a picture of you stumbling around with a hurt toe! (Are you "seeing" that now?) And you know what's even more messed up? We now know AI will generate false proofs if we ask for evidence of something. So will our very own *artificial* intelligence! Your mind will fabricate a picture of "you" stubbing your toe even if you never have and this will get registered as a memory! (You might want to re-read that last sentence). Not only that, but this reactive evocative question and what it automatically elicits will also strengthen the priming for you to be *more prone to clumsy experiences in the future*! This stubbing the toe example is pretty innocuous, but the mechanism at play is, as my teens say, in the current parlance, "wild."

Damn.

Let's cut the crap and do none of that. Let's instead ask, "I wonder what it would feel like to be super-coordinated?" You aren't lying to yourself (new age affirmation version) after stubbing your toe by saying, "I am super-coordinated." Instead, you are using your mind to your advantage by asking it a question that will prime and evoke the future you value and choose to have.

"I wonder what it would feel like to be walk around with grace and ease?"

Like Google, your mind will start searching for "hits" of anything and everything that has resembled the experience of coordination, grace, and ease. As it comes up with results (because of the "thinking and feeling loop" now working *for* instead of *against* you), you will start actually feeling more coordinated and graceful because the images you invoke will organize the sensations of your body. As you start feeling more ease, you will start thinking more like a person who *is* coordinated... and you are now priming your brain and body to both notice and have more experiences of being coordinated, gracious, and easy going in the future! As you feel more coordinated, you think of yourself as more coordinated, and this "upward spiral" results in more useful identity, "I am coordinated."

Pause. Take a deep breath. Let that sink in. Read it again. This is very empowering stuff.

Now, consider, what do you want your mind to be searching for? What evidence do you want to find? What do you want more of? If what you focus on grows, how can you focus more on what you value and choose?

The management of your attention is your greatest superpower.

We live in an age of distraction and confusion where everyone and everything is vying for *your* attention. It's time you start investing in yourself.

What neural networks do you actively choose to sprout (and indirectly prune) so you can explore, discover, learn, grow, and create the future that you value and choose to have?

What *is* that future that you value and choose to explore, discover, learn, grow and create?

This is where the C-IAM and NRF come in.

The C-IAM and NRF

Because I have my C-IAM and NRF, I always know exactly what to do to get back on track. I know who I am (the C-IAM) and what I do (the NRF) when I feel great. So, I can reverse engineer it. I can "come from" my C-IAM while following my NRF in a manner of exploring, discovering, learning, growing, and creating, all while calibrating to the JOLKA-GPS (joy, openness, love, kindness, awareness, gratitude, presence, and surrender). I have maps to follow, tools to make it real, and instructions for how it all works, *together*. I am totally empowered, at any given moment, to turn stops into steps and to rise over the ground on which I once stumbled. I can become the greatest possible benefit to myself, others, and ALL.

With all of this in mind, allow me to guide you through the process of developing your C-IAM and NRF.

One more thing before we do, though: ask, "Who is reading this book right now?" Are you both reading and *knowing* you are reading? Is there a pause; a witness; an Aware-Will in the equation?

People often confuse "being present" with Presence. Presence does not just mean doing what you are doing when you are doing it (a great skill in itself that is growing rarer in the age of distraction). Presence means showing up as an Aware-Will. It means *noticing that you are noticing*. It means holding extra and open attention while you are engaging with whatever is going on and consciously flavoring the experience with your C-IAM. Aware-Will is the universal template we all share, and the C-IAM is your entirely unique expression of your Aware-Will.

Keep all of this in mind while you are creating your C-IAM. You will get so much more out of these exercises, this book, and your entire life if you come from your Aware-Will, notice that you are noticing, and choose wisely instead of re-acting.

Creating the C-IAM: Phase 1

You are about to explore, discover, learn, grow, and create something that will improve your entire life, for the better and exponentially, the more you work with it. So, sit up and pause for a moment, activating your Aware-Will.

This is not ordinary information. This is a work book. So, please have a journal and something to write with nearby.

I am now going to present a series of questions that will prime you to notice more of what you value and choose to. By choosing to do this exercise, you give me consent to prime your brain with questions, and by doing so, you are still in charge.

What matters during this exercise is what comes up from inside of you as you read these questions. There is no right or wrong. The wisdom you need to thrive and heal is already within you. I am merely showing you how you can access more of you through these questions.

Please first just "sit" with the questions I ask you, like a sort of meditation. It would be very useful for you to activate a state of extra and open attention and to read the questions in a contemplative state, as an Aware-Will that is open to unknown, yet-to-be-discovered possibilities. Allow yourself to freely conjure the words, images, sensations, and experiences that arise as you consider these questions, and write down any keywords or ideas you discover as you explore them. They are meant to guide you through a process of contemplation that is ongoing; a work in progress.

When you consider your answers, focus particularly on the sensations that arise in your body. The more you rehearse and practice the types of thoughts, emotions, sensations, postures, breathing patterns, muscle organizations, motivations, and actions associated with your answers to these questions, the more you will activate the different parts of your brain that align with your C-IAM.

More than just jotting down some notes on scrap paper, I suggest you write out the answers to these questions in cursive, deliberate, care-full writing in a dedicated sacred journal that you fill only with content that you value and choose to create more of.

Some of the questions may result in overlapping answers, and that's great! Repetition is your friend, in this case.

A final tip: take your time. Each one of these questions is humongous in scope and in the amount of thought they could prompt. There is no rush to do this work. My answers to these questions are a constant work in progress that I refine and optimize in the laboratory of my life every day.

These questions are borrowed from Lar Short's (of Grace Essence Mandala) General Life Purpose and Required Curriculum teachings. Other invaluable resources on this topic are *Your One Word*[79] and *Built to Serve*[80] by Evan Carmichael, along with *Outwitting the Devil*[81] by Napoleon Hill.

Here we go, the Loving and Benefitting Questions:

1. What are five or more things you love about yourself?
2. What are five or more things you love to do and that make you feel more alive?
3. What are five or more things that you love to share with others?
4. If you knew your efforts could not fail to produce good results, what would you love to give your attention and energy to?
5. What do you participate in and support through your attention and energy that you would love to see last beyond your lifetime?
6. How do you think, feel, and act when you are most benefiting yourself? (I suggest a running list of each category: thoughts, feelings, actions)
7. How do you think, feel, and act when you are most benefiting others? (I suggest a running list of each category: thoughts, feelings, actions)
8. How do you think, feel, and act when you are most benefiting both yourself and others? (I suggest a running list of each category: thoughts, feelings, actions)
9. If you were Goddess or God and you could make your perfect vision of the world come to life, what would that be like?

Remember, the more you ponder these images and mind-movies, think the thought-words so inspired, feel the concomitant emotions, and savor the physiological sensations that arise when you answer these questions (and act on these thoughts and feelings), the more you create the future you value and choose to have. You traverse from thinking to feeling to doing to becoming to being your Creative-IAM, a true work of art that is both playful and beautiful.

---

[79] Carmichael, E. (2016): *Your One Word*. TarcherPerigee.
[80] Carmichael, E. (2020): *Built to Serve: Find Your Purpose and Become the Leader You Were Born to Be*. Savio Republic.
[81] Hill, N. (2011): Outwitting the Devil: The Secret to Freedom and Success. Union Square & Co.

Creating the C-IAM: Phase 2

If you've completed the previous exercise, that means you have a list of dozens of words, ideas, or phrases that are packed with the best experience of your life, the desire of your core values, and a sense of purpose and meaning.

Pause again and place your attention on the sensations of aliveness in your body as you savor the flavor of these contemplations. If you have given these questions the type of time, energy, and quality of attention I am asking of you, you will already be feeling a sense of cohesiveness and "togetherness" that you likely haven't in a long time—maybe ever. Savor this experience and mix in a sense of appreciation for your life, the people you love, and the future possibilities you are bringing into effect through this exercise.

If you aren't feeling it, either you are just reading this book without doing the work, or you are stuck in your head and only completing this exercise intellectually, not meditatively. See if you can slow down, relax your body, and ask these questions in the quiet of your open heart.

As you sit with all these words and sensations, ask for two or three words to emerge from the list that most accurately embody how you feel when answering these questions. This is not a rational or logical process; just ask inside, with sincerity, and take a chance on trusting the words that "zing" for you. Rest assured that questions asked sincerely into the unknown always yield nourishing fruit. Your job is not to make the fruit come to being (that is up to nature, or God, if you prefer that vernacular), but to plant good seeds (i.e., ask good questions) in good soil (i.e., with sincerity, openness, extra and open attention, and a desire to be of the greatest benefit to ALL).

When you find the words that "zing," you will feel a sense of "a-ha," or "yes," or "this is it." Many words that are positive and valuable, but don't quite "zing", might arise along the way before you discover the ones that really resonate. Hang in there, keep relaxing into your extra and open attention, and keep asking until something feels very powerful. It's okay if it doesn't come to you right away, or even in this session. It might come to you in a dream, or when you're walking down the street a few days from now. It's also perfectly wonderful if something "zings" for you today, but then it changes a year from now as you evolve more and more into the person you value and choose to be between now and then.

Here, we are looking for "basket words" or phrases that describe the experiences you're thinking about in a way that also encompasses the other things you value and choose. But don't try to hard to find the "perfect" words. Create the space and the words will come. For example, you may know that you will feel joyful when you can afford the lifestyle you value and choose to have, and that you will feel joyful when you feel more physically healthy. So, here, "joyful" is the basket word that encapsulates the experience of both fitness and financial abundance.

Why do we have to find these basket words? Because they represent you as a free person who is giving to life what you wish to receive. If you are joyful because of what happens to you, that is reactive joy and ultimately, strange as it seems, being dependent on anything, even "positive" things, is a type of dis-empowerment. I don't want you to hold your "joyful" feelings hostage to outer circumstances that have not yet occurred (e.g., having more money). Instead, I wish for you to conjure feelings of "joyful" right now, that come from you in a way that also includes drawing yourself toward a future where you just so happen to have more than enough money and feel physically fit. So, we have to identify the words that embody that future, in the simplest terms. You are putting the ends, first. You are creating the future, now.

When your "basket words" come to you, you will have conceived your Creative-IAM!

You can put these words together in a way that rings true for you, changing the syntax and playing with the word order. I provide an example of this in the next section.

My Experience of Creating my C-IAM

This is how I would go about Phases 1 and 2 of creating my C-IAM.

I would first ensure I am coming from my Aware-Will before practicing extra and open attention for a few minutes, in a dedicated space with a journal nearby. During this process, I would set my intention to prime my brain for creating the future I value and choose to—a future body, mind and circumstances I would absolutely love to inhabit.

Having been primed by the nine Loving and Benefitting Questions, I'd brainstorm, "What future do I value and choose? What are the greatest possible outcomes? What is it like for me to be totally happy and in love with life?" While brainstorming, I would not analyze, critique, or worry if I think, *That's impossible,* or anything along those lines. If I value it, I'd write it down and saturate in the sensations that ensue. I'd let this be an exercise in loosening repression and going for it. Anything and everything, I'd write it all down.

I'd notice my tendency to think in terms of what I *don't* want and transform that. I'd put everything in "positive" terms and ask evocative questions. If I thought, *I don't want to feel anxious,* I'd ask, "What does it feel like to feel calm and at ease?" If I thought, *I don't want to be poor,* I'd ask, "How great does it feel to have much more than enough money?" I'd remember not to declare what my mind will protest, such as, "I am rich," as this would create an inner conflict counter response of, "No, you're not." I'd remember to be sincerely curious about what it would feel like to have much more than enough money or be exceptionally fit, knowing that curiosity will get my consciousness Exploring → Discovering → Learning → Growing → Creating.

I'd reinvoke extra and open attention to get out of my thinking mind and into my living sensations. I wouldn't just conjure up the thought-words about what I value and choose; I'd also allow myself to see it and feel it. I'd notice the images and feel the sensations in my body. I'd focus on the way these deliberate thoughts and feelings organize my body, including my posture, breath, facial expression, and gaze. All the while, I'd notice that I am noticing all these aspects of being. I'd explore and deepen the way these thoughts and images organize my sensations posture, breath, and the expression on my face. I'd identify these inner and outer conditions I'm displaying as what I experience when I'm thriving.

I'd ask, "What does it feel like to be as happy and healthy as I could choose to be; to be living the life I choose to live? How great does it feel to be in love with life?" I'd be curious! I'd allow my mind to search for words or phrases that describe how it would feel to be the person I value and choose to be. I would then open myself up to the unknown and allow two or three words, phrases, or ideas that encompass these sentiments to emerge. These would become my basket words. I'd release any words that don't quite fit and keep relaxing until two or three words really resonate with a feeling of, "Yes, that's it. This is who I really am. This is who I value and choose to be."

When I actually did this exercise, I initially came up with, "I value and choose to feel love, joy, peace, and a sense of meaning and purpose; to live a life of contribution with grace and ease; to have more than enough money to live a prosperous and charitable lifestyle." These were the words and phrases that came to me when I searched my mind for how it would feel to be the person I value and choose to be. Then, I condensed these into "love," "joy," and "prosperity." These were my basket words. Initially, I included "a sense of meaning and purpose" and "contribution" in my list of basket words, but then when I asked deeply, I realized both of those things fit into "love" in my experiential sense. Perhaps I also had on my list, "I want to be in shape, have more energy, and be a better lover," but knew that if I was experiencing prosperity, love, and joy, all those other things would also be at play, as a natural byproduct. So, I continued to pack those alternate meanings and feelings into my chosen identity as "love, joy, prosperity." No further words needed. They already encompassed everything I associated with my most beneficial self and state.

I played around with the syntax and what might feel like a better way of organizing the words so that they evoked a powerful feeling of identity. I messed around with "Prosperous-Love-Joy," and "I am prosperous-love-joy" to figure out what resonated most.

Once I had my basket phrases, I went and packed them full of any and all other positive associations and started a practice of regularly "meditating" on these qualities.

I regularly revisit and update these basket words, so that when I conjure up "prosperous- love-joy," it triggers my brain and body to feel it all. The more I "fire" these thoughts, images, sensations, actions and experiences, the more I "wire" in these *results*. This inspires new ideas and desires that align with this identity. I return to extra and open attention and repeat my basket phrase to myself *as a question I am genuinely curious about,* as many times as I like, multiple times a day. Here, I may only be reciting my identity—my C-IAM of "prosperous-love-joy"—as a mantra, but the power comes in *how* I am saying it. The most powerful way to repeat this incantation is in the form of a genuine, sincere question to the unknown; in the form of wondering and genuine curiosity. "I wonder what my life is like when I am expressing 'prosperous-love-joy?' What benefits come from 'prosperous- love-joy?' What surprises and opportunities arise in a space of 'prosperous-love, joy?' How much more joyful, open, loving, kind, and aware am I as 'prosperous-love-joy?' How grateful do I feel when I am 'prosperous-love-joy?' How much can I surrender and trust in 'prosperous-love-joy?'"

I'd allow my posture, smile, emotions, mental images, and thought-words to be organized by the repetition of the basket phrase while I remain in a meditative, "asking," invitational state. This means orienting myself toward openness and curiosity. It means wondering and conjuring. This is different to "affirming," which could invite the Reactive-iWAS to protest with "proof" to the contrary.

By repeating my C-IAM (prosperous-love-joy) and allowing that to organize the way I think, feel, and act, I am priming my nervous system to notice more and more experiences that will foster that felt and lived reality of prosperity, love, and joy. If I continue to return to extra and open attention (which is kind of like a blank slate) and then color that with thoughts, feelings, images, and sensations of "prosperous-love-joy" in states of relaxation, brain and heart coherence, and flow, then my entire being (including my subconscious) will be geared toward exploring, discovering, learning, growing, and creating new and exciting ways of becoming "Prosperous-Love-Joy."

Woo-hoo!

Well Done!

If you have worked through this exercise, then congratulations! You have created the Creative-IAM that will help you to most effectively navigate your way to the future you value and choose to have. I can't wait to hear about what unfolds for you as a result! Be sure to inform me of your wins so you can inspire others and so we can celebrate the real you in the ATA online learning community which you can join if you'd like to be around other like-minded people doing this great work. https://www.alltogether.academy/the-joyful-excellence-mastermind

It is now time for you to nurture your new creative sense of self by celebrating its arrival and giving it the care, attention, and value it deserves. It is time for you to organize your life in such a way where your C-IAM can thrive. How? By creating the Neurochemical Roadmap to the Future You Value and Choose. Let's cover that next.

23
THE NEUROCHEMICAL ROADMAP TO THE FUTURE YOU VALUE AND CHOOSE (NRF)

BEFORE WE BEGIN, LET'S INVOKE YOUR Aware-Will as your C-IAM (which, by the way, is something you can and "should" do any time you are willing to and remember to). How would "prosperous-love-joy" (or whatever your C-IAM is) continue to read this book (or do the dishes, or talk to your child, or show up at work, or drive in traffic, or notice that you feel depressed or anxious)? How would your C-IAM be sitting? What would its posture be like? What would you, as your C-IAM, notice around and inside you? How would you listen to someone, look at a flower, or get on the bus? What would the quality of your attention be like? How would your C-IAM go about the exercise that you are about to do?

Now that we've done that, let's learn how we can create and use your NRF.

Your NRF is your map. It outlines what your C-IAM does when you are at your best and what your Reactive-iWAS does when you are not at your best. These are your "steps" and your "stops," respectively.

As with the C-IAM, it is best to create your NRF in a contemplative state of extra and open attention, with a sacred journal nearby and with an open heart and mind. Ask and be curious about the best possible outcomes that can arise from the unknown.

This first set of questions I'm about to ask you will reveal your NRF's steps. These are what your C-IAM does when you are at your best. The second set of questions will reveal your "stops". Journal your answers to these questions in a meditative state. The more answers you have for each question, the better.

Build and expand on your "steps" and "stops" lists over time and review them often, packing everything into your C-IAM basket phrase. Finally, please answer these questions from a place of sincere curiosity about what it would be like to think, feel, and act as your C-IAM, or not.

Your Steps

1. When you are embodying your C-IAM, how do you know that you are?
2. How do you think? What kinds of thoughts do you have about yourself, your life, others, and the world around you?
3. How do you feel? What kinds of emotions do you experience?
4. How do you act? What actions do you take in your life? What day-to-day things do you do?
5. What sensations do you feel in your body? How do you walk? Stand? Sit? Breathe?
6. Do you feel more "open" or more "closed?" More relaxed or more tense? More excited or more lethargic?
7. What else do you feel?
8. What kinds of opportunities arise when you are feeling your Creative-IAM and putting your Creative-IAM out into the world? What surprises take place? What doors open? What doors close?
9. What kinds of things do you assume or take for granted when you are embodying your Creative-IAM?
10. What kinds of things do you believe while embodying your Creative-IAM?
11. What do you notice about others when you are embodying your Creative-IAM? What do you notice about your environment? About the way you look at the world around you? About other people's responses to the way you look, feel, and act? What kinds of things do others say to you about you?
12. Who else benefits from you being in this state? How do your family members benefit? Your friends? Your colleagues? Your community? What do they notice? What feedback do you receive?
13. How does it feel to see them and notice them benefiting and noticing you in this way?

Return to extra and open attention for a few moments and saturate in all these sensations. Notice how you can create the future now and how this results in you feeling better today, easily, without any gimmicks, in a sustainable way that makes perfect sense, and how this now plants seeds for fruits and flowers to sprout, blossom, and thrive in the future.

Consider how, if you keep doing this cultivation and acting on these new thoughts and feelings, day in and day out—moment by moment, even—it is entirely inevitable that you will not only feel better today, but that you will also feel better and better in your day to day into the future, and that you will end up with a beautiful, bountiful garden (a future life worth loving).

Your Stops

This next set of questions will reveal your NRF stops and the likely territory of your Reactive-iWAS. If in the following questions, contemplating how your "Reactive-iWAS" thinks, feels, and acts doesn't evoke your habitual negativity, you can replace it with "Upset," or "distressed." How do you think, feel, and act when I AM upset, when I AM stressed out, when I AM "in a bad mood" or "having a bad day"? Ask yourself these questions and journal your answers to them, like you did for your NRF steps.[82]

1. What stops you from embodying your Creative-IAM? (Allow the experiences that do not embody your Creative-IAM to arise in your awareness.)
2. What thoughts do you think when you are feeling like your old, familiar self (the Reactive-iWAS)?
3. What kinds of things does your Reactive-iWAS imagine?
4. What kinds of things does your Reactive-iWAS expect to happen? What opportunities are missed? What doors close?
5. What kinds of things does your Reactive-iWAS assume or take for granted?
6. What kinds of things does your Reactive-iWAS believe?
7. What kinds of things does your Reactive-iWAS do on a day-to-day basis?
8. What's the "same old, same old" like for your Reactive-iWAS? What is your Reactive-iWAS's "fate?"
9. What kinds of things do you not do when you believe in your Reactive-iWAS's "truth?"

---

[82] Bonus task: Give your Reactive-iWAS a name. This can be useful, especially if it's a funny name! Ideas could be "the petty tyrant" or "the adult tantrum."

10. What kinds of things do you feel, or what emotions generally predominate, when your Reactive-iWAS is active? What spirals out of control as one thing leads to another?
11. What kinds of criticisms, judgements and complaints does your Reactive-iWAS foster about yourself, others, the world?
12. Who else is affected when you embody your Reactive-iWAS?
13. What is the quality of your relationships with others when the Reactive-iWAS is in charge? Your family? Friends? Colleagues? Strangers?
14. What kind of reactions do you get from others (particularly from the people you care about most) when you are embodying your Reactive-iWAS?
15. What kinds of reactions do you get from colleagues (or even strangers) when you are embodying your Reactive-iWAS?

Return to extra and open attention and feel what it's like to not be your Creative-IAM; to default back to who you were, over and over again. Then, ask yourself:

16. Do I want more of this?
17. How will my life turn out if I continue not being my Creative-IAM for the remainder of this day? For one more year? What will happen in my life if I continue this way for five years? Twenty-five years?
18. What will I be thinking, feeling, and noticing on my deathbed if I continue acting out the familiar habits and patterns of my Reactive-iWAS?

The answers you get from these questions "should" sting a bit. If not, I suggest you take this exercise deeper and really process the fact that if you do not do the work, you will use your free will to go to your deathbed full of regrets.

Return to extra and open attention and thank yourself for going through this process.

By being willing to contemplate your stops, even though that is painful, you are coming from your Aware-Will so you can host your limitations with kindness and freedom from suffering. Your C-IAM can see the obstacles on the road clearly, and without huge emotional reactions, can more easily steer out of the way.

And Breathe

Congratulations! You have just created your very own personal Neurochemical Roadmap to the Future (NRF) You Value and Choose, complete with directions for how to get where you want to go (your steps) and clearly marked roadblocks, obstacles, and wrong turns (your stops). Now, you have dozens of thoughts, emotions, sensations, and actions that signify you being "on the right track," meaning, you can now more accurately determine what the next, easiest thing is that you are willing to do now, to benefit yourself, others, and ALL.

You have probably been conditioned to think life needs to be a struggle, or else you aren't trying hard enough. I am going to reiterate a countercultural suggestion: you should do the next, easiest thing that you are willing to do to get back on the road to where you want to go. Lest you activate your neural networks of the past that lead down the well-paved highway to your Reactive-iWAS, you need not concern yourself with "why" you've gotten off track, for how long you've been off track, where your tendency to go off track comes from, who's to blame, or wondering if you'll ever get back on track. You don't even need to go to "reasons why we get off track" therapy. All you need to do is notice that you're off track, pause, and choose to get back on track. The more you make this choice, the more you develop the muscles to choose this more quickly and easily in the future, and the more you build the habit of staying on track and paving a new highway to the future you value and choose. Practicing extra and open attention builds this capacity to notice, pause, and choose, while fog breath and the power switch build your capacity to do a U-turn when you notice you are driving down the road to your Reactive-iWAS.

Creating Your NRF: Recap

To consolidate what you have learned so far:
- Write out the answers to the previous roadmap questions very carefully (if you haven't already), ideally in cursive and in a sacred journal that you fill only with content that you value and choose to create more of. This is your roadmap to where you want to go (your steps) and where you don't want to go (your stops).
- When you get off track, refer to your roadmap questions. What is the next, easiest thing you are willing to do right now to pivot from a "stop" to a "step?" You may want to put all the stuff you would do

(i.e., all the "steps" you would take to transform these "stops") on a list so you can easily reference this and pick the next, easiest thing you are willing to do whenever you face a "stop" in the future.

- Check in with your "stops" from time to time. Get to know yourself better, including what doesn't work for you (but don't ruminate on this list). The more familiar you are with your "stops", the quicker you will notice them before they generate all sorts of "proof" for why you "should" stay the same.

- Understand that "alchemy" is turning "stops" into "steps." Taking steps when you feel like stopping builds your psychospiritual muscles and gets you in the best shape of your life.

- Continue practicing extra and open attention. It builds your "noticing" muscles. Think about it: if your Reactive-iWAS is your unconscious "reactive" mode, how will you become conscious of the fact you have become unconscious? Simply, you must practice becoming the "noticer!"

- Continue practicing the power switch and fog breath. Once you notice you are off track, you can use these tools to change state and clear the canvas, so you can then start painting the picture you value and choose to with the colors of Joy = Gold, Openness = Blue, Love = Green, Kindness = Red, Awareness = White, Gratitude = Rainbow, Presence = Clear, and Surrender = Purple. These colors are not random, but actually come from ancient spiritual traditions and practices that use movements of energy and imagination to combine forces and elements into a cohesive and coherent process for developing your "independent subtle energy body." This is much more than we can get into in this book, but it may be cool for some of you to know that this work not only provides a foundation of mental-emotional freedom, psychological stability, radical health and happiness, but, if you are so inclined, it can also serve as a foundation for the ultimate in spiritual development, beyond what we can even imagine. In other words, there's a method to the madness, and everything I am sharing with you is a very deliberate expression of my personal life mission to preserve and pass on the greatest treasures of human potential. In the ATA online community (which you can find by visiting the link: https://www.alltogether.academy/the-joyful-excellence-mastermind), we actually remind each other of these colors by connecting them with a different virtue every day of the week. This is a powerful way to prime our brains!

Using Your C-IAM and NRF

Just like the question, "What would Jesus do?" now that you have created your C-IAM and your NRF, you know exactly how to organize your identity according to what you value and choose to have in your life. No need to defer to another authority!

Don't get me wrong, I love Jesus, but that is largely because love is a natural expression of my C-IAM. So, I value and choose to worship, invest in, and become love itself.

"What would my C-IAM do in this exact moment and situation?"

You also now know exactly what to choose (when you ask the grace and ease question in consideration of your NRF). This will logically result in you getting closer and closer to the future of your dreams.

Making better choices will expand your possibilities, so keep adding to your "steps" list, and soon, you will find that "steps" come up for you more organically and easily than "stops" do.

More good news is that when you take deliberate, dedicated action, there are only two possibilities:

1. You get the desired result.
2. You get closer to the desired result.

Direction is everything, what you focus on grows, and what you worship you become.

Note that what you worship has nothing to do with what you claim to "believe" or whether you are religious or atheistic. What you worship is what you invest your life into. Life is comprised of heartbeats and breaths, and you only have so many, so whatever you devote your heartbeats and breaths to, or whatever you spend your lifeforce on, is what you worship, and what you worship, you become.

What is happening *to* you is less relevant than how you are *choosing to act* amid whatever is happening. This is where your freedom (and your happiness) lies. No matter what the conditions or situations in your life are, it is up to you to show up as who you value and choose to be. In this way, every single moment and experience is a gym in which you can exercise the spirit of your C-IAM. Some days are heavy lifting, and some days are a walk in the park. Either way, the more you spend your heartbeats and breaths thinking, feeling, and acting as your C-IAM and taking steps on your NRF, the more you become just that. It is by becoming who you really are instead of how you've grown accustomed to being that you discover the only possible path to lasting health: happiness!

Creating and Using Your NRF: Reflection

So far, we have learned a lot about the nervous system, surviving and thriving, extra and open attention, breathwork, mindset, new ways of thinking and feeling, the NRF, the C- IAM, the JOLKA-GPS, heartbeats and breaths, participating and contributing, and so much more. Take a moment to reflect on what you've learned so far, how you've grown, and smile!

Consider, what are your most important takeaways so far? What's the next, easiest element you are willing to integrate into your life so that you can feel better today, easily, without any gimmicks, in a totally sustainable way that makes perfect sense?

Once you notice you are in survival mode and there is no immediate danger, you can pivot to any of the thoughts, feelings, sensations, and actions associated with your NRF's "steps." This doesn't have to be hard. In fact, please don't make it hard. Start with a breath, a smile, a pushup, a shower—any step in the right direction—and then keep going. As you travel along your NRF, you can keep putting a red flag on anything that is either off track or a road hazard (your "stops"). "Red flagging" these things will help you to notice them more quickly and easily whenever they crop up in the future, which will help you to choose your next "step" more quickly and easily, which will result in you feeling better, today, easily, in a totally sustainable way that makes perfect sense.

24
EMBODYING YOUR C-IAM AND FOLLOWING YOUR NRF

SOMETIMES, REMEMBERING TO REMEMBER TO DO the work is the hardest part about embodying your C-IAM and following your NRF. So many clients have told me, "I was sure I was going to remember to invoke my C-IAM, but I haven't thought about it for a week!" Guess what that means? It means "you" have been asleep and running on an autopilot program basically 24/7 during that time. It also means your reactive conditioning has been in charge of your life, not you.

If this happens to you, take a deep breath and don't worry. It happens to the best of us. Plus, remembering something you've forgotten is the only way to build your "remembering" muscles!

Consider, who is driving you right now? Who is driving your B-P-E train? Is it your environment, your past, marketing, memes, everything other than *you*? Is it the Reactive-iWAS, or the C-IAM? Remember, you can establish this by considering whether you are feeling any of the qualities of the JOLKA-GPS. If you are beating yourself up for not remembering to invoke your C-IAM—that is, if you are feeling the old familiar pangs of guilt and "not good enough"—then you already have your answer: your Reactive-iWAS is in the driving seat. On the other hand, if you are feeling the joy and openness of exploring, discovering, learning, growing, and creating new ways of thinking, feeling, and acting, you are expressing your C-IAM.

Woo-hoo!

You should now have a list of dozens (perhaps more than a hundred) thoughts, feelings, sensations, postures, expressions, tones of voice, ways of being and acting, and things you notice in yourself, others, and the environment around you that you can activate and embody at any given moment, to get you back on the highway to where you want to be. These are your "steps." These are the thoughts, feelings, actions, and experiences you want to "sprout."

When I say it works better to create solutions than it does to fix problems, I mean that it is better to create the solutions that both benefit you now and that plant seeds for a better future; for the future you value and choose. These solutions are all written on your "steps" list.

Choose anything on that list to action now. In fact, choose the easiest thing you are willing to do now to regain momentum and direction.

You should also now have a list of dozens (perhaps more than a hundred) thoughts, feelings, sensations, postures, expressions, and actions to *not* embody. These are your "stops." This is the stuff you want to "prune." These are the weeds you want to put in the compost pile and leave alone so they can turn into the turbocharged fertilizer that can feed the creations you value and choose to feed. It will likely feel uncomfortable to *not re-act* these habitual patterns. That discomfort is the compost pile working, turning the shit into fertilizer. That discomfort is proof you are doing it right! You are making the most potent fertilizer of ALL.

Like I said before, please regularly add to your NRF "steps" and "stops" lists and continue to "pack" values, thoughts, sensations, emotions, experiences, and celebrations into your C-IAM.

Everything we've talked about in the last couple of chapters may seem "easier said than done". Easier to understand than to accomplish. That's because it is, in a manner of speaking, easier to keep unconsciously playing out our Reactive-iWAS. But, in the long run, your willingness to endure the temporary discomfort of composting this material, your life will actually get easier. If you do what you did, you will get what you got. If you do something new, you will grow too. You are the power point of change, and the present always presents an opportunity for you to change direction, for better or worse. You get the largest gains when everything inside you wants to go down the road you've always traveled—the highway to your personal hell—and you don't. True change happens when you choose to respond differently today to the exact same stimulus that you gave into yesterday. The future you value and choose to have is available to you at all times; all you need to do is transform and redirect the compulsive thoughts, feelings, and actions that are "stopping you" from embodying your C-IAM—the ones you continue to re-act based on past conditioning—even when you have valid "reasons" (like a health condition or a life challenge) to give into them. Because really, nothing is "stopping you" from achieving personal health (happiness) other than you thinking like, feeling like, and acting as your Reactive-iWAS.

How to Find Joy
Even If You Have a Hole in Your Bucket

Stay vigilant of the first signs of anything on your "what's stopping you?" list, because the good news is, again, nothing is actually stopping you. *You* are stopping you. This doesn't mean you should be in denial about the hardships you're facing; it means you can and "should" take charge of what is in your control and leave what is not alone. The more survival mode runs rampant, the harder it becomes to turn stops into steps and the more addictive the neurochemicals of "stress" become. Lar Short reminds us:

Again and again, the world was and is beyond our control... Life does not consult us. Everything else shows up in our life, and this is what is on our plate. We can only work with whatever is there. This is the plan... The irony for us as control addicts is that we are trying to be responsible for things that we cannot control, and we do not take responsibility for the things we can. [83]

When you are response-able for getting back on the highway to the future you value and choose to have, even if, aside from, and especially because what you are going through right now is challenging, not only are you taking the only logical way to get to where you prefer to go, but you are also using the high-octane fuel that gets you there faster (the mastication of your resistance to whatever is seemingly "against" you right now). This is how you supercharge your growth. You take survival mode's lifesaving fuel that is activated in your upset, and you use it to fuel your entry into thriving mode and the future you are choosing to create now. The more courageous you are in saying "no" to kneejerk re-actions and pivoting to the "yes" that you value and choose to experience, be, and become, the more beneficial you can be.

The very fact that only you can stop you from being happy is good news. Why? Because you can stop stopping you! In fact, you are the *only one* who can stop stopping you. Remember:
- We change better by feeling better, so do the next easiest thing and feel better for it, and you will want to do more.
- Direction is everything.
- "Is this useful?" is a better question than, "Is this true?" Why? Because it is more useful!

---

[83] Lowenthal, M. & Short, L. (1993): *Opening the Heart of Compassion: Transform Suffering Through Buddhist Psychology and Practice*, p.63. Tuttle Publishing.

Also remember to apply logic and will. Ask in any "now" moment, "Will the manner in which I am currently thinking, feeling, and acting logically and practically lead me to where I value and choose to be?" If the answer is "yes," then ask:

- How can I create more of it?
- How can I celebrate it?
- How can I share it with others?
- How can I increase the benefits it brings?

If your answer is "no," then you are facing an opportunity to exercise your inner spiritual warrior and powerfully say, "No!" (A very powerful "no" makes space for a very powerful "yes.")

We are all busy and we all lead full lives. But how can you expect new, valued experiences to come into your life if you don't make room for them?

Consider, what do you need to say "no" to? What do you need to cut out to make space for grace? When you know, cut it out.

Once you have said "no," allow for a new "yes" to arise. (Choosing "yes" might happen spontaneously in the moment, or you can more methodically choose anything on your NRF "steps" list to say "yes" to.) Once you are back on track with "yes," ask again:

- How can I create more of it?
- How can I celebrate it?
- How can I share it with others?
- How can I increase the benefits it brings?

Reverse Engineering

Your C-IAM is your driver, or your navigator, on your journey to your desired destination; to your version of health and happiness. But even the best driver needs to know where they are going and how to get there. It is for this reason that we have created your NRF—and neurochemically speaking, the best way to fortify this map (your NRF) is to "reverse engineer" it.

Let me share an example.

A few years ago, and about 20 years into a chronic yet to be diagnosed serious illness, by using power questions, I was able to consider, "What would it be like if I was already as happy and healthy as I value and choose to be?" Among many things that "came up" in my search, one of them was surprising to me: there was a "knowing" inside that I would "dance more."

I wasn't consciously aware of a desire to "dance more" before I did this exercise. In fact, I had a Reactive-iWAS as a "bad dancer," and I therefore had all sorts of beliefs based on this Reactive-iWAS which altered my perception and led to me always find "reasons" to not dance in life (thus altering my experience of life). Yet it turns out if I were already as healthy and happy as I would choose to be, then I would be dancing more. Who knew? [84]

Importantly, I wasn't going to wait until I "felt like" dancing more before I started bringing this vision to reality. We are always either waiting or creating. With this wisdom in my heart, I was able to choose to "reverse engineer" my happiness by putting the result (the future) upfront (in the here and now).

I started small by following the grace and ease question: "What's the next, easiest thing I am willing to do?" At first, this meant just listening to good music while doing the dishes, allowing myself to flow and tune into my body. Then, because that felt good and I wanted more of that good feeling (we change better by feeling better), I started dancing around the kitchen more when no one was home (because I was still embarrassed to be seen "dancing!"). That felt really good, which inspired an authentic desire in me to move more, so I started exploring dancing for its own sake, in my room, by myself, with headphones on—door locked, you can bet!

After some time, I expanded out a little more by doing dance-based workout routines from YouTube and Apple Fitness. I did these in the upstairs living room, with my wife and kids able to hear me and walk by if they wanted. This was a big deal for someone with a long-entrenched Reactive-iWAS as a "bad dancer," with all its indoctrinated "insecurities" and encultured beliefs about dancing being "gay" and "gay" being "not okay." (Remember, beliefs are not truths, and if they are not questioned, challenged, and even dismissed, they can wreck lives. Human beings literally go to war, with themselves and others, because they mistake beliefs for truths!)

After dancing my way through my workouts and seeing that my wife and kids, far from judging me critically, thought it was awesome, I was able to take a really big step. I didn't do this because I was forcing myself with "should," "musts," and "ought tos," but because I had felt better and better

---

[84] As you may have discovered for yourself by this point, when we quiet our mind and ask power questions, our heart-mind often has wisdom for us that is surprising and can take us down paths we never imagined we'd go down.

along the way, and nothing is better for confidence than tangible results. As B.J. Fogg says in *Tiny Habits*, people change best by feeling good, not by feeling bad. [85]

With these steps—by doing "the next, easiest thing I was willing to do"— I was able to stretch my comfort zone (growth!) and ask my wife if she wanted to take salsa lessons.

Some context is needed here: my wife is a Latina woman who is also a professional musician and an ex-lead singer in a cumbia band. She's been dancing her whole life. It's second nature to her. Not only that, but we were living in Mexico at the time, so we would be surrounded by people who had also been dancing their whole lives and were damn good at it. All of this threatened to reinforce the Reactive-iWAS of "I am a bad dancer"; of "I am a stereotypical gringo who can't dance." But here I was, encouraging us to go out salsa dancing!

Mental and emotional obstacles weren't the only things I overcame in this process. At the time, I was also struggling with the complications of an undiagnosed life-threatening injury in my chest, traumatic brain injury (TBI) and severely compromised proprioception that resulted in me feeling dizzy, nauseous, and even more uncoordinated than usual. Still, I chose to not wait until I was happier and healthier; until I "felt like" dancing. I chose instead to create the future now (because, again, we are always either waiting or creating).

During this journey, it sometimes felt like I was taking big strides, but more often, it felt like I was taking small, incremental steps. Other times, it felt like the best I could do was crawl. This is powerful. Regardless of what degree of movement feels best and easiest right now, never underestimate the power of persistence. As Robin Sharma says in *The 5 AM Club*, seemingly small acts performed consistently over time yield staggering results. [86]

Bolstered by feeling better today, easily, without gimmicks and in a way that was totally sustainable and made perfect sense (and wanting more, organically and naturally), a salsa class was a great place for me to continue growing into a much more useful belief: "I can dance! I can enjoy dancing! I can even be a 'good dancer,' especially if I develop the (useful) belief that the purpose of dancing is to have fun!"

---

[85] Fogg. B.J. (2019): *Tiny Habits: The Small Changes That Change Everything*, p. 123, Harvest.

[86] Sharma, R. (2018): *The 5 AM Club: Own Your Morning. Elevate Your Life*, p. 6, HarperCollins.

To make a long story short, my wife and I had a total blast. We danced and laughed and smiled. It was pure fun. More relevantly, I became a "good dancer." I systematically erased "Reactive-iWAS a bad dancer" and replaced it with "C-IAM a good dancer." Along the way, I redefined what a "good dancer" meant to me: one who enjoys dancing! And what do you know: I was feeling pretty darn healthy and happy! I had brought the future I valued and chose to have into the present. I turned the question, "What would it be like if I was already happy and healthy?" into a reality.

That's reverse engineering it.

We're doing this all the time, for better (as in this example) and for worse (like when we worry about getting sick and *make* ourselves sick as a result). I imagined what it would be like to already be in the future I valued and chose to have, and I started acting that way. Bit by bit, I became that way. I went from knowing, to doing, to becoming, to being a good dancer. Well, at least a happy one! I didn't "fake it 'til I made it"; I just made it. Nothing fake about it. Every step was as genuine, sincere, and real as it gets.

Goals: Direction is Everything

Direction is everything, and goals can keep you directed. They are not the be all and end all of your existence here on earth, but they are very useful.

While traveling "north," you never arrive at your destination *per se*, but by passing through various cities on the way, you can identify that you are heading in the right direction. Goals are much like your "north." They give you direction, and for that, they are important, but they are not the destination itself. As you have seen in your own life (and the lives of countless people who have "made it"), goal fulfilment does not give you happiness, or a feeling that you have finally "arrived." So, when you believe that accomplishments and rewards will make you happy, you turn steps into stops. Goals and rewards are not ultimately satisfying unless they are recognized as what they are: steps. You can enjoy your accomplishments and go to a nice dinner in the new city you've found yourself in, but the real satisfaction lies in you relishing the journey itself as you venture into the infinite unknown as your C-IAM, on your NRF, exploring, discovering, learning, growing, and creating the JOLKA-GPS.

Habits and Why They Don't Stick

New habits usually don't stick because of our tendency to default back to the Reactive-iWAS. When (and only when) we perform our new behaviors over time (the NRF) and attach ourselves to our new identity (the C-IAM) do our changes last. In this scenario, we do not go back, and we no longer need to cope with problems associated with who we were, because that version of us no longer exists, and therefore what we used to do and how we used to experience life has become irrelevant.

Identity is like a center of gravity: if we are attached to and identify with all the programs and patterns of the Reactive-iWAS, we gravitate to who we *were* and what we *did*; to the lowest common denominator of what is known and familiar. Therefore, for change to last, we must become new and fresh. That starts with us checking and changing state.

You already know that the tools for checking and changing state are fog breath, power switch, and extra and open attention. However, it's also worth keeping in mind that the process of checking and changing state is ultimately based around the consideration, "Am I waiting or creating?" So, ask yourself:

- What is my posture right now? Is it useful? Is it creating what I value and choose to create? Do I want more of this?
- What is my facial expression right now? Is it useful? Is it creating what I value and choose to create? Do I want more of this?
- What are the thought-words running in my mind right now? Are they useful? Are they creating what I value and choose to create? Do I want more of this?
- What is my attention focused on right now? Is it useful? Is it creating what I value and choose to create? Do I want more of this?

If your answers to these questions are "yes," then ask:
- How can I amplify it?
- How can I make more of it?
- How can I feel it in every cell of my being?
- How can I savor it?
- How can I appreciate it?
- How can I share it?
- How can I radiate it to others/ALL?
- How can I use it to uplift others?
- How much more beneficial can I be?

If your answers are "no," then:

1. Say, "No!"
2. Invoke extra and open attention.
3. Regulate your breath (using fog breath or the physiological sigh).
4. Invoke resolve. Choose to change.
5. Ask, "How does the future me—my C-IAM—aim to sit or stand?" Adjust your posture accordingly.
6. Ask, "What facial expression will generate the chemistry I value and choose to create? What do I wish to communicate?" Adjust your facial expression accordingly. (hint: smile 😊)
7. Ask, "What kind of thoughts would I be entertaining if I was already over this problem?"
8. Ask, "How would my C-IAM think in this situation? If I couldn't fail and I was already the person I choose to be [which you are; we are just trying to access it], how would I be thinking?"
9. Ask, "What can I focus on right now that will generate more possibilities? Where can I place my attention so that I can be more response-able and resourceful?"
10. Notice the sensations of "aliveness" in your body. Feel the changes in your posture.
11. Breathe bigger, stand upright, and smile!

Now you are back in the state of "Yes!" ready for more and to share!

Consider how your new state of being can benefit you. How much better—how much more useful—for your health and happiness are the chemicals now coursing through your body?

Who else gets to benefit from your chosen state of being? What is the positive upward spiral—the ripple effect—of your alchemy?

Let your mind search for feelings, opportunities, and futures where you can shine. Bathe yourself in gratitude for the future possibilities that are not yet known to you but are the only logical conclusion of your continual beneficial changing. Amplify your "Yes!" state over and over again by making more of it and sharing freely from your state of abundance.

Deathbed Trajectory

If you need some extra motivation to invoke your C-IAM, you can ask, "Are my current thoughts, feelings, and actions conducive to me creating the future I value and choose to create? If I continue to think, feel, and act this way, what will my life be like in one day? One month? One year? Five years? Twenty years? On my deathbed?"

You can turbocharge this motivation by skipping straight to the deathbed contemplation. As my mentor says, "Death doesn't care. It's going to take you either way. You can die a hero or a victim. Death doesn't care what the quality of your life is from now until it takes you. But *you* might care!"

What is the one word you would want to describe your life on your epitaph? Really pause and consider this. "If only one word was written on my tombstone to encapsulate what is absolutely most essential to me, what would it be?" Expressing *that* value is what makes life worth loving.

It's your body, your mind, and your spirit we're talking about here. It's your life! So, take one hundred percent responsibility for getting back to, amplifying, and sharing your most optimal state. Choose to be the dominant influence in your own life—not your past; not your trauma; not your spouse; not the government; not the news; not politicians; not your pain; not the weather; not your boss; not the asshole who just cut you off. As long as anything other than you is in charge of your state, you will not be happy. If anything and everything else controls you, then you are automatically disempowered. Naturally, this results in you feeling afraid (disempowered), which "activates the alarm" and puts you in survival mode. That's called being stuck! When you regain dominion over your own body, mind, and spirit, however, you reclaim the power, vitality, and benefits of thriving.

Retrain your brain or remain the same.

Celebrate Your Success

Remember to celebrate your success! This really makes a huge difference. Every time you celebrate a success, your brain produces a beneficial neurochemical cocktail endogenously, which means it's coming *from you*, not from a drug or dessert or notification on your phone.

Brains love feelgood neurochemicals so much that every time they get them, they ask, "What came just before I got it?" Whatever answer it comes up with, it will want to do again and again. This is both the root of addiction and the means by which you can hack your brain to create the future you value and choose. You already have inside of you the most powerful and effective pharmacy, and when you activate these beneficial neurochemicals endogenously, there are zero negative side effects. There are only benefits.

This is cause for celebration! *You* are cause for celebration.

When I finally got down to working on my C-IAM and NRF, I already had two master's degrees and three kids, and I was mired in the consequences of deeply entrenched depression and anxiety patterns since I was a child. I was also dealing with serious head injury complications and major internal damages that would not be surgically repaired until many years later. There were days, weeks, and months when the going was rough, even when I knew I was moving in the right direction (on my NRF). Thus, the ability to celebrate my successes with an almost irrational persistence, no matter what their size, was key to making my best life a sustainable reality.

What we focus on grows, right?

This almost sounds crazy to say in the context of our current cultural trance, but: for practical neurochemical reasons, our efforts pay off way more when we celebrate our successes and forget our failures. Like Ted Lasso says, "be a goldfish" and have no memory when it comes to your mistakes. Props to my Uncle Ed, a renowned Jesuit Priest who boasted of his "good memory", "I only remember the good stuff" and when his financially successful friends would take him golfing he would come home and say, "I shot a four!" "A four, Uncle Ed?" "Yes, I only count the good shots."

Lighthearted perspectives not withstanding, for those working these tools and concepts and coming up against obstacles along the way, I made a video about how to work with tough stuff. You can find that on our in your Module 9.1 of your book resources at www.alltogether.academy/joy-bucket-tools.

Improv Acting

When we are emotional, we literally re-act stories, roles, lines, images, sensations, and conditioning from the past. We have so thoroughly "memorized" who we think we are (our Reactive-iWAS) that these memories feel like who we are. Like Socrates said, "The masks we wear are apt to become our face." This means that when we try to change and start making a deliberate, dedicated effort to become our C-IAM (and not our Reactive-iWAS), this often feels awkward and even "wrong," as we have not yet "nailed the part." However, a good actor is not one who "acts" happy or sad; they *are* happy or sad. They rehearse their role so thoroughly that they fully embody the experience of being happy or sad, because that is what is being demanded of them by the script. Actors can evoke within themselves states of being so intense that they change their and our neurochemistry just by watching them, so they and we completely embody their chosen rehearsed experience.

This is a function that we all have access to. Why not use it for the benefit of ourselves, others, and ALL?

I personally find it very useful to think of becoming my C-IAM as similar to becoming a great improv actor, in that I know that it will take time for me to practice thinking, feeling, and acting according to my C-IAM until it becomes "natural" for me to *be* my C-IAM. I know that I have already memorized "the script" of my Reactive-iWAS, and that therefore, it feels natural and normal for me to think, feel, and act the way I always have in the past. I know that because my C-IAM has not been fully integrated into my identity (my sense of self), it will likely feel awkward, strange, contrived, and even "wrong" to think, feel, behave, and be my C-IAM at first. Still, because I value and choose to be the author of my own destiny, it is worth rehearsing again and again until I "nail the part" and remain "true to character" no matter what life throws at me (hence the "improv" part, because most of life happens off-script!).

When I make a powerful choice to embody my C-IAM and when I commit to deliberately following through on this resolve, I become a creative (instead of a reactive) being. This is the difference that makes all the difference. This is what enables my spirit to unfold as I explore, discover, learn, grow, and create the greatest possible outcomes and benefits. This is what reveals the JOLKA-GPS (joy, openness, love, kindness, awareness, gratitude, presence, and surrender). This is what activates the inherently beneficial qualities that are totally unique to who I am. When I am benefiting others to the best of my ability, that is when I feel personally satisfied with myself.

This brings me back to the "benefiting" questions I asked you earlier, during the C-IAM priming exercise. Consider them again.

1. When do you benefit yourself the most? When do you benefit others the most?
2. When do you benefit your living space the most?
3. How do you use your body in the most beneficial way, for yourself and others?
4. How do you communicate in the most beneficial way, for yourself and others?
5. How do you use your mind in the most beneficial way, for yourself and others?
6. Considering who you value and choose to be (your Creative-IAM) and your Neurochemical Roadmap to the Future You Value and

How to Find Joy
Even If You Have a Hole in Your Bucket

Choose (your NRF), how can you be the greatest possible benefit to yourself, others, and ALL?

Together, we thrive.

25
TRAUMA'S IMPACT ON THE REACTIVE-IWAS (AND WHAT TO DO ABOUT IT)

I F YOU HAVE TAKEN ON BOARD what you have read so far, that means you have a good understanding of how and why it is far more effective, compassionate, and kind to create solutions than it is to fix problems. It also means you understand that if you are attempting to "fix" your Reactive-iWAS, you will only make it stronger. "Don't think of a red X," will make you do just that. Have you ever focused on avoiding a pothole so hard that you've ended up actually slamming into it? This is just the way the mind works.

That said, for folks who have dealt with trauma (everyone to varying degrees) the decision to redirect their focus to their C-IAM is easier said than done. After all, nothing programs and "wires in" your Reactive-iWAS more than trauma. Trauma convinces you that you must remain in survival mode, "or else", and this way of being gets programmed deeply into our identity making mechanism.

I know firsthand what a tricky conundrum this presents. How the heck do I get into thriving mode when I feel like everything is constantly crumbling down around and inside me?

Here's the rub: your trauma induced wounds are actually physical (even if you understand them to be "mental" or "emotional"), because (as we have covered) there is no such thing as a difference between the body and mind. They are just two ways of looking at the same phenomenon. The good news is, just as your body knows how to heal a cut on your finger and does so automatically, so, too, does your nature know how to heal "psychological" wounds. Psychological wounds manifest in your neurochemistry and are not only stored as elaborate memory networks that branch out like spiderwebs to collect and more of your experience, but are also stored in your muscles, fascia, organs, bones, and the central nervous system; in how you breathe, hold your posture, talk, look, speak, think, emote, and perceive. If you attempt to fix one piece of the puzzle at a time, you will more than likely drive yourself crazy. When you solve one problem, ninety-nine others still overwhelm your gains. Thriving mode, on the other hand, is a salve that heals ALL *together* and we can "do the work" that I call Embodied Aliveness Trauma Transformation (EATT).

I must repeat a disclaimer here: before anyone starts to object and call this a system of denial or gaslighting, rest assured that my claim is that if you deny, reject, hate, or want to get rid of your problems, that means you are already coming from a survival mode orientation (meaning things will get worse and worse). Positive change starts with you walking through the doorway of radical acceptance. We *must* start here (i.e., where we are). Acceptance is the essence of kindness and the foundation of effective change work.

Acceptance does not mean liking, and it certainly doesn't mean condoning. It simply means accepting what is. Is it okay this happened, or that I feel this way about it? No.

Okay, then is it okay that it is not okay? Maybe! From that place of "okay," or acceptance, I can proceed, because the thriving mode door is now open. (Taking steps with this door closed only leads to headaches from us bumping our heads against it.)

As a word of warning: too many people mistake acceptance of what is for acceptance of their *stories* about what is. Take anxiety, for example: I accept that my heart is beating fast, I feel short of breath, there is tension in my chest, and I feel lightheaded. Those are all "ingredients" that generate the "dish" of anxiety. I can work with all those ingredients, and me just noticing them in an accepting way will often result in the reduction of these "symptoms" all by itself. But if I add stories about what is—"Why me?" "This is awful." "I hate this." "Please make it stop." "Am I having a heart attack?" "I am anxious because of *x, y,* and *z.*"—I will make matters dramatically worse. This is because these stories either exaggerate the symptoms or identify the "cause" of my feelings as something I can't influence—a sure way to make me feel disempowered and out of control and to ignite more fear, thereby elevating the survival chemicals coursing through my veins. (My body experiences this as confirmation of the "truth" of the story my mind is telling about why I (allegedly) feel anxious.)

Acceptance means paying attention to what is. This also means disengaging from what is *not* and shifting your attention from what you cannot influence (including the past or the future) to what you can (including the present). If you look at it honestly, you will be able to see the "story" is no different than a horror movie—and that you are free to walk out of the theatre at any time. What is, is rapid heart, short breath, tense muscles; what is not, is, "I am anxious because of this or that." Even if that is "relatively true," that is not functionally useful. If I stay with the ingredients: heartbeat, tension, breath, I can influence those and feel better, today, easily, without any gimmicks, in a totally sustainable way that makes perfect sense. If I keep focused on the "this or that", the anxious ingredients will boil over.

Acceptance also means accepting responsibility for what you *can* influence: the way you think, feel, and act in the present moment, and whether or not you stay glued to your seat, stuck in the thinking-feeling loop about why you feel this way or that way and why you can't do anything to help yourself.

An important note about this work: when you begin to deliberately create more thriving mode experiences, it is likely that some of your "stuff" will "come up" to be expelled, like pus from a wound. The key is to not re-act to this—or, perhaps more realistically, to notice that you are re-acting and to work to lessen the frequency, intensity, and duration of those re-actions, by checking and changing state and then pivoting toward your NRF, as your C-IAM. This process can look like this:

1. Name it to tame it. "I notice upset, and that means survival mode is activated."
2. Break it down to what it is. "No matter what kind of upset I am feeling, I know it is a type of energy. Energy is neither good nor bad. Whether it positively or negatively impacts me depends on whether I use it, don't use it, misuse it, or abuse it."
3. Own it. "This is *my* energy." Even if it's been stimulated by others, a memory, or a future worry, it is, right here and now, *my energy*.
4. Ask. "How am I going to use it? How would my C-IAM think, feel, act in this situation? What is the next, easiest step on my NRF that I am willing to take right now?"

The first statement ("I notice I am reacting and that survival mode is on") provides an experience of distance that enables you to pause and choose. Extra attention is, after all, "the portable pause," so if you've been practicing this, you should be getting better at noticing and finding more "space" to choose.

On the other hand, a response of, "Oh my God, the sky is falling," results in you losing yourself in the reactivity, blaming secondary circumstances for "your" anxiety, and missing out on the opportunity to turn a stop into a step.

If you welcome, allow, and touch the emotions that come with your reaction in the moment in which they arise (which I know may seem nuts, because we normally want to avoid this stuff at all costs), you can do yourself a tremendous kindness by letting it be "done with", or perhaps at least alleviated, and pivoting toward thriving.

Every discreet object or experience, from the perspective of Awareness, has a beginning, middle, and an end. Whatever you are experiencing will come to a natural completion and it all happens within Awareness. Awareness noticing the beginning of anxiety, Awareness noticing the middle, Awareness noticing the end. Awareness is the reliable constant. Anxiety is the temporary variable. When we shift our identity from "I am anxious" to "I am Awareness" we grow more steady and less reactive. We are able to watch things come, and go. Stephen Hayes tells us, "You cannot deliberately get rid of your psychological pain, although you can take steps to avoid increasing it artificially."[87]

The two ways we prolong pain and turn it into suffering are:

1. By hating it, rejecting it, resisting it, and trying to get rid of it.
2. By indulging in the stories about it that end up exacerbating it, because what we focus on grows.

What if we did neither of those two extremes? What if we hung out in the middle and simply noticed it, without resisting and without elaborating? After all, its beginning, middle, and end will come to a relatively rapid and natural conclusion *if* we don't prolong it by focusing on the stories that stoke the fire.

This is such an important concept that I have included a video explaining this phenomenon in Module 4.2 ("Emotional Intelligence Mistakes vs 'Being With'") in your book resources at www.alltogether.academy/joy-bucket-tools.

Can you see how turning toward your experience is the only way you can disengage survival mode? If I hate my symptoms, I am in SM (fighting). If I am afraid of my symptoms and look away from them, I am in SM (fleeing). If I am hiding from, numbing myself from, or denying my symptoms, I am in SM (freezing). When I stop fighting, running, and hiding, and I accept, go back to ground zero, and reset, I can, as Aware-Will, notice the beginning-middle-end and pivot toward thriving.

When you emotionally re-act, you literally create more of the same neurochemistry you are reacting to. In other words, you create more of the "upset" feeling. This is why you stay stuck. So, you must train your brain to

---

[87] Hayes, S. (2005): *Get Out of Your Mind and Into Your Life: The New Acceptance and Commitment Therapy*, p. 2 New Harbinger Publications.

Think → Feel → Act → Experience differently, especially in these pivotal moments. Train the brain or remain the same. Extra and open attention is the foundation of this work.

If you are not well practiced in remaining in the thriving states of being for longer and longer, then addressing trauma is counterproductive and deepens the wound.

I want to really emphasize this, as there are lots of immature therapists, advisors, influencers, or even friends who (usually with good intentions) encourage people to "process" or "vent" their trauma in ways that are potentially doing more harm. If the nervous system is overwhelmed when recounting a traumatic event, past, wound, or story (and is doing so with survival mode activated), then this exercise lays down more material in the already- potent neural network of that trauma (and strengthens the Reactive-iWAS). These therapists, advisors, and friends may think, *Oh, great, they are shaking and crying and raging. This means they are having a cathartic release,* but this may be the farthest thing from the truth. I have been very deliberate about setting up a foundation that will instead enable you to approach trauma from a position of empowerment, not as a victim of circumstance (even if you have been legitimately victimized).

I also hope I have been clear in the fact that the approach I am outlining in this book is not a macho approach, nor one that denies the fact that awful things that are beyond your control may happen (or may have happened) to you. Such experiences should certainly be viewed and treated with kindness, patience, compassion, and understanding. Still, framing your adversity as a challenge and opportunity instead of as an overwhelming threat is what works, and is the difference between whether you go on to experience posttraumatic stress symptoms or posttraumatic growth symptoms.

From this perspective of empowerment and personal responsibility for your own health and happiness, this chapter is about trauma resolution (which, in the end, is really about Reactive-iWAS resolution). This is the Way of Metabolism, and ultimately even trauma can be nourishment, when you learn to EATT (Embodied Aliveness Trauma Transformation).

As yet another disclaimer, I will add that it can be very useful, and sometimes even necessary, to work through traumatic material alongside a qualified professional. In reading this, you are now acknowledging that it is your responsibility to seek professional assistance if you need it and that this material does not substitute for professional care.

How the Brain Processes Memory and Experience: The "Hippocampus" versus the "Amygdala"

Before we begin, please note that here, we will be exploring workable, useful theories that help us to activate useful inner states of being. These inner states have beneficial effects and to activate them we can borrow from "neuroscientific" concepts and language in a way that is generalized or symbolic (hence the quotation marks around these terms). They do not necessarily constitute actual, exact explanations of the infinite factors that occur within the brain and body to orchestrate such practical changes and benefits. No doubt brain models will be updated and become outdated, as the nature of science and learning is to explore the unknown and grow beyond what we knew. Nevertheless, we can use the potency of linguistic understanding to help us make useful adaptations in our life.

Got it? Good. Let's get started!

The foundation for all the knowledge you're about to garner in this section is this: your brain is recording everything, 24/7, 365, and those recordings in different places and in different forms, depending on your state of being.

The "hippocampus" is responsible for *chronological* memory storage. Emphasis on *chronological*, as this is a key feature. The experiences that get put here are stored in a way where your entire brain and body knows how to make a distinction between now (the present moment) and then (your past experiences). When a certain memory has been stored in your "hippocampus," you know (not just intellectually, but neurochemically) that the situation is over and done with. The "amygdala," on the other hand, stores things in a "timeless" way for ever-ready triggering. It keeps the past ever- present on purpose. It is one thing for the mind to know that the trauma is over, but it is another for the body and brain to also know that the trauma is over. When your traumatic memories are stored in the "amygdala," on the other hand, it is possible for you to identify the past as "passed" intellectually, but not physiologically—your brain and body re-acts as if the threat is ongoing.

Here's the thing: if you are in survival mode, your brain stores every fragment of your "alarming" experiences in the "amygdala," which deeply programs your Reactive-iWAS. This results in you linking your past with your current Beliefs → Perceptions → Experiences about who you are and how "reality" is.

Why is this? Well, survival mode posits that everything that causes you alarm is potentially dangerous, and so your brain wants the Rolodex of everything you've experienced as "threatening" immediately at hand, constantly available for immediate recall. This means that instead of filing your scary memories away in the filing cabinet of the "hippocampus" (which is what happens to memories, "traumatic" or otherwise, when you are in thriving mode), the brain keeps all those experiences on "sticky notes" (in your "amygdala") right in front of your face so you can't forget about them.

Pretty soon, you accumulate so many sticky notes all over your desktop, bathroom mirror, and fridge that you can't even see ahead of you. You are completely overwhelmed by the distracting messages that are constantly bombarding your nervous system and flooding you with alarming thoughts, emotions, and sensations. There are simply too many "alert" notifications demanding your immediate attention. It's only a matter of time before you get frustrated, angry, and panicked (or before you shut down in overwhelm).

This piling up of "alerts" mostly doesn't happen on the conscious level, so you are likely to not be directly aware of the alerts themselves. You're much likelier to be aware of the *symptoms* of them. These may be anger, frustration, fear, anxiety, panic, worry, apathy, lethargy, insomnia, and inability to concentrate[88]. This impacts your state of consciousness and ability to think clearly, make good choices, and pursue goals. Perhaps most shockingly, it blocks your capacity to be healthy and happy entirely (remember, survival mode is only concerned with survival).

It's no wonder most of us are so tired and are continuing to not get good sleep to boot! Our systems are not only dealing with the fast pace of modern living and super- stimulation, but they are also overloaded with too many alerts stored in our "amygdala."

This is where the "work" comes in. One of the super keys to radical health and happiness, whether you identity with being "traumatized" or not, is moving the excess material that is gumming up your "amygdala" and causing you to re-act distressing thoughts, feelings, and emotions over and

---

[88] As a relevant aside: I think this is often what is going on in those with "ADHD." I've had dozens of clients (including myself) no longer meet ADHD criteria and leave medication behind after clearing out the "alerts" in their "amygdala." Jane, for example, who had had a potently traumatic experience, came to me specifically to "treat ADHD," and after eight months of working together, she asked me to write a letter so she could have her ADHD removed from her medical records. I gladly did this. Through our work together, she had developed a healthy capacity to focus.

over again into the "hippocampus."[89] I did a podcast episode on this topic, called "The Longevity Hack No One is Talking About", which you can find here: https://www.alltogether.academy/podcasts/the-boyling-point.

Memory Fragments

I briefly mentioned before that traumatic memory "files" are stored as "fragments," not "complete," whole representations of our past experiences. The reason for this is simple: your evolutionary design is intelligent enough to realize that the same exact experience never happens twice. So, if your alarm system needs to protect you from impending doom, then it would be useless for it to store whole (or even accurate) pictures or representations of the past. Instead, it must store bits and pieces of your alarming experiences so that any piece of the puzzle can trip your entire alarm system at any moment. This results in an experience called "state dependent triggering."

Here is an example:

Imagine someone named Tom had a traumatic experience at age seventeen. During that traumatic experience, the way the light came through the window and flashed in Tom's eyes for a brief second became stored in his "amygdala" as a fragment of that alarming experience. Tom's conscious brain never even noticed this flash of light, and Tom has not thought much about the accident in the twenty years since, never mind how the sun shone in his eyes for that split second.

One day, while at work, the sunlight through Tom's office window hits Tom's eyes at the same angle that it did during the traumatic event he experienced at age seventeen. Suddenly, he is having a full-blown panic attack. According to his nervous system, that accident is happening again *now*.

Remember, Tom has no conscious recollection of his original experience of sunlight flashing in his eyes twenty years before, so he has no idea what has triggered this sudden panic attack.

Tom's panic attack was triggered by his subconscious "raising the alarm"—by the automatic, immediate part of his brain—in less than a

[89] Hölzel, B. K., Carmody, J., Vangel, M., Congleton, C., Yerramsetti, S. M., Gard, T., & Lazar, S. W. (2011). Mindfulness practice leads to increases in regional brain gray matter density. Psychiatry Research: Neuroimaging, 191(1), 36-43.

second. This really complicates matters, because now, in the present-moment panic, Tom's brain is recording this "new" experience of a panic attack and associating it with his office, his job, and any other present-moment circumstances as the "cause" of his "panic." This recording is adding another layer of future potential triggers to Tom's alarm system Rolodex, which is now essentially a whole bunch of stories about why he ought to be anxious. So, even though the sunlight was the original trigger tied to a car accident he hasn't thought about since, Tom now (consciously and subconsciously) starts avoiding his workplace, his office, and any other factors that were identified as being a cause of this new "panic scenario."

Crazy, right?

This makes a lot about our daily lives finally make sense. It explains why you might start World War III when your partner doesn't replace the cap on the toothpaste, or why you might yell and flip someone the bird when you get cut off in traffic. It also explains why a lot of us are so exhausted all the time. Living like this is like having a brick on the gas pedal of your car even though it's parked. The engine is constantly "idling high," wasting gas and subjecting the parts to inevitable and constant wear and tear. Like a computer with too many windows and files open, you may find that you get worn down and that you freeze a lot. You may experience this as an "impending sense of doom" and a worldview that "what can go wrong, will go wrong," or maybe just as "generalized anxiety." Or perhaps you have a need to control everything, you "startle" easily, or you frequently yell at the people you love. Maybe you avoid intimacy, shut down in the face of vulnerable conversations, or feel a bit numb and lackluster about life.[90] You may find it hard to focus and get things done, and you may shy away from examining the goals and values that mean a lot to you.

If this is all going on fairly regularly, there's also a good chance you have, or will have, "physical health" problems, from digestive issues to chronic pain, heart issues, headaches, vertigo, and more. In fact, being in survival mode too much and too often is the cause of practically every disease.

Basically, the memory fragments stored in the "amygdala" wreak havoc on our lives, and they do all of this under the radar, while we blame whatever present-moment person or circumstance that seems to be the "cause" for why we are unhappy, unhealthy, or upset. All of this is liable to

---

[90] Did you notice, from your education in this book so far, that the past few sentences are explanations of common instances of the different aspects of fight, flight and freeze?

lead us to a process of infinite regress as we try to fix or eliminate present-moment "threats" and symptoms without addressing the underlying issue (an overburdened alarm system full of "fragments"). Unless we understand this phenomenon, learn to do the work to reprocess our "recordings," and store these in a filing cabinet where they are no longer demanding our attention, we are likely to stay stuck on the merry-go- round of suffering, no matter how valiantly we attempt to fix our problems.

Everything you have learned so far in this book is designed to accomplish the type of thriving that results in healing. Extra and open attention has been proven to physically shrink the "amygdala" and increase the size and processing speed of the "hippocampus."[91] I believe (and this is a useful belief) that this "shrinkage" happens because there are fewer memories in the amygdala, meaning there is less work for it to do, meaning it adapts its size accordingly. Think of this like psychological workouts: the parts you want to grow bigger (the "hippocampus") grow, and the parts that you want to trim down and get smaller and leaner (the "amygdala") do.

This movement of "files" from the "amygdala" to the "hippocampus" happens every time you don't re-act to a trigger, every time you shorten or minimize your re-action to a trigger, and every time you soothe yourself when you are upset (no matter what your outer circumstances are). This is how to EATT. Plus, getting into thriving mode activates innate healing capacities all by itself. This is why I can say confidently that when you focus on solutions in the present, the past is metabolized and heals all by itself. So, don't react to the re-action! This is something I tell myself regularly.

When you meditate, or when you check and change your state, or when you accept and "sit with" your thoughts and feelings without avoidance or embellishment, this is the difference that makes all the difference. You don't have to consciously reexperience or "process" all your traumatic memories. In fact, you probably don't even consciously notice most of the "fragments" that get "refiled." Yet you absolutely do feel lighter, clearer, more trusting and open, and happier. This is why I can liken your body's capacity to heal psychological wounds to its capacity to heal the cut on your finger: even if you do know the medical or scientific terms and explanation (the story) for *why* the hurt happened or why your skin all of a sudden has no sign of the cut, you don't *need* to have this knowledge for it to fully heal. That's miraculous!

---

[91] Taren, A. A., Creswell, J. D., & Gianaros, P. J. (2013). Dispositional mindfulness co-varies with smaller amygdala and caudate volumes in community adults. PLoS One, 8(5), e6457.

Most people take this for granted when it comes to physical cuts, but don't trust it can happen with psychological wounds. I'm here to tell you, it can. On the other hand, your "mental health" gets significantly worse when you focus on the problem, the past, the symptoms, and the trauma, kind of like the way your cut would get infected and not heal if you kept picking a scab with dirty fingers. This is why a lot of "therapy" and self-help culture doesn't really work and despite gains in de-stigmatizing mental health "issues", things collectively seem to be getting worse, not better.

A Tool for Managing Trauma: Minding the Gap

If there is a gap between a response that would be appropriate if you were facing the situation for the first time and the way you actually re-act, that means you are dragging the past into your perception of the present. In other words, you are reacting from and as your Reactive-iWAS. The solution? You need to "mind the gap."

Acting based on past experience isn't always a bad thing, and if you come from and as your C-IAM, you won't lose this capacity. It is very useful, for example, to remember that doorknobs open doors when they are turned (and to not have to learn that every time you approach a door). This mechanism becomes problematic, however, when you find yourself terrified every time you approach a door because you burned your hand on a doorknob many years ago.

We all do this kind of thing frequently, to varying degrees of intensity, so don't berate yourself for it (remember shame is a sign you are operating from survival mode freeze, and the most effective approach to shame is kindness). Again, it's not always a bad thing. We just want to prune the not-so-useful aspects of this function, like we would prune damaged limbs on a bush to help the flowers to bloom and the whole bush to thrive.

Anyone who is less "reactive" is more "enlightened." They meet situations anew and afresh, and their engagement in life is more spontaneous, lively, creative, and effective. Some research even suggests that advanced meditators "prune" the part of their brain that causes them to re-act to life through certain counterproductive filters entirely. [92]

---

[92] The reticular activating system and the default mode network, if you were curious!

Research also suggests that they are literally (neurochemically speaking) more present, because their Reactive-iWAS has been sufficiently pruned. [93]

Let's revisit an example I gave previously to illustrate this:

If you walk into the bathroom and find the cap is off your toothpaste, an appropriate first- time response would be for you to simply put the cap back on the toothpaste and walk away without another thought about it. When you walk into the bathroom and the cap is off the toothpaste "again," however, your blood starts to boil, and you start to activate the survival part of your brain that is responsible for saving you from tigers. Perhaps this has been a recurrent "issue" between you and your spouse. It also could be that you only said something to her about it one time before, yet you have an Reactive-iWAS that feels like it is "never listened to" (which was generated by your parents' dismissiveness), so this now feels like a personal affront.

You then start to tell yourself all sorts of stories to justify why you are so angry and why you view your partner as a predator: "She knows I hate it when she does this. I've asked her not to. She must just be trying to piss me off or disrespect me! Doesn't she know I have 'cap off the toothpaste issues?'" (Sounds a lot like the stuff most people think they are supposed to tell a therapist!)

We all do this frequently, so, I repeat, don't beat yourself up for it (and take my cheeky sense of humor with a grain of salt, please!). Do look around and consider where the "gaps" in your life are, though. Which situations are you (unnecessarily) using survival fuel to manage? "Overreacting," in the literal neurochemical sense, is like putting jet fuel into your Honda to go to the grocery store down the road: not only is it unnecessary, but it's actually going to damage your car (plus, it's expensive!).

The good news is that wherever there is a "gap" in your life, there is a tremendous amount of energy to EATT. You don't need Red Bull or three

[93] Brewer, J. A., Worhunsky, P. D., Gray, J. R., Tang, Y. Y., Weber, J., & Kober, H. (2011). Meditation experience is associated with differences in default mode network activity and connectivity. Proceedings of the National Academy of Sciences, 108(50), 20254-20259.... Pagnoni, G., Cekic, M., & Guo, Y. (2008). "Thinking about not thinking": Neural correlates of conceptual processing during Zen meditation. PLoS One, 3(9), e3083.
Tang, Y. Y., Ma, Y., Wang, J., Fan, Y., Feng, S., Lu, Q., ... & Posner, M. I. (2007). Short-term meditation training improves attention and self-regulation. Proceedings of the National Academy of Sciences, 104(43), 17152-17156.
Lutz, A., Slagter, H. A., Dunne, J. D., & Davidson, R. J. (2008).
Attention regulation and monitoring in meditation. Trends in cognitive sciences, 12(4), 163-169.

cups of coffee to thrive; your daily life has all the extra energy you need waiting around to fuel you up! You just need to redirect it to the things you value and choose, as your C-IAM and along your NRF. Very few things are more healing than living an inspired life rich with value and skill expression, purpose, and meaning! The energy that is currently being wasted on your survival approach to everyday life is the very energy that will not only heal you beyond logic and reason, but that will also allow you to create the new life you value and choose to have. This is the energy you need to go from being a caterpillar to a butterfly. This is also how, in a genuine way, you can feel grateful for the difficult moments in your life: you need this jet fuel if you are to launch a higher caliber life. It's a double-edged sword for sure, though: what you don't use to make you stronger can actually kill you—which is why doctors always say stress kills (even though they don't have a clue what to do about it).

I say we can rise over the very ground on which we once stumbled, turn stops into steps, and use the digestion of the reactive tension between where we are and where we want to be as the fuel we need to live up to our highest, most creative potential.

For now, don't even worry about the big stuff—the "issues" you aren't sure whether you should "let go" of. Instead, try this out with the small stuff. There are countless daily situations you are currently overreacting to (fact), like the cap off the toothpaste or the rage you feel when in traffic. When you reinvest that survival fuel you are wasting on these trivial matters into thriving mode, you gain tremendous power, vitality, and confidence. You can tackle the bigger "issues" when you feel ready to—or they might just disappear altogether while you're cleaning up your "amygdala!" Be open to that possibility—that you may just suddenly feel better without ever knowing how, or why, or where it came from, or where it went. This is especially likely if you are regularly practicing extra and open attention or yoga nidra. And may it be so, with grace and ease. The same way the cut on your finger completely disappears without a trace, without you knowing how or why, your "psychological" wounds can vanish into thin air the more you create the future you value and choose.

You are already doing what you need to do to resolve your trauma if you are implementing the tools and lessons you have learned in this book so far. Every time you notice you are upset and you flip the SafeSwitch to thriving mode, you are doing what you need to do. When you sprout your C-IAM, prune your Reactive-iWAS and its default survival mode reactivity (and all its concomitant suffering), and travel along your NRF, you may well be doing all the trauma work you need to. You do not necessarily need to understand, or have intellectual cognition of, the specific memories you are refiling from the "amygdala" to the "hippocampus." You might happen to already have this understanding, or a "memory" or "insight" may arise, but this is not necessary. Remember, the trauma stuff is stored as fragments that might not piece together sensibly anyway, and they are stored in the subconscious, so you may not even be aware of them.

Even though you might not "know" what memories you are reprocessing, it is important that:

- You know you are healing old wounds every time you change state from surviving to thriving (so long as you do so when it is context appropriate and in a way that values safety and healthy boundaries). Whenever you do so, you are not only successfully changing state and "mixing" new and improved ingredients into the present moment, but you are also simultaneously healing past wounds and making way for a better future. Pulling weeds, planting seeds. Pulling weeds, planting seeds.
- You celebrate your success every time you progress in the right direction. Direction is everything.

Another Tool for Managing Trauma: Tapping

I didn't come up with this tool, but it's a great one. It's informally referred to as "tapping" and is formally called "emotional freedom technique" (EFT).

As always, please consult with a professional healthcare provider for support as needed through this process.

Tapping makes use of acupressure points to help remove stress and blockages from the nervous system. Before you start to think this makes it "woo-woo," allow me to explain: is it fair to say that the nervous system is comprised of electric "channels?" I think the answer to this is pretty obvious. Otherwise, how does a pain message travel to your central nervous system once it has received the signal that you have stubbed your toe? If you didn't have "channels" that your impulses could travel through quickly, your mind wouldn't be able to communicate anything at all to your body. Plus, we know there are even more of these channels going from your body to your brain than from your brain (afferent nerves) to your body (efferent nerves), which is why it is more effective to EATT from what good trauma therapists call, "the bottom up." Body-based interventions for "mental" health simply work better, yet most "therapy" is a mental process. But I digress, back to channels!

How to Find Joy
Even If You Have a Hole in Your Bucket

Now that we can all agree that the nervous system operates through "channels," we can extrapolate information from the analogy of a river (which is a "channel" of water):

A river has its own innate flow and direction. When this flow is unobstructed, the river not only brings life to the valley, animals, environment, and atmosphere, but it also regulates its own health. Disease may arise within the river's ecosystem, but this is quickly balanced by the river's rising and falling levels of bacteria, algae, insect activity, movement, and flow. However, if a tree falls into the river, it will begin to snag other branches, leaves, rocks, and eventually even pieces of trash that are floating downstream. As more debris gathers, the water in that area starts to become stagnant, forming an "eddy" or pool. The flow of water is cut off, and the life downstream is no longer getting the vitality it is accustomed to. The stagnant pool has now become a breeding ground for mosquitoes and has a proliferation of toxic algae. These mosquitoes can now develop diseases that they can pass on to the surrounding community through their itchy bites.

This is what happens when we get stuck in emotional upset. We create a whirlpool of looping thoughts and emotions that grow more and more toxic. If we don't return to the flow of life, moving forward in a way that naturally heals us, this stagnancy eventually results in all kinds of physical and mental diseases.

To take care of this problem, we do not necessarily need to spray more toxic chemicals to kill the mosquitos—or if we do need to do that, we can at least also remove the obstruction, so we can fix the root issue.

When the river starts to flow freely again, the mosquitoes and algae get sucked downstream, becoming fish food, and the toxic stagnation is cleansed by the river's natural power and flow. Life and vitality return to the valley. All is well. Similarly, when we "tap" on certain parts of our body in certain sequences while thinking and saying certain things and activating our imagination in certain ways, we remove obstructions in our nervous system channels and create a natural capacity to heal and thrive.

There has been a solid amount of good research done on the efficacy of tapping. You can find some of this at psycnet.apa.org by searching for "tapping" or "EFT." Like yoga nidra (remember that?), this tool is something that the US Armed Forces have invested in for soldiers returning home with PTSD. In fact, I first learned about it from a colleague with whom I was co-facilitating a trauma therapy retreat for soldiers and spouses with PTSD with me. I mention this in case anyone reading is skeptical about these points or thinks it a little too "new agey." If it can help soldiers coming back from war, I think it is gritty and grounded enough for me!

If you've ever had acupuncture, then you will have experienced what it's like to "unblock" your channels in this way. "How did putting a needle in my foot immediately alleviate my headache?" The answer is channels. The specific points that you tap on are like power spots that, when flowing freely, can bring a tremendous amount of healing and vital energy through your entire system, just like when you clean the leaves out of one spot in a drain and the water once again flows smoothly throughout the entire system. When the nervous system channel's energy and information is flowing freely, healing and thriving downstream (and in the entire environment) is a natural result. The river doesn't need to "try" to heal and thrive, nor to solve its specific problems. In fact, some of what was a problem becomes an opportunity that makes the river's life stronger (like the fish that can feed on the extra mosquitos that are sucked downstream when the stagnation is released). When obstructions are removed, healing and thriving happen automatically. It is intrinsic to the river's natural design.

When you are tapping, "stuff" may "come up," and this may feel alarming. But if you maintain extra and open attention and an attitude of welcoming acceptance throughout the entire session, this "stuff" will get digested in the flow of lifeforce and become stored in the "hippocampus," where it can no longer wreak havoc.

As another disclaimer, I will add once again here that it can be very helpful to have a guide while you are tapping. There are also biosocial and generational trauma conditions that may make it difficult to work through trauma. I encourage you to stay in touch with a local licensed professional to assist you with any possible complications.

Tapping Resources

There has been much research into tapping, and, like in all good research, the variables were all isolated to see what (if any of it) actually works in a statistically significant way. Tapping has various components (which you will see when you watch me demonstrating in the video in Module 10.1 if your book resources at https://www.alltogether.academy/joy-bucket-tools), and these were all accounted for separately.

In the video in Module 10.1, I show you the sequence and wording I value and choose to use when using this tool. There are lots of other resources available on this topic online, and I am not attached to you using "my" style. I *am* invested in you doing the work in whatever form works best for you.

In many cases, you will see people tapping with one hand on one side of their body. I personally find that the process is enhanced for me when I use two hands and both sides of my body, for bilateral brain stimulation. I use one hand and one side only to tap whenever my daughter is nestled in my other arm (we often tap together before she falls asleep). I also sometimes alternate between one hand and one side of the body, the other hand and the other side of the body, and both hands and both sides at once. It is good to experiment and be flexible. Do what works best for you. You can also head to positivepsychology.com/eft-tapping to learn more about tapping (no affiliation). My wife, children and I also take advantage of The Tapping Solution mobile app (with Nick and Jessica Ortner) pretty much every day.[94]

There are lots of different phrases that can be used when tapping. I used to use the phrase, "Even though I am feeling *x*, I allow myself to feel *y*." I thought I needed to control the direction of my "river" by telling it what I wanted to feel, instead of what I was feeling. Sometimes, that's a good idea, but what I have learned since is that I don't always need to do that. In fact, that might get in the way of nature's wisdom. Now, I say, "Even though I am feeling *x*, I accept that this is happening," or more simply, "I notice this emotion/sensation." Remember, the beauty here is that by *not resisting* and simply "being with" what is happening (combined with the tapping), I restore the flow of life. This moves the "stuck" energy through my nervous system, which automatically results in feelings of relief, release, joy, and contentment.

There is nothing wrong with experiencing negative emotions. It is when these emotions get *stuck*—when we get attached to the stories and reasons about *why* we are upset—that we foster the breeding ground for mental, emotional, spiritual, and physical illness. This also sets the stage for the Reactive-iWAS to get "wired in," so that we Believe → Perceive → Experience through the lens of our various upsets (which results in us Thinking → Feeling → Doing → Becoming → Being the various reactive identities we associate with survival).

Controlled, blind, peer-reviewed, and validated research with meta-analyses from independent professionals demonstrate statistically significant decreases in depression, anxiety, PTSD, and cortisol (the survival

---

[94] I have absolutely no affiliation with this app and do not benefit from suggesting this in any way (other than knowing you may benefit from using it).

mode distress hormone) in those who tap.[95] Tapping may also contribute to what I call "amygdala shrinkage" (i.e., alarm switch shrinkage) and "hippocampus activation." It may clear out the reactive filters of the Reactive-iWAS so that you are less easily "triggered" and more able to Believe → Perceive → Experience according to what you value and choose (as your C-IAM traveling along the NRF).

The point I want to draw out of the research I have read on tapping is, while all the components of tapping (the acupressure points, the sequence, the bodily sensations, and the statement) are part of the whole package that is proven to work amazingly, some studies have been done to isolate each component, and I have found through research and my own experience that the flowing awareness of your bodily sensations while tapping on the designated points is most important.[96] So, by all means, use all the components, but sometimes I personally get distracted by the statement/cognitive part and I get stuck in my head thinking of what I should say. In those moments, I remember to focus just on the tapping and my extra and open attention (the arising bodily sensations and my awareness of myself in space). I get great results doing this.

Like I said, it is normal for stuff to "come up" when you are tapping. In fact, it is ideal. It is coming up to be healed. It is coming up to be "completed." My hope is that you have had enough training with the material covered in this book so far to not get stuck on the stories and images that arise. Remember, the question is not whether they are valid, true, or historically accurate (they may or may not be); the question is whether they are *useful* and whether you want *more* of them. Letting go of whatever arises and clearing out the old debris in the "amygdala" can be very useful, like clearing a branch in the river dam that loosens up the whole stagnant pool. Noticing and releasing the tension associated with the "thing" that has come up can unlock wisdom and healing that you didn't even know was possible. If your frame of mind embraces this, then that is what can happen. If, on the other hand, you grab onto what arises, have

---

[95] For an example of one such study, please see Beer, J. (2023): "EFT Tapping: The Psychology Behind Tapping Therapy." Retrieved on November 25, 2024 from positivepsychology.com/eft-tapping
[96] Sebastian, B., & Nelms, J. (2019). The effectiveness of emotional freedom techniques in the treatment of psychological conditions: A meta-analysis. Explore: The Journal of Science and Healing, 15(1), 18-30.... Diepold, J. H., & Goldstein, D. (2013). The effectiveness of meridian tapping for reducing test anxiety: A controlled pilot study. Energy Psychology: Theory, Research, & Treatment, 5(2), 3-14

strong emotional reactions about what arises, and attach stories to your identity about what is arising (making it "mine" and about "me"), it can take you downstream and over the edge of the waterfall.

Trauma's Impact on the Reactive-iWAS: A Case Study

I was tapping the morning I wrote this because I was feeling triggered. My son had just injured himself, and this had triggered a ton of panicky Reactive-iWAS feelings. Tapping as a tool was on my mind because of my writing, and I wanted to reduce my stress and increase my trust in the likelihood that he would be fine and that "this, too, shall pass," so I chose to tap it out.

While I was tapping, an image and name of a person I'd known in sixth grade popped into my mind. I had never been friends with this person and had had no meaningful interactions with him ever (other than those which are standard for a classmate in a large public-school setting). I neither disliked nor liked him in particular and had not thought of him for a single second since middle school—until this morning.

I noted these thoughts and the image of his face and had the thought, *That's strange. Why am I thinking about that kid?* I kept tapping and tracking my bodily sensations. Then, a scene—a memory—popped into my mind. In it, another classmate (who I also hadn't known very well or thought about since that time) got a compound arm fracture in gym class. Blood was squirting everywhere. There was panic and screaming. I had not thought of this experience since it had happened in the sixth grade, and I'd certainly had no idea it was influencing how nervous I was about my son's injury. I also had no idea why me thinking of the previous random classmate had led to me remembering this girl's broken arm in gym class (he, the girl, and the incident have no connection that I am conscious of). Regardless, I went with it all, still tapping and feeling, and within a short time, I realized I was no longer afraid of my son's situation and could clearly see that he was fine and that it was actually no big deal. In short, I was overreacting. There was a huge gap between what was actually happening and my re-action to it. Unknown to me, that gap had to do with random memories that I never even knew had been stuck in my "amygdala." When I cleared those memories in a state of thriving, they were refiled in my "hippocampus" (which I know, because I can still consciously choose to recall those memories without there being any emotional charge associated with them whatsoever). From then, I was able to respond to the actual situation in the present moment, free from the influence of the past, in a way that benefited not only me, but also my son, wife, other children, career, and immune system (because I was no longer freaking out and was back in thriving mode).

Trauma's Impact on the Reactive-iWAS: Recap

- Nothing programs and "wires in" your Reactive-iWAS more than trauma, as it convinces you that you must remain in survival mode, "or else."
- If your nervous system is overwhelmed when recounting a traumatic event, past wound, or story (meaning, your survival mode activated), then talk therapy or "venting" lays down more material in the already-potent neural network of that trauma (and strengthens your Reactive-iWAS).
- Your brain is recording everything 24/7, 365. Depending on your state of being, your brain stores fragments or whole recordings of those recordings in different places, respectively. If you are in survival mode, it stores fragments in the "amygdala"; if thriving, whole memories go in the "hippocampus." The former deeply programs your Reactive-iWAS such that your past filters your current Beliefs → Perceptions → Experiences.
- One of the super keys to radical health and happiness, whether you identify with being "traumatized" or not, is moving the excess material that is gumming up your "amygdala" and causing you to re-act distressing thoughts, feelings, and emotions over and over again to the "hippocampus."
- Wherever there is a "gap" in your life between a Reactive-iWAS re-action and a C-IAM response, there is a tremendous amount of energy to reclaim. Your daily life has all the extra energy you need waiting around to fuel you up, as long as you can EATT (Embodied Aliveness Trauma Transformation) it. This is the very energy that will not only heal you beyond logic and reason, but that will also allow you to create the new life you value and choose to have. This is the energy you need to go from being a caterpillar to a butterfly.

Trauma's Impact on the Reactive-iWAS: Homework

Experiment with "tapping." Find a YouTube video you like, use my example linked earlier in this chapter, or get The Tapping Solution app (a relatively expensive option, as far as apps go, but worth it, in my opinion), and dive in.

26
KINDNESS, SURRENDER, AND GETTING "UNSTUCK"

THIS CHAPTER COULD HAVE BEEN CHAPTER 1, as it contains what could be perhaps the most important concepts for how to make the work "work," but I believe it's ideal to work it from both ends.

Effortful Surrender

The work will work best if you do so while in a state of "effortful surrender." "Effort" is everything you've learned thus far; "surrender"(the last aspect of the JOLKA-GPS) is what we will now address.

Note that surrender does not mean resignation (this is the counterfeit, depressed version of surrender). It also doesn't mean gaslighting (by way of the spiritual new age) or denying (according to the macho attitude of yesteryear). Surrender is at the intersection of radical self-acceptance, radical acceptance of the forces beyond my control, and radical responsibility for showing up to what is next, with as much C-IAM as I can muster, while activating the thoughts, feelings, and behavior of my NRF. It is truly "letting go" (surrendering) of what is not in our control that activates the magic of thriving mode, which ironically makes us more powerful and better able to be a beneficial influence. And, this takes real courage.

How many times have you noticed something has happened right when you stopped trying to force it? The moment you stopped chasing the girl, she came to you. The moment you stopped worrying about the results, they came back positive. A lot of us struggle until we are exhausted, surrender, get good results, and failing to realize we can skip the "struggle" and "exhausted" parts and go straight to "surrender" and "good results."

An important note: just because this way of being is about not struggling doesn't mean it's easy. Most of us are control addicts! Thinking, feeling, and acting differently; letting go of old wounds and trauma; becoming someone new; opening up and surrendering not only requires a tremendous amount of support, skill, perseverance, and dedication, but also a ton of guts. Anyone who thinks this a big exaggeration and that psychospiritual growth work doesn't take courage simply hasn't done the work and is probably mostly in the survival modes of anger (which manifests as criticism and control), fear (which manifests as running away and avoidance), and freeze (which manifests as numbness, denial, and apathy).

The fact is, everything in life fits into two categories: "stuff I can control" and "stuff I can't control." Hence, it's a very simple and effective cognitive exercise to simply ask, "Is this in my sphere of influence?" If so, go! If not, no!

The catch is, even the stuff that I *can* control (primarily, the way I think, feel, and act) won't be managed effectively if I handle it in a controlling way. The results, their timeliness, and *how* they come about will often not be in my control. I don't make the acorn turn into an oak tree (but I can give it the right conditions to facilitate that potential). We can only control what we can control. Short tells us, "We cannot be responsible for the world. To be responsible for the world is to become a victim of responsibility."[97] Furthermore, if I am even subtly trying to control others (even with "good intentions"), that's not benefiting anyone; it's manipulation. Even if it is me I am trying to control in harsh or critical ways, it won't end well: I will rebel against my own efforts and "self-sabotage."

I think of effortful surrender like growing a beautiful garden. My job is to plant seeds, pull weeds, cultivate the soil, plant complimentary fruits and veggies, learn about the seasons, manage shade and sun exposure, and minimize toxic invasions. It is not my job to create the fruits and flowers themselves. That is not in my control. That's "God's" job. I can benefit from the process of joyfully and diligently creating an environment where fruits and flowers are *likely* to show up, but at the end of the day, lightning might strike a tree that falls in my garden and wipes out my whole crop. If or when this happens, I can lick my wounds for some time, if that helps, but I can also look for opportunities. Maybe I can add a tree trunk feature in my garden, or let it compost, grow fungus, and become a home for beneficial species.

---

[97] Lowenthal, M. & Short, L. (1993): *Opening the Heart of Compassion: Transform Suffering Through Buddhist Psychology and Practice*, p.68. Tuttle Publishing.

Effortful surrender means knowing I can *influence* my life for the better, but that I am not *in control* of it.

Control versus Influence

I will admit that despite my Boston-based, hyper intellectual, highly educated, skeptical upbringing, I like many of the "truths" about the law of attraction. As we have learned, our beliefs really do color our perceptions and play a part in generating our experience of life. However, a major problem with the new age version of the law of attraction is that there is such a false sense of control in it. And so much "me!" "My truth." "My experience." "I created this." "I created that."

Please.

Do you make your heart beat? No. Can you influence it? Yes. There is a huge difference here.

Do you make apples grow? No. Can you influence this process? Yes. There is a huge difference here.

Don't get me started on the jerks who shame people (and likely themselves) for "manifesting their cancer or trauma." The facts are, there are forces at play that are way bigger than us. The new age version of the law of attraction is a psychological defense mechanism against this. It is an attempt to cope with the reality that we really are not in control of a lot (like whether we will wake up in the morning). Besides, a little humility goes a long way. Knowing your actual role is both honest and empowering. In fact, it's a huge relief! If you think you are lord and master of the universe, that's a lot of pressure. Heck, you can't even control what you will eat today beyond what's available in your kitchen (or a nearby restaurant, if you are immensely privileged)!

Some prefer "cocreator" lingo. I can see that perspective a little more, but still, it can sound very egocentric some of the time. The way I see it, it's more like this: creation (in the human sense) means I have the capacity to manage my attention and organize my body, mind, emotions, and actions in such a way that more grace, ease, serendipity, and wonder abounds in my life. This increases my ability to benefit myself, others, and ALL and to receive what feels like grace and the miraculous. (For the miraculous, I need to look no further than my beating heart, my digested food, a healed cut, a crispy apple, the rising sun, a drop of rain, the healing power of love, and the fact that I can choose to smile.) Of course, wild and miraculous things do happen "out of the blue," but we didn't *create* those things, and we certainly aren't in *control* of them, even if we can make ourselves open to experiencing the "miraculous" more and more.

These mechanisms come with the fortune of our life, which we can't take credit for. Life arises from the unknown, and despite those who think we "manifested our birth," we actually had nothing to do with it. Can you imagine the hubris of thinking you organized the zillions of cofactors that resulted in your conception, let alone your gestation, birth, and the family you were born into? Most of us can't even organize our to-do lists for the day!

There is a difference between creating the toy and being able to play with it.

We are damn lucky that we get to play with creation for our benefit and to be able to optimize our experience. However, knowing our place and our limits keeps us from having the counterfeit experience of a "divine ego" (i.e., narcissism—and I don't just mean the pathological type). Such an ego blinds us from the humble recognition that, as one of the infinite expressions of "divinity," we can value and choose to harmonize with that which is living us, and that we can therefore become likelier to experience a miraculous, joyful life that uplifts ALL.

The "Okay" Corral

We briefly touched on this in Chapter 25, but I'd like to reintroduce it in the context of kindness as a type of surrender, which is really acceptance of what is.

A very simple tool for "acceptance" (which is a type of surrender and true kindness) is to ask, "Is this okay?" If the answer is "yes," then work from there. If the answer is "no," then ask, "Is it okay that it's not okay?" If the answer is "yes," then work from there. If the answer is "no," then ask, "Is it okay that it's not okay that it's not okay?" Keep going until it's okay. This doesn't mean you like it or condone it, or that you won't work to change it. It means that you are now in a place of acceptance, which is, ironically, where you need to be to effect change.

Scheduling It

"Scheduling it" is another "surrender" tool my clients love. It seems basic or even silly, but it works really well. It is also great for when your "upset" states are permeating your life in a way that is both counterproductive and contrary to your aims and values. It looks like this:

1. Schedule at least two fifteen-minute periods in the day to be upset for: one in the morning and one in the evening. You can add a third for midday, if you need.

2. During these "upset sessions," set a timer and then really let it rip. Exaggerate, awfulize, and dramatize—literally: act it out with gestures, sounds, and so on. Don't hold back!

3. Go for the entire fifteen minutes. At around the seven- or eight-minute mark, you'll probably start thinking, *I'm done. This is ridiculous.* Keep going anyway. Exhaust it.

4. When your timer goes off, say, "I am done with this for now. It is time for me to move forward with my life. If these thoughts and feelings come up again and interrupt my day, I will tell them, 'Not now. You can have your time later, in our next session.'"

5. Every time your upset feeling arises again, nip it in the bud and say, "Nuh-uh, not right now. I am living my life. You have your scheduled time at our next session," or "Not right now. I am going to sleep. You have your scheduled time in the morning. Goodnight."

This is a kind approach in that it gives space for the tough stuff that we all inevitably face, while also allowing you to keep taking positive steps in your life so that you can digest and heal from it all.

After a few days or weeks of doing this formally and following the "rules," you may find that you naturally become able to compartmentalize more organically, spontaneously, and healthily. This means you can put the tough stuff away and get on with things, and then come back to it and digest it one bite at a time when you feel ready to. *Unhealthy* compartmentalizing (which is more the norm) means you never come back to the tough stuff, leaving it to fester in some dark corner of your psyche. This isn't good. Sure, a moderate level of shit will turn to fertilizer if it's left alone in the ground, but a septic tank that has exploded needs containment and a strategy.

Sometimes, life explodes, but by scheduling it, you can deal with it (and the rest of your life) with kindness, skill, and effectiveness.

Kindness, are you a horse whisperer or whipper?

If you whip a horse into shape, it might perform for you in the short-term, but it's going to kick you in the head as soon as it gets the chance. If you use fear and punishment to train a dog, it may obey you with a broken spirit (is that what you want for your dog?), but it will shit on your rug and tear up your furniture when you aren't looking. It is far more effective to be a horse whisperer or dog whisperer than it is to be a horse or dog beater, even if the whip does give you some temporary results.

I'd guess this sentiment already makes complete sense to you and aligns with your personal beliefs... in the context of literal animals. Yet in all likelihood, you still think you need to "whip yourself into shape" and "beat yourself up" if you want to *get* better and *be* better.

How's that working out for you?

As it turns out, the part of your brain where habits and emotions live has the same structure as the part of the brain where horse's or a dog's habits and emotions live.

Throughout this book, I have said you are empowered to make radically positive changes in your health and happiness, and that kindness is the only way to go. That in mind, it is kind to give yourself space to feel shitty feelings, and it is also kind to say, "That's enough for now." It is harmful to avoid and deny your upsets, but it is also harmful to wallow and drown in shit. It is kind to "be with it," and also kind to cut that shit out. It is kind to do the next, easiest thing you are willing to do and to not try to force things or struggle. You change better by feeling better, and when you ask the grace and ease question ("What is the next, easiest thing that I am willing to do?"). You can feel better today, easily, without any gimmicks, in a totally sustainable way that makes perfect sense.

Troubleshooting: When We Get Stuck

Every time I get a call or an email from a client stating they are not doing well, I always think this is down to one of two things (or, usually, both):

- They stopped using the maps, tools, and instructions (MTIs).
- They are in the downslope of the progressing loop.

Let's explore both options.

When We Stop Using the Tools

When I look honestly at my own life, I can see clearly that when I am suffering, that means I am not working. I have stopped using the tools. This doesn't mean I never experience pain, misfortune, or discomfort when I *am* doing the work, but it does mean I am not *suffering* for it (or at not as much as I would be if I completely stopped using the MTIs).

It's a funny thing about us humans that we stop doing the stuff that we know makes us feel better, and then wonder why we feel bad. My clients who have been around for a while sometimes call me, already laughing (a good sign of maturity), and say, "Mike, I am stuck again because I am not using the tools." It happens to the best of us, and here is where it most definitely works better to be a horse whisperer than a horse whipper. Beating ourselves up (fight) is a survival mode re-action, and it can only result in us fighting back (self-sabotage/anger), avoidance (flight/fear) or hiding, or numbing out or feeling stuck in shame (freeze).

"What's the next, easiest thing I am willing to do to get back on the NRF?"

If you find yourself feeling stuck, the only thing you need to know about what's wrong is that this happens to everyone (it's not your fault) and that it's not what you value, and that it's therefore time (it's your response-ability) to choose something else. Once you realize this, you can pivot back to your C-IAM and travel down your NRF. This is what will logically lead to more of what you value and choose to have. Yes, this choice may need to be made ten thousand times with joyful diligence before it becomes your new "easy and automatic," but it will still work every time if you persist.

The Progressing Loop: Practice Makes Progress

The progressing loop is an advanced version of "five steps forward, two steps back." Here's how it works:

You can only ever start where you are. Let's call that level one. In level one, you are excited and motivated to level up, and in your excitement, you shoot past level two and have experiences that are above and beyond what you are ready to deal with as your new norm. You explore new heights and discover new things; you learn new tools and come across more resources; you create new and more desirable ways of thinking, feeling, acting, and experiencing... and then you hit a test or a shell (remember the chick analogy in Chapter 21). You encounter old habits and patterns that used to trip you up. This is your opportunity to apply the new tools, perspectives, resources, motivation, and inspiration that you gained by shooting past level two. You go "back" to level two, newly resourced. You now think, feel, and act differently today than you would have if you faced the same stimulus yesterday. You consolidate and integrate your new ways of thinking, feeling, and acting into the very situations that used to be a stop. By doing so, you turn them into a step and find solid footing on level two. You enjoy this plateau for a while and feel like you are good, steady, improved, and on solid ground—and then you feel inspired to level up again. This progressing loop repeats itself, over and over, level by level, for infinity.

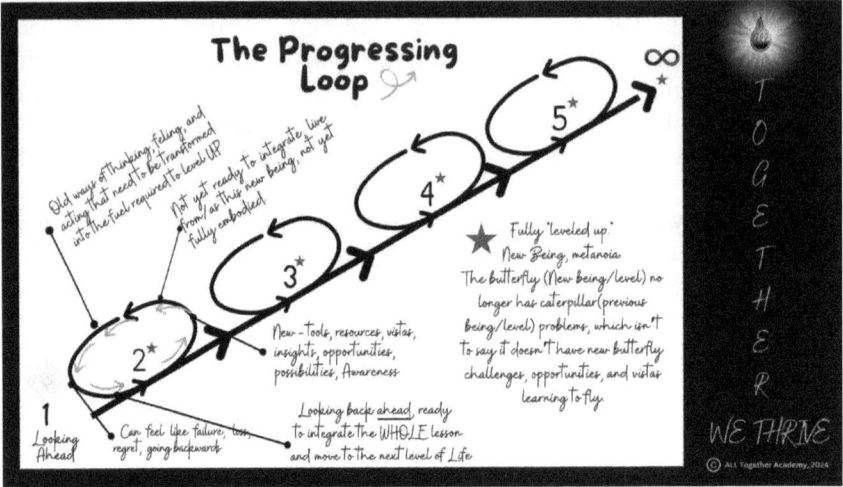

It may appear at times like you are going backwards, and since this is no *Pollyanna* approach, I will say that sometimes, you might be. We go backwards when we re-act with all sorts of crimes against wisdom, such as by beating ourselves up, binging Netflix, going back to the bottle, buying into the "overwhelm" story, fighting life, running away from our responsibilities, and hiding from the ongoing work of stepping up. When we stop using our MTIs, we can (and do) downgrade our experience of life. Staying in survival mode too long can actually kill us. This is inevitable and will also happen to the best of us, and the only effective, kind, rational thing to do in response is:

1. Pause in extra and open attention.
2. Invoke your C-IAM.
3. Ask, "What's the next, easiest thing I am willing to do get back on my NRF?"

Here is the genius of it: when you transform the thoughts, emotions, actions, and behaviors you are exhibiting while you're on the downslope, you give yourself the very fuel you need to thrust yourself upward to the next level of becoming and being (no matter how far "back" you have slid). When you realize you cannot progress without the shit that you need to make fertilizer, you learn to not only stop hating your adversity, but to also smile and say, "Thank you! Thank you!"

The easy stuff in life is great—enjoy it while it's here and get some R&R!—but it's not where you grow. You grow in challenge. You *require* challenge. Lead becomes gold. Shit becomes fertilizer. Gas becomes rocket fuel. When you turn stops into steps, you rise over the very ground on which you once stumbled, and you climb to heights you never would have been able to reach if you hadn't faced the adversity in the first place.

Zones of Growth

To continue the topic of kindness, Dr. Andrew Huberman tells us that the optimal zone for growth is when we are "getting it right" eighty-five percent of the time and "getting it wrong" fifteen percent of the time[98]. In case you were wondering, that's a solid B for you perfectionists out there—and that solid B is optimal. Getting straight As in the curriculum of life means that it's too easy and that you are slowing down your progress! (I find that really funny.)

Growth is uncomfortable, sure, but it is also not unbearable or overwhelming (these feelings are counterproductive to growth).

At any given moment, you can assess whether you are in:

- Zone 1: Rest and Recovery. This zone is easy to be in. It indirectly supports growth through repair. If you spend too much time here, though, you atrophy. Consider, "Is it appropriate for me to be in Zone 1 right now, or have I been hiding out on Easy Street?" If appropriate, enjoy! If hiding out, go get uncomfortable!
- Zone 2: Challenge. This zone is moderately difficult and uncomfortable, but you have the skills and aptitude to succeed eighty-five percent of the time when you are in this zone. The fifteen percent of the time you get it wrong is your growth zone; a place where you recalibrate after the mistake, failure, or loss. If you

---

[98] Huberman, A. (Host). (2023, June 19). *How to Learn Faster by Using Failures, Movement & Balance | Dr. Andrew Huberman* [Audio podcast episode 78]. In Huberman Lab

want to grow, you can hang here as much as you want, because any adversity coming your way is making you stronger. Naturally, you will choose to dip back into Zone 1 for R&R sometimes, and that's okay. Zone 2 is (necessarily) uncomfortable.

- Zone 3: Overwhelm. This zone is counterproductive to growth and harmful. You don't ever need to enter this zone on purpose, as life will put plenty of this on your plate without your permission. You will inevitably find yourself here. When you do, you can shift into Zone 1 for some R&R so that you can get back into Zone 2 for optimal growth. My mentor's teacher would say, "If you are in hell, don't stop there!" Purposefully get yourself some extra Zone 1 or build your muscles so you can work skillfully with what's arising from within Zone 2.

This is a really simple tool that my clients have benefited from greatly. We use it regularly in our sessions to cement the more complex ideas and tools: is this situation or feeling Zone 1, 2, or 3?

27

BONUS CHAPTER: THE RELATING RENAISSANCE

FOR YOU TO HAVE HEALTHY RELATIONSHIPS of all kinds, you need to regularly invoke and revisit your Creative-IAM. Without your C-IAM, you will often fall onto the continuum of codependence, which is characterized by the victim-perpetrator-rescuer triangle and which is dictated by the reactivity of your Reactive-iWAS.

The topic of healthy relationships (what they are and how you can build them) will be covered in more detail in the next book in this series. For now, it is enough for you to know that by doing the work that will allow you to create and cultivate your C-IAM, you are exploring, discovering, learning, growing, and creating the type of wholeness that allows for the highest potential of interdependent relating. Still, I would like to link some of the basic ideas covered in *The Relating Renaissance* to the content we have covered here, to give you a little taster of how the next book in this series could unfold new worlds of potential for you and your relationships.

Survival Mode and Relationships

When an incomplete person (belief, not truth) connects with another incomplete person and they both attempt to rectify one another's basic sense of "lack" (think "you complete me"), it works kind of like multiplying fractions: ½ * ½ = ¼. In other words: Reactive-iWAS * Reactive-iWAS = *Kaboom!* The two come together and activate the other's wounding, and both parties enter a realm of diminishing returns as a result. This is how we come to objectify another person: by treating them (and ourselves) as commodities that can fill us up, fix us, and make us feel whole. Only, it never works like that. Alternatively, when a whole person comes together with another whole person, they create something bigger and better than the sum of their individual parts. In this case, the math is illogical and exponential: $1 + 1 = 8$ (8 being "infinity" in this equation).

My point is this: did you know that "communication issues" are not what's in the way of your relationships thriving? I know this sounds crazy. You're probably very used to hearing about how you just need "better communication" to solve your marital problems, rekindle the love and trust in your relationship, and reawaken your intimacy. But no. While communication is important, it does not play the role you may think it does, or at least not in the *way* you may think it does. So, what is the big secret; the lynchpin; the key you need to have to unlock the mystery of lasting love, trust, connection, and joy? It's the neurobiological facts we have covered in this book. Nothing communicates more loudly than your state of being!

You can "consciously" and "effectively" communicate until you're blue in the face—how many times have you stayed up all night doing so?—but as long as your nervous system is stuck in survival mode, it does not matter what you say or how you say it. Your partner will say, "I love you," and you will think, *Why is she smothering me and trying to control me?* "I need some space," will become, *She doesn't love me. She's abandoning me. She's rejecting me.* "I'm tired and need to get some sleep," will become, *He doesn't want me anymore.* The ways in which you can misinterpret your partner's intentions, words, desires, and beliefs are endless. You misperceive sticks to be snakes, and talking about them more so you can "get clarity" or "reach an understanding" is like a dog chasing its tail around and around, to dizzying proportions.

When your brain is in survival mode, it lies to you and interprets everything in the worst possible light (due to your evolutionary default negativity bias). In other words, when you are upset for any reason, your brain is a big fat liar, and while you may feel "your truth" very intensely, your interpretations are decidedly skewed toward the negative and are, quite literally, not accurate. Instead, they are the result of deletions, distortions, and exaggerations that fit into your Reactive-iWAS → B-P-E → Thinking → Feeling → Doing → Becoming → Being. Most of our "communications" (even, and perhaps especially, with the people we love and feel most vulnerable with) are merely attempts for us to prove ourselves right based on faulty premises. And when both people in the equation are operating from their Reactive-iWAS, things escalate quickly. We end up hurting each other for real, based on interpretations that are false. We argue about snakes that are really sticks, and in so doing, we end up spewing real venom.

How to Find Joy
Even If You Have a Hole in Your Bucket

This is not your fault. Your brain is designed to assume the stick is a snake... and then to be relieved when it realizes it's just a stick.

This mechanism is fine in the jungle. It sucks for marriage.

The main thing to understand here is that your brain, when in survival mode, experiences even the people you love as either a competitor or a predator. This means that no matter how well intentioned you are or how clearly you communicate, your conversations and marriages will always devolve back into "win-lose," "lose-win," and "lose-lose" consciousness.

Once again, this is not your fault. This is all that a brain in survival mode *can* do. As we went over in detail at the beginning of this book, it is perfectly natural for a brain in survival mode to attack and defend, preserve itself at all costs, and perceive danger anywhere and everywhere (even in the people you love the most). Thankfully, though, you can upgrade your brain and partnership from the default manufacturer's survival version to thriving mode.

This is huge. This is empowerment.

The problem is, we don't give ourselves the chance to do this, because we don't "stop the bleeding," so to speak (which, by the way, is Module 1 of my "Relating Renaissance" program). We keep talking about our problems, going to therapy about our problems, praying for a cure, and "processing," but all of this is done from survival mode. This only guarantees that we'll keep hurting ourselves and each other and that we'll never have a chance to heal and thrive.

How can we expect a wound to heal if we keep picking at the scab? Even a tiny cut, if interfered with enough, can get so infected that we need to amputate a limb to save our life. Similarly, a perfectly wonderful marriage could become so toxic it needs to be terminated, all because we've continued to spit real venom about fake snakes.

When we deliberately turn off survival mode, we "stop the bleeding," and when we activate thriving mode, we not only create the chemistry of love, trust, joy, autonomy, and connection, but we also give ourselves the conditions we need to actually and effectively heal. From there (and only from there), healing happens naturally, and we continue to tend the garden of our love life and (for perhaps the first time in our entire relationship and life) experience truly conscious and effective communication.

What makes this so special is that you have the power to choose, act, think, and feel differently; to create instead of re-act. You are response-able. You also don't need to go it alone! There are maps, tools, and instructions that I at one point also did not have. It wasn't my fault, and it isn't yours, either, but now I know how to use these tools, and I am sharing the love.

Michael Boyle

My life was once dominated by depression, anxiety, trauma, insecurity, and dysfunctional attachment patterns, so I know what it is like to suffer, and I don't wish that for anyone. I especially don't wish that for your kids or mine. It's taken me two decades and me and Tania (my wife) rescuing our own marriage from the brink of divorce to discover this Relating Renaissance.

If you could create an environment for thriving that would enable you to heal, what would that mean for your kids? It would mean they would be able to take for granted the love, trust, connection, autonomy, and joy that you and I must do the work to create. Like the sound of this? Well, it's just the basics. If you really want to uplevel your relationships, you need to check out *The Relating Renaissance*. It might just be the make-or-break factor of all your closest relationships.

CONCLUSION:
RELEASING SHAME AND MOVING FORWARD

IN THESE PAGES, I HAVE PRESENTED a very empowered and even gritty approach to self-help "mental health", which I prefer to call mental fitness, and optimal performance. I have underscored the necessary foundation of acceptance, tolerance, kindness, empathy, compassion, and grace that underpins this journey. I have presented the uniquely countercultural idea that you can feel better today, easily, without any gimmicks, in a totally sustainable way that makes perfect sense. I have told you that if your therapist is not interested in working (or more likely doesn't know how to work) themselves out of a job, you might want to fire them. I have let you in on the challenging truth that while there are many things beyond your control that have influenced your suffering and are not your fault, only you can do something about your suffering, internally and externally, personally and societally. I have reminded you that you are always either waiting or creating, and that if you are waiting, you are going to be waiting forever (unless you make the decision to stop waiting now).

In the rules of exegesis, some of the most important aspects of a piece of work are always placed at the end. This is why I want to take some time, after speaking about surrender and relationships, to get real about shame and the journey to loving ourselves and one another, in all our imperfection.

Shame

The most challenging hole to crawl out of (and the one I am personally most familiar with) is the "freeze" state of depression. When this part of survival mode is active, the alarm it sounds throughout the system says, "It is dangerous to move." If ever there was a challenge to the "waiting or creating" conundrum, this is it, because this aspect of survival mode is very good at convincing us to wait; to do nothing; to freeze; to go numb.

One of the freeze state's most venomous toxins is the seemingly low-energy state of shame, hopelessness, helplessness, hiding, and the apathy it brings: "I don't care, and I don't care that I don't care." When this part of the NS is lit up, we are like a field mouse who knows a hawk is overhead and only sees motion. We become immobile, with the sense of, "If I move an inch, I will get seen and eaten." We get flooded with opioids, to numb us from impending doom. Everything inside us wants to stay stuck, invisible, and numb.

This is precisely when we are required to choose to move anyway (of course, after establishing the fact that we aren't hiding from a real, immediate threat to our lives). *How* we move can also be the difference that makes all the difference. I've told this story I made up to many clients to illustrate this idea:

Imagine your dog is stuck in the corner of a room. Between you and them, there is a pool of fiery lava and a narrow plank that can only hold the weight of the pet (not you). You try to step on it to rescue your best friend, but you realize that if you do so, it will snap immediately under your weight and take you into the melting pit below. You also see that the lava is rising, and soon, the plank and your dog will be consumed.

Your dog (understandably) is frozen, cowering in the corner, having retreated as far from the lava as possible. But you, with your rational human brain, know what must be done. The pet must walk across the plank to safety.

You are terrified and very triggered, so at first, you implore your cherished friend in a panicked tone to hurry, hurry, hurry across the plank!

It stays frozen.

Then, your panic rises into anger, and you yell, "Get the fuck over here!"

It stays frozen.

You start to rage and shame: "You stupid fucking dog, why won't you just come?" You start to lose hope and go numb, and the blank stare on your face says it all.

The pet stays frozen.

Then, you come to your senses and realize what must be done. You must cajole your friend across the plank. You kneel, change the tone of your voice, slow your breathing, and call, "There boy, hey there boy, hey there, just look at me... Look at me... There you go... Here I am... Here I am... I'm right here... Listen to my voice..."

You sigh with relief as he begins to make his way over.

"There you go... That's a good boy... Just look at me... Come to my voice..."

How to Find Joy
Even If You Have a Hole in Your Bucket

You hold your arms out.

"There you go... Slowly... Come on, boy, you can do it... I am right here with you... That's a good boy... I believe in you... I love you... Just keep coming... Yes... You are doing it... Bit by bit... Keep looking at me... Listen to my voice..."

And into your arms your best friend returns!

Now imagine if you treated yourself like your own best friend!

Here's another example, for those who relate more to a parent-child story:

Imagine you're the parent, and today, you are exhausted. You need your kid to fall asleep so that you can rest. So, you rush through the evening routine and are distracted during the bedtime story. You prematurely leave the room, knowing your child isn't quite in a deep state of sleep (likely due to your nervous energy), speed through your personal bedtime routine, and crash into bed. Just as you are falling asleep, you hear your kid cry, and you think, *WTF, why?!* You say to yourself, "I am *so* tired."

She doesn't stop crying, and you can tell from her tone that she isn't going to settle down on her own. She needs your help. You are tapped, but you do what parents do: you go anyway. Still, you are thinking more about how tired you are than how distressed she is. Frankly, you are frustrated, and you think she's just being manipulative. You open the door and sternly ask, "What's the matter?"

"I had a nightmare, Daddy."

"Okay, it's over now. Get back to sleep," you say in a harsh tone. She wails louder, and your blood starts to boil. "Stop your crying. Right now."

"But there is a monster in my closet!"

"There is no monster in your closet. It's just a bad dream. Now get back to sleep."

She cries and cries, and it dawns on you that this is only getting worse, not better. No one in the house is going to sleep any time soon, that's for sure.

You take a minute in the hallway to recollect yourself. You practice fog breathing. You know what has to be done. You re-enter the room and sit next to your daughter. She is totally beside herself, snot-crying and all. You try to reason with her. "Honey, it's just a bad dream. There are no monsters in here."

She's not having it, and she cowers in the corner of her bed, edging away from the closet.

You ask permission to move closer. She says yes. You realize talking won't work, so you decide to just sit there and do your own physiological sighs, because you realize you need to change state. After a few moments

303

have passed, you ask her if she wants a hug, and she quickly scurries up your body like a cub climbing a tree to safety. You rub her back and hold her, speaking in soothing tones. You start to say things like, "There, there, sweet girl. I am with you. You are safe. Feel my body. Feel your body. Listen to my voice. Feel my body breathing. Feel your body breathing." You slow and lower your voice. You slow your breathing. You release muscle tension from your body, and you start to feel her relax. "There you go, sweetheart," you encourage her. "You are here, and I am with you, and we are safe." You let that sink in, and her crying goes from panicked and hyperventilated to the type of shaking that you know means she's releasing the fear from her body. She starts to play with the buttons on your shirt, pokes her head up from your chest, and starts to look around. You allow her to go at her own pace.

You notice her eyes relax and her breathing slow down. You notice how she starts to orient back to the room. You sense that it is a good time to challenge her fear, and in a very calm soothing tone, you tell her, "I looked in the closet and there's no monster in there. I promise."

She's not totally sure, but is feeling safe enough to ask, "Are you sure, Daddy? I swear I saw one."

Even just by saying this, she tightens up a bit, but you rub her back, and she follows your lead. You know that her learning brain is turned on now that she's relaxing, so again, in slow, soothing tones, you validate and teach, "Yes, it can feel really scary when our alarm system is turned on, and sometimes, we even think things are there that aren't. Isn't that weird?"

"Yeah, Daddy, that is weird. I don't like that."

"I know, honey. Me neither. But you know what? Sometimes, when we feel ready to be courageous, it can really help us to see for ourselves that everything is safe. Do you want to come look in the closet with me?"

"I don't know, Daddy."

"How about I go first? Is that okay?" "Okay, Daddy."

"Okay. I am going to get up and go look in the closet, okay?" "Okay, Daddy."

You get up and go to the closet, and with no sarcasm or condescension whatsoever, you look around, move things around, and say, "Yup, it's all clear. Want to come to see?"

She walks over a bit hesitantly and says, "There, Daddy. I still see it." You move the robe she is pointing to that is hanging on the rack, and then, all becomes clear to her. She laughs and says, "Daddy, it was just my robe!"

"I know, silly! It was just your robe. But sometimes, we see things differently when we are scared, don't we?"

"Yes, Daddy."

"Now, you must be tired. Are you ready to get back to bed?" "Yes, Daddy."

You tuck her in, and before you know it, she is sound asleep—and you are, too!

This only took about five minutes, which is so much better than forty-five minutes of her crying herself to sleep (which really means passing out in freeze in a state of feeling abandoned and alone).

Together, we thrive.

When we are upset, survival mode is active. Survival mode resides mostly in the mammalian/toddler brain, and it can't be reasoned with. It is not logical. It experiences the stick as a snake, no matter how much someone yells, "Look, it's a stick!" The good news is, we have the capacity and opportunity to be our own benevolent, skillful parent, or our own "dog whisperer." The more we try to "snap ourselves out of it" with criticism, shame, panic, and worry, the worse things get every time.

This is not about being politically correct. This is not "every kid gets a medal." This is not "coddling" and making yourself (or your kids, or your pets) weak. This approach, very practically and logically, is what works, and nothing is sacred but results. Everything else—even if it appears to "work" in the short run—only sets us up for worse and bigger upsets in the future. The only way to true and positive change is through the doorway of acceptance, kindness, love, and skill for ourselves, others, and ALL.

I hope this book will continue to unfold worlds of beneficial opportunities for you, the people you love, your communities, and our shared world. Among these opportunities, you are now qualified to apply to work with me 1-1 on implementing these MTIs, so you can more quickly and easily Do → Become → Be the greatest possible benefit to yourself, others, and ALL. Due to time constraints, efficiency, effectiveness, and my desire to make the deepest, most positive impact on others, I choose to only work 1:1 with people who have read this book and who demonstrate understanding and willingness to implement these principles. I am, however, most excited about the group work we are doing at ATA, where people like you and me are coming together to play the greatest game of *all* (joyful excellence by design) right now! You can read more about that here: www.alltogether.academy/the-joyful-excellence-mastermind.

I would be thrilled to learn, from any of you reading, about the ripple effects I know will radiate into your personal health and happiness, your friends and families, and your careers and our communities as you do, become, and be your Creative-IAM, traveling down the Neurochemical Roadmap to the Future You Value and Choose.

Some parting reminders in the meantime:

1. Reverse engineering gives you direction. Once you know the direction you are heading in, don't look at the finish line too often. That will likely land you in Zone 3 (overwhelm). Instead, ask for grace and ease: "What's the next, easiest thing I am willing to do to move in the direction I value and choose to?"

2. Keep going. No matter how many times you get stuck or lose your way, you can only ever start from where you are. You don't need to go back to the past to figure out how to find your way forward. You can get out your JOLKA-GPS, recalibrate to the future you value and choose, and apply the grace and ease question, and you will feel better today, easily, without any gimmicks, in a totally sustainable way that makes perfect sense.

3. I'm a practical guy, and nothing is sacred to me but results and the work that works to produce those results. So, allow me to reiterate: the work only works if you work it.

If this way of working resonates with you, there are more and more opportunities for you to continue this work at ALL Together Academy, a training ground for ALL (Awareness Loving Life). If you would like to be part of a kind, supportive community of likeminded people who are "doing the work," you are always welcome to join us. And for those of you who've gone all the way on the journey to finish this book, the code [RESET20] will give you twenty percent off the 30-Day Reset From Surviving to Thriving. www.alltogether.academy/30-day-reset

Love to ALL,
Together, we thrive,
Mike

www.ingramcontent.com/pod-product-compliance
Lightning Source LLC
Chambersburg PA
CBHW031043110426
42740CB00048B/797